MY CONTINUING JOURNEY—

INTO SPIRITUAL, ARTISTIC & REVOLUTIONARY THOUGHTS

RED JORDAN AROBATEAU

MY CONTINUING JOURNEY—INTO SPIRITUAL, ARTISTIC, & REVOLUTIONARY THOUGHTS

JOURNEY Volumes 11-13.

Any resemblance to any person living or dead is purely coincidental.

Cover Art by Red Jordan Arobateau; Home Sweet Home/Self-Portrait-The First, 2008; Oil on Canvas, 15" x 30". Artists Collection, San Francisco.

ISBN: 978-0-578-00682-6

**Published by RED JORDAN PRESS
484 Lake Park Ave. PMB 228
Oakland, CA 94610
USA**

My Journal continues. A kind of Dreamtime For The Every Day Revolutionary.

--Obedience To The Call Of Art, 2007

If you've ever been down on the abject bottom of society you will be looking up, as if out of a deep pit, towards a faint lighted window exit and know, absolutely, from within the chilly bones of your being, that this situation is wrong; that this situation needs to be turned up-end, reversed; so that all of us down here clamoring and crawling over each other in mayhem, in the slime of the refuse pit would be suddenly sitting on top—out in the clean air, the free air, with food, with plenty, with peace, and the few ghouls; bloodsuckers who are our jail wardens, as their fortunes necessitate it, *they* would be cast down into this uttermost bottom.

My journey into revolutionary thoughts begins here, at the bottom of the pit. While struggling to have a life—me being a lonely soul who makes few friends, and none easily; a fine arts painter to the best of my abilities, and writer of a very good if not great, degree. I am recounting my life's journey as of the last age which began concurrent with my sex change—starting around 1998, in which I deal with the elements of painting rediscovered after 40 years in which slaving on the time-clock for pay lost in the maize of Kafkaesque bureaucracy; dizzy, cycling endlessly on a treadmill rat race of the kkkapitalist system in which I could not paint for lack of time, but only wrote, and between the pointers and observations of a fine arts are these *gestures* of a revolutionary, nascent, pacing in the pit down here in the bottom, in the flesh, in barely a crack of light from that far-off window to give me hope we might one day escape.

2008

Index:

MY CONTINUING JOURNEY—
INTO REVOLUTIONARY THOUGHTS

Volume 11.

Many of us are doubly driven to the desire for change—which is what revolution means—, because of a bad current life, which has arisen out of a nightmarish early childhood. Hence, an examination of personal problems under the light of psychology is necessitated. Too long some supreme terrorists and revolutionaries have cut out psychology, personal problem solving, not to mention art, love, religion—as in worship of a deity (not a humanbeing)--- as petty and of no consequence—how wrong they are!

If a revolution is to successfully elevate the human systems from a bad, intolerable condition to one workable, just, and humane, all elements of the human being, its psyche, mental processes, as well as its community and social dynamics must be dealt with!

If we can't get our personal problems straight, how are we going to straighten out the New Order?

144.

AM May 28, Wednesday

Its quite clear. The young generations honor themselves w/no thought for us FTM oldsters. Participated a panel 'fireside chat' with myself, James Green, and 78-year old retired teacher, Jeffery. The usual group of 5 to 7 dike/Transman pre-transitions didn't show. Thanks for the support buddies. I guess you all have a good excuse; don't expect me to give much heart to your tired problems in the future!

AM Wednesday May 28

As I have said before, when you enter the fine arts, you enter a more physical discipline—then as a writer. Especially oils/acrylics, and medium-size to larger canvases. Find myself lifting canvas back and forth, on/off easel, cleaning bushes, getting up, backing away from it to get perspective; moving about constantly. Also, Jasmin does her watercolors on a table, or her lap looking down upon them—and they are regular watercolor size sheets of paper, which she can manipulate with two fingers.

Where does art come from—out of myself. *My self!* Must keep up the brush & paints, no matter what!

If I ever get famous, rich, all those who ignored me, passed my product over—they will realize they bet the wrong horse. I'd been on the scene dangling myself deliciously in front of them, hopefully waiting to be acquired. My paintings, writings; the work of my hands & mind.

The old mans body was a mass of aches and pains. He did not use the medical painkillers prescribed to him by his doctor, only one small aspirin per day, which was for his heart. By evening this is the though he would have:

> Did you know in heaven we are perpetually young? Old women, with crease-lined faces will be forever young no matter what great age they had obtained on earth. We will have many romances. Each woman will be given a bouquet of red roses. I know for the Spirit of the Lord(ess) has told me so.
> --Spirit of God to the Prophet Red Jordan Arobateau

Later that day, as he went racing about the studio, and off into the streets about his errands, he reflected on Catholic Saints; about abortion issues, plus many other disagreements he had with them. Yet, he thinks of Mother Teresa possessing only 2 shifts to cover her body, for a lifetime. One she washed out at night, and hung out to dry, while wearing the other. The nuns of her Order bathed, laundered, using cold water. —So as to live closer to the very poorest persons on earth. Her vow of total abstinence. As Transman looked with anger, resentment at the rich who get more and more; who get anything they want for all their lives—those who have sold out; & here, so severe a life; it didn't stick—his anger. --- His resentment falls away from her, cannot be placed on her. So he looks at Mother Teresa without hate, or anger, nor bitterness, looks at her as someone pure.

But for now, today on earth, 2008, very real time, it was a long cold walk thru the Tenderloin. 2 blax street men holler on the windy street corner of Hyde & Turk:

$10,000! Psyche the nigger out!

They don't have a product—so they find a hustle.

Its 3PM. Just as the old black-clothed man limped vigorously up the hill towards Trans, its Lunching Ladies group ends. T girls scatter out of the center in all directions. Spreading the vision of transsexual women into the environs.

Trans Space is an education about those of us men-women, women-men into all unaccustomed places; to neighbors, shopkeepers, markets who surround us. By now they have seen not simply one lone apparently 'crazy' transgirl, or the hardened man-dike, scowling, who, protectively, like a hermit crab, goes scuttling thru the streets; today they see dozens and dozens of us en-masse; sometimes 100rds; summoned up for one of our events. They encounter planet transsexual in the elevators, in restroom mirrors, in corridors…

Tomorrow afternoon is to be an event featuring Dr. Lori Kolher:

Red: oh, an event for you girls—about getting tits.

Toni: No its an event for girls who need tits! I got mine! (Cupping her brown hands under her tits, jugging them.)

Girls acting out @ trans space. Another argument. *I hate you! You're a dog! Why are you laughing at me!*

Some times my children run so afraid—they break out in anger.

@ Trans Space; a community gathering. Speakers inform us of the latest HIV statistics among trans—both MTF & FTM. Never been any other project like this in the world. Rest of the country & the world looks to SF for guidance.

The audience sits here today, some because they have no home. Lean black hands, my sisters, beside me at trans center. Slowly relaxes, falls onto the sofa, she is sleeping.

> 37-69% of trans have been in jail.
> 1 out of 50 inmates in the prison system is TG.
> 1 in 15,000 people is MTF out of the birth male population. Yet 28% TG is HIV infected.

> FTM's with HIV, 1-3% have HIV. If you are having sex with a population which has a high rate of HIV, (FTM's having sex with gay men) you increase your chances of becoming infected.

> 55% depressed FTM's with no access to T and services. This greatly drops when they have these services.

Small Transman sat upon the couch beside a larger trans sister who was catnapping—being homeless; --- all her worldly possessions in a brown paper bag. His art and writing weighed heavily on his soul, and sat in a backpack, besides hers. And he vaguely wondered in the sunlit day, listening to the presenters drone statistics, about himself, in his own Spartan situation: 'But a problem is when lack of resources, and poverty impact the extraordinary artist? What happens to the homeless if they're a potential writer? Are we swept up with everyone else in criminalization? Due to laws supposedly to our favor which have failed, us, and we remain outsiders; not worked into their system…'

People are much too quick to try to categorize us trans into slots they are familiar with—male or female, and nothing else! Can't understand why a FTM transsexual would transition to male—and then like men! The ignorant say, well why go to all that trouble, just stay a 'woman' its easier to get men that way! Likewise, an MTF. They don't have a clue about the division between gender and sexual preference. Anyway, there's another workshop coming up in Trans Space on FTMs and *men*. which includes FTMs with other FTMs, FTMs with bio men, including gay men, straight, and bi men. Lets see if this one is better attended then our comparatively small aging fireside chat.

I might as well confide in you, set upon the backdrop of my life is the ongoing, ever-encroaching fact, starkly becoming apparent, that I no longer belong here in the city has which has harbored me, and seen me grow since I was 23, and now I'm 64.

Again the old mans thoughts turned to revolution, to actively step out of the hopeless mode of one who cannot make the rules of society with their lone vote, overpowered by the egregious cunning of the rich, and the apathy of his fellow poor:

> In our circumstances a person who suffers, but knows that he is completely innocent, sometimes has no place to lodge a complaint and no way to receive satisfaction.
> --Notes Of the Fatherland (Russia), 1878, Quoted in Angel Of Vengeance

And so was poor, elderly disabled Transman's lot.

So now I learned a lesson in not just knowing the Word, studying the Word, but *doing* the Word. This is what all these nuns & priests attempted to do, some thru sacrifice, others thru activism. Carrying the meaning of the Word thru to its natural conclusion—which results in a kind of socialism or communism or mass world collectivism—so no one is hungry, afraid, un-housed, or poor. This means giving up a great portion of the hogs-share the U$A has—and which some newly developing countries are beginning to frantically grasp at, because like a displaced tidal wave on one shore; it also wreaks havoc on the opposite shore across the globe, so, our massive engine of economy is wrecking havoc on lesser nations. Engulfing their frail infrastructure. The USA has shown all others the way, China, India, they are rapidly climbing up the ladder too, and all of us big fat cats are crushing the small mice of the earth; who squeal horribly in distress—then die.

If the Word must be *done*, then what do people of these privileged countries realize now? How their actions infringe on the very existence of those not so well off?

Play cousin Angelo (alias, Carlos) has come to town on his yearly vacation over dinner at Lorrie's restaurant ('50's oeuvre) he says:
> In China and India, people who were eating just once a day are now eating 3 times a day. People who were just eating 3 times a week are now eating every day. But somewhere in Africa, or Southeast Asia, or South America people who were eating 3 times a week are now eating once a week, and slowly starving to death.
> --Carlos.

Well, says Red, a mouth full of spaghetti tails dangling out of the red sauce on his mouth:
> At a major political summit somewhere in Europe this dignitary from Africa said, about the growing depression in America, and gas shortage here, he said 'what is discomfort in your country is killing most of the people in my country'. And he said this real simple with no malice, like its just a fact.
> --Red, repeating a news brief.

Instead of sitting here in bookstore reading revolutionary books, to Do Something. Like Billy in STAGE DOOR. *
*Billy Bradford shot & killed the realestate agents who were a part of the reason he was being kicked out into the street.

Friday, May 30, AM
I was a lonely child and for years words & writing were my only friend; this skill evolved fairly recently in human civilization—about 7,000 years ago—whereas the human race is carbon dated back to its pre-humanoid cut-off at around 68,000 years; and early paintings existed even that long ago on the cave walls, chiefly of bison and other animals our ancestors hunted for food to supplement a diet of foraging nuts, roots, fruits, & scavenging carrion. (The pictures might have been magical rituals to ensure a good hunt.) Words. My friends. And now 80-books accompany me on my voyage thru this bitter earth, often making a space for me at social gatherings—around the ancient campfire –transposed up 68,000 years to today's modern

12

drawing rooms. My ex-lover Jasmin does an even more ancient art form---the dance, --which predated everything! That and drumming—ancient tribes people's palms of hands beating rhythms of the heart on hollow logs they'd found, and later crudely crafted; the swaying bodies of dancers in the moonlight/starlight, when the human family assembled itself in a tight circle, to prepare against the coming night, darkness, fear of wild animals and natural disasters; huddling together for mutual protection and reassurance. Where is that huddling together in this modern age? Where the reassurance? Where is family, and who is family? This is the struggle of the modern person; ---in gaining individuality, we have isolation. One gift displaces another! Words are my friend, and magically so. I have told this to you little ones, so you will feel more at home around my ancient campfire as I lay dying in our modern world!

Cousin Carlos is in town, and it's good to have him here. A few more days, then he creeps back to Madison WI, snail like, by Greyhound bus—a surface traveler-- another like myself, Jasmin, Nicole, etc., who do not like flying. Nicole flies anyway. She's recently been to Florida, and next to Europe—making pit stops in Finland, then to Spain, where she will go to school in Madrid. Jasmin flew to Los Vegas with her lover L., and also down to Southern California, where they met the Lesbian Boat Cruise & sailed down to Mexico. And they flew back. But this was under duress. I have flown 8 times in my life as documented previously in AUTUMN CHANGES, and, yes, truth is that my pretend-cousin Carlos (formerly alias Angelo, ((AUTUMN CHANGES)) has never flown in his life!

Nice thing is, Red wouldn't be alone all weekend, because of Carlos being in town. Oh, PS, cousin purchased the remainder of my fine arts posters, which he didn't already have--$140 worth—also a copy of RETROSPECT.

As far as Mr. Growley, the bookstore Proprietor is concerned, Red had a story to tell about their disastrous argument. Concerning how Red showed-out at a nearby neighborhood establishment, when refused admittance to their Opening Party. The last scene of the last book of my JOURNEY pictures him shouting, standing under streetlight, waving his cane in the air! Hurling epitaphs against the

encroaching rich and would-be rich poseurs against the poor! Alas
Babylon!

Destruction. Creation. Rebirth. If the tools of suicide are right there,
it enables the suicidal human to proceed with their plan of self-killing;
and the tools of suicide are always right there, and have been, down
thru beginning of time—the lovers leap off a cliff thousands of feet
above sharp rocks. The ocean. Some deep dark well in the
farmyard…

Transman preferred the creative process, and found that it steadily
pushed aside the blue cloud of his depression.

I want to share my vision with you, you, & you.

Its difficult to make yourself get started to create. Creation is one of
the most difficult things. More so then repetitious laboring in a form,
which is already there, each morning, set up for you. In addition to
getting up out of a safe, warm bed, you have to go to a place of work,
your desk, easel, barre, and stand there—creating something, which
did not exist moments before. Where as in regular labor, those boxes
come tumbling down a conveyor belt; those old people lay there
comatose, bodies waiting to be turned lifted wiped, refreshed; the
paperwork of sales, invoices en, rushes out at their victim in a
constant stream that must be processed. You sit at the writing desk.
You stand at the easel. A blank page. A fresh canvas—WHAT!

Some are conflicted:

> My hand is heavier on some.
> --Hashem.

Brokenness? Brokenness.

I had a certain amount of mental problems, because of my mother
being mentally ill and me being forced to live in that atmosphere as a
child; which evidentially restructures the physical brain, setting into it
post traumatic syndrome for the future—irreversibly. This was a
handicap to me going on to higher education. I couldn't concentrate,
found it impossible to sit trapped in a classroom. Some might have

overcome this handicap; gone on to achieve high scholastic marks, a long work history at higher pay, hence greater security. But in addition, discovering I had artistic talent, I followed the path of least resistance. Not forcing myself to do what was extremely difficult— fitting into a established social pattern that the vast majority of my family had done before me--- but instead went off on the maverick road of self discovery to the extent art would take me—and am still going upon that path 60 years later.

Dear Lord, let me drink of Living Water. I want to repair myself. I want to be whole. Drink deeply of Your Living Water.

I've lived a hard life, and continue to live a hard life; so anything that makes my life easier is a blessing to me. Must say that this guy Sean has been a blessing to me. He has helped me. He is able to do these maneuvers on computer, and as a person friendly to me, all of which helps my life, which is difficult, so his effect is to make things better, and I am thankful for this.

AM May 31, Saturday
Its not only themselves the artist counts on; some try projects with others. Facts to mention regarding collaborations; difficulties can and do arise because of people they work with—especially people that hold the purse strings. Those who have the expertise, when you do not. People die, they get sick, they loose their funding; they change their minds.

Several young photographers/filmmakers @ bookstore have become embroiled in a project in which the major funder and supplier of the necessary cameras is changing his part of the original plan, and throwing everything into a tailspin. It is difficult for a creative artist when their own art moves out of their control, and becomes subject to the whims of others.

RE: Revolutionary Thoughts:
Don't get me wrong, I'm not advising terrorism; it is not the best way. Revolution must happen by the masses of people all refusing to work inside the corrupt machinery, refusing to pay rent, refusing to do anything. To sit down on the system of capitalism, to boycott our oppressors. To no longer be the muscle and energy that runs the evil

15

apparatus. To demand, set up, and administer a new order of justice, equity and an equal share in the profits of all the goods they produce by the work of their hands, and a free decent house, education, medical services. They should not stop the work of cultural enrichment, but stop the work of corporate capitalism, this advanced capitalism, this gargantuan capitalist slave-wage system, just as our political ancestors dethroned the kings and queens of old, and overthrew the control of the monarch and the papistry.

I have spoken of my bad childhood and how it informs me as an adult, let us go a step further.

Only by analysis of personal problems in conjunction with the desire for revolution can we move along with revolutionary practices. The radical must look into self and see just how much of their rotten lousy childhood is going into desire to change the system—to insure their vision is not clouded. Maybe some things they hate about the system don't need to be changed at all, but kept and reinstalled upon the rise of the then New Order, but personal problems block the view. I.e. The unloved child declares love to be superfluous, bourgeoisie, a middle-class privilege which the poor can't hope to indulge in and the rich distain from indulging because it siphons off their power and control—so upon the rise of the New Order, once this radical and his/her thinking is installed, love being abolished, the New Order, it is bound to crack apart and begin to fall immediately as so much of the natural human race and natural people love; experience love, seek love, give love, and hold love as the paramount emotion given to human and animal kind and that is what makes life worth living—not all the revolutionary doctrine in all the books in heaven or hell!

The above is just an example of what I mean.

Many of us are doubly driven to the desire for change—which is what revolution means—, because of a bad current life, which has arisen out of a nightmarish early childhood. Hence, an examination of personal problems under the light of psychology is necessitated. Too long some supreme terrorists and revolutionaries have cut out psychology, personal problem solving, not to mention art, love, religion—as in worship of a deity (not a humanbeing)--- as petty and

16

of no consequence—how wrong they are! (E.g., Mao's cultural revolution. The revolutionary Russian Serfs distain for the fine arts of the Hermitage.)

If a revolution is to successfully elevate the human systems from a bad, intolerable condition to one workable, just, and humane, all elements of the human being, its psyche, mental processes, as well as its community and social dynamics must be dealt with!

If we can't get our personal problems straight, how are we going to straighten out the New Order?

I mean how crazy can you get! To try to set up an order where every social foible is dictated from above! For instance the Russian Communists plan was to—demand all comrades partake in mass dinners together nightly, instead of each cooking in their individual kitchen; to demand collective farms where no one personally kept one stalk of corn, where no one wrote books nor painted art any more (as bourgeois luxuries) a true failure to grasp the importance of some vital human needs was not assessed! The need for individuality, for privacy, and some ownership and some control over their private space and effects and creations of their hands! --This vastly different from the monstrous, corrupt corporate or and gargantuan capitalism of one owner who extends their borders of personal control so that soon it envelopes his or her whole neighborhood, her whole city, his whole nation. ---One is a deadly animal, destructive to life; the other, what a human being is.

AM Early June 1, Sunday

> Red: Dear Jesus please set things right.
> Jesus: Its easy.

Dear Jesus, thank you for your help in the past. --& in the future.

Underwent Kinko's torture. Blurb, and Lulu tortures, —all in a single day. Then went home, pigged out over burrito, slept 5 hours straight.

This means my first fine arts painting (Ho's Bath) is now available for the public to purchase on line. And RETROSPECT.

The system kills and murders and we must be ready for it at every twist. It takes away your apartment because of money issues—the most important thing then, is to preserve your relationships you have established with family, friends, loved ones, pets; and to preserve your belongings. The system has the potential to destroy, and we must be prepared! Even the rich sometimes are shafted severely by circumstances coming from outside themselves, which tear them apart, their belongings and lives—although this is very unlikely. It is the spiritual things, the emotional things, the family ties between friends and animals and beings we love which are paramount! To fashion a life which can evade this murderous system and preserve what is important and centermost to you life is vital!

The Hawaiian people were stripped of their land. It is foreigners, intruders, conquerors who today own those islands—all tourists who flock there are complicit in their little whore-mongering of native Hawaii—for she is an occupied nation! Her once-people dispersed, murdered by arms and by foreign invasions of disease. In the churches of today do you hear from the pulpit the preaching of justice and fiery diatribes calling for these ugly misdeeds of the past to be addressed? The native people of North America—the Indians have made a long stand against white injustice, and now many tribes are being funded by the allowing of gaming on their land—the reservations. They are doing better then the native Hawaiians—who are all but gone. A matter of justice would be to assemble a tribal structure of surviving persons of Hawaiian blood, and deed a portion of *their own land back to them*. This land could never again be sold or taken. The native people of the island of Palau have such a rule. All those of Palauen blood own their own homes on that affluent little island in the far South Pacific---now also an American air base. The Americans pay rent to the Palauens and have a lease, but they do not, cannot own the island. The Palau people have a fierce tradition, religious and cultural, that their land may never be sold to any one for any reason. Likewise the Hawaiian remnants, of that desecrated tribe must be granted back a large portion of their land, to be administered justly by the remaing persons of Hawaiian blood. This is how it would work. All person of full Hawaiian blood lineage. Very few left. Persons who are half-Hawaiian native blood. Persons who are one-quarter Hawaiian native blood. All have a share in the administration according to how much Hawaiian they are. None of them either individually are given the land for individual use, but to administer it, for the enrichment of the tribe; and none of them individually or collectively can ever again sell the land out of Hawaii control! This is a matter of justice! Are the churches of today speaking of this justice? No! The Word of God plainly states, I am a Just God, and enjoins us to study God's Word and to make and mold our lives to be like God---which means that we should study the meaning of, and how to, and then practice *being Just* Individuals! Yet the churches seldom are heard saying this! No—what comes out of their mouths of the church—**"Yo' gowin' to hell! Yo' gowin' to hell fo' dis' 'n dat'!"** These are the churches of ignorance! The churches condemning the stranger, and those they don't like—like queers—like me!

"Yo' Gowin' to hell!" Over and over from the moment they can talk to the day they die! And that's all they ever do! Where is justice? Where is the true word of God!

The feisty old man muttered these thoughts to himself with vehemence as he puttered around delicately moving some prints of his paintings. *Inventory! I'm doing painting inventory! Hateful count of fine arts posters; how many in tube, in storage, in display book. 1 Oyster Eater. 5 Pigs. 3 Ho's. 1 Arab. 1 Madman, etc.*

I promise you, I promise you; you are not going to be chosen for their 'feature book' of the month. I promise you, you will never be their 'pick of the week' of new material submitted. Because you are an embarrassment, you are an outsider they would rather forget, and happily go about pretending they never saw, nor heard of you at all! Straight, gay, it was all the same! That's what they thought of me! Black as well as white, they'd shove my books under the rug or hide it behind the curtain at a book fair, as if it accidentally dropped there.

Thru the ages my people worked hard, --they were blacks, whip driven, laboring for white slave masters; they were un-empowered, working for rich bosses for very little money. They always had to work; and I work. I keep on, non-stop.

I ran; I mean honey, I *ran* down the track!

People can be very discouraging; 2 friends have said, one today, the other last week; 'you shouldn't write if you can't get an editor.' As the spelling and grammatical mistakes get on their nerves so much they won't read my stuff. So that means if I had taken their advice I would have written 10 books—which were edited—and not 80 that today exist, which for all their typos, grammatical errors exist, and are not simply *dreams* never materialized, like the work of so many would-be authors.

Sunday, condo-showing day in The City. A rich young man—many of them gay—cruising, turns the corner, curious at FOR SALE sign. This sign is placed on one of the ancient stone buildings built 60 years ago, which has been condo converted, totally remodeled. This means its 28 units which may have housed 140 people has gone off the rental market, disgorging hapless tenants, many of them seniors, disabled or poor into the vast unknowing; for a small fee per head, and now will sell to single, or two person couples most likely, at prices zooming astronomically to $755,000 for a two bedroom 1 bath unit---three-quarters of a million dollars. Now housing just 40 owners of the affluent class.

I feel I am not to the same degree dedicated as a Mother Teresa, a St. Francis Assisi. I am more in the style of these well-meaning priests who go running around here, and running around there, trying to do good—you see them dishing out food at the food bank, you see them avidly attending labor union sit ins wearing sincere smiles, they sprinkling their presences around, here and there—but they never go all the way on any one cause—they can't go all the way, very few humans can; if we could we'd all be saints, this world would be closer to Gods perfection. So—after 3 days missing, I gave up on cat. Haven't been there since Thursday when Carlos and I went up—and cat was nowhere to be seen. After weaving surreptitious path between gossipy BART police, and Bart construction workers, saw some uneaten pile of shriveled up food from two days past, semi eaten—maybe by rats, walked around, feel cat has found strength from my previous food to go seek greener pastures, hope and prey this is the case. I love you cat.

AM Tuesday June 3

The young rich upper middle class they step out of fancy new cars, at the curb, they wear leisure wear and thongs on their bare feet, bodies are perfect; toned in the gym, tanned in a sun lab; their faces and hair groomed perfect, they are well taken care of, they are displacing us.

In gender divide heterosexuals have avenues between them where they come together in community, and as individuals but in gay life— there are 2 separated worlds, polarized ones; one gay men, the other lesbian women. You can have some of the most polarized men, off into their exclusive gay male galaxy of bathhouses, hotels, bars, restaurants. And the most fringe-dwelling dike women, coupled off, living isolated lives. The rise of a plutocratic gay male class into power a'la the Greco-Roman Empires. A well dressed, suited out-of-state gay; lean, exquisite built figures sculpted by upperclass diet (costly protein & health foods) and gym training. This speaks to a small segment of queer world---the privileged class-- and not to the rank & file gay man; nor to the underprivileged trailer park gay, or dispossessed senior grey haired man, no longer desirable, far fallen from the beauty of youth, perhaps living in poverty and isolation.

I am thankful when me & and gay men have a friendship, such as Richard who has helped immensely with the photographs of my fine arts paintings. Met for dinner to give him a copy of RETROSPECT; he was pleased, a smile spread on his face. He has said to bring him the next batch paintings when I have five—that's 1 & ½ more to go.

He & Richard speak of Red's transsexuality, the gay-bi man curious: We must go thru many evolutions. Many butch dikes somehow found themselves fucking men; underneath a man, lovemaking, had to fight for his/her identity as a masculine being. To turn the tables from bottom to top. Although these dikes enjoyed the sex, greedily, these pre-transition men were not happy with the identity it illustrated. Although his physical being as a female was intact and well delivered its orgasm, he wanted to be the one doing the fucking with his dick, and so this was a gross mix-up in the physical-mental, and a problematic situation waiting off in the future to be remedied by some means, of which by now he had a clue—transsexual change.

One of the dangers for the artist, Dear Children is this: many middle class European artists of the 1700rds first lived in poverty as fine arts oil painters/poets/sculptures because their middle class parents decided to cut off their inheritances & allowance funds to 'teach them a lesson' so they had to live by the brush, the pen, the sculptors chisel to earn a living. For many this tactic worked—they couldn't survive, and so returned to lives of professors, bankers, industrialists, manufacturers, alongside their fathers—so we haven't heard of them today, 200 years later. However a very few did squeeze thru the trap and they are the Monet's, Gauguin's, of our art history. It is not unusual for an artist to dwell in ignominy and poverty for a measured time then break into prominence on the art field—and dwell there in the limelight for a generation—before they are overthrown by some modern school which forges ahead, using the ideas and techniques the master originated as a spring board for their own imaginings. However, for some, like Monet, fame returns in yet the 3rd generation, in which they are rediscovered. The lesson being, never give up hope!

PM

As I said in LEADER OF THE PACK the Spirit informs Angel, one of the heroes of that dike biker novel; **I will show you what tribe you should be committed too**—and I see, as of yet I have not found that tribe. As a couple, Jasmin and I went thru several such communities—but never were totally received, nor befriended nor made our home in any of them—so we moved on. Here are some of them:

> Dike society
> Neighborhood dikes homeowners group where we lived
> SM players
> Cliques of writers/dancers/performance artists

Individually I have been thru several more on my own—Jasmin stopped trying, and devotes all her energy to her partner, and to herself, dog, birds, & plants, with no outreaching but for the sake of her career--dance. You can put all the blame on me, and or on Jasmin personally, but I don't think so. Incidentally, I have been thru the following tribes, with disastrous results to minor nothings:

> Trans community (FTM, and MTF respectively)
> Jewish temple/community
> Christian church/community

Now, today, here's these poor street queer kids, disfranchised, many of them homeless, who seem to be interested in me, and whom I am frankly 'above' status-wise; in that I'm housed, sane, have an income (albeit tiny) and a career (albeit barely a success in any sense of the word). This rag-tag bunch. One black brother-sister, his/her long lean ebony frame in a pink dress and azul blue gymshoes peers in window of establishment at a space vacated by a commercial display. It is 5' by 4' square, with clean carpet; additional wall socket; he/she states:

> I'd be glad to sleep right there, —its more then I have now.

> Yes Transman added, and it's got a electric outlet you could plug in a computer and write a novel right there!

This stark reality of poor queers really does call me into account about my self-orientated ambition to have my 'dream' --a condo here in the city!

> I hold all the cards.
> --Hashem

So, in the meantime, we all sit on a precarious fault line leading to the future, the goal? --to create as much art as I can—despite semi-depression or financial straits, or lack of 'connections' before death or abandonment on some poverty ward. Like Bozo Texicano, who tagged every boxcar which came under his jurisdiction at the railroad yard at the early part of 1900rds, in a desperate effort to make my mark in life, to help dislodge this impure Empire from its position of greed & war, and inform the public about all which I know.

> My children love the Light.
> --Hashem.

Often the secret police found the authors of letters to the editor of newspapers supportive to Vera K., the attempted assassin, yet the secret police had no political prior record of them, they were simply ordinary Russian citizens; to which furious Czar Nicolas us wrote: who are these people!" --From Angel of Vengeance. This is precisely what revolution takes—all the people together.

Speaking of The People, here are 2 more appropriate quotes from Angel Of Vengeance:

> Was it really true, she (Vera --) wondered, postulating to Karl Marx, that the Russian rural peasants needed to first become landless workers "thrown onto the streets" of Russia's cities, at the mercy of the rising capitalist class, in order to become true revolutionaries?

> For radicals in particular, wither European or Russian, she radiated a pure untainted, commitment to socialism, in all of her theoretical writings, editorial work, and organized activities, her only thought was to encourage the oppressed to revolt and to gain their freedom.
> --From Angel Of Vengeance, by Anna Siljack.

There's many activists of different kinds. Some just dropout of the system, not adding fuel to its evil machine; living as Spartan as possible to do so.

AM Wednesday June 4

Thus this loss of what would have been the first female candidate does damage me somewhat. (Senator Hillary Clinton in failed bid for the white house presidency.)

Females undergo a degrading process in life, whereas they are told constantly, shown that they are second class citizens, inferior to men, and continuously 'put back' into this position, no matter how hard they try. Women's rights are something which must be fought for non-ceasing, it s a full time strain which men are liberated from, from birth, and thus able to shoot up higher; as shooting stars.

Young people involved in the anti-gentrification social action group use the words *resist cultural erasure*. This is what I feel about my old lesbian genre, which was a fringe success. The mainstream shuns and passes by, and thus it dies—from lack of support. Eventually by lack of support from even the people it portrays. Cultural erasure. Also feel the omnipresent burden of anti-feminism, which pervades all stratums of cultures worldwide. Hilary Clinton's loss only exemplifies this. Reminds me that early in the 20th century, tho women (chiefly white women) and black men fought side by side to get the vote, once black men were granted the vote, they forgot about women's issues entirely, and the cause of women's sufferage was set-aside for another 60 years. This Hillary Clinton stuff has made me

24

depressed—in a slightly different way then when George Bush won his *second* term election despite how awful he'd been at the first term. At that point I withdrew my interest in TV politics, switched off the TV set (5 of them in my house, 2 used for my sex videos exclusively) and only watch when some news of magnitude as Hurricane Katrina or the election primaries comes on, so yes, I am depressed about the first women candidate for president running—and apparently loosing. Again vow to withdraw from world political interest like a turtle into its shell—for emotional survival!

Frankly, its important for me to be holistic, I value myself, and if the news is damaging to me, I must withdraw from it. I wonder how many millions more humans all over earth do the same!

PM June 4, Wednesday

I hear the smallest voice, says the Lord(ess).

I still hear the loud arguing, shouting we did, about the 2008 political candidates. Eventually this will pass away, into the eternal winds. One day this bookstore will close its doors for the last time. I will stand upon the street facing the anonymous row of buildings across this street, which rise to 4, 5, and 6 stories. Its architecture grey white, pink painted brick, their windows, housing various inhabitants behind blinds, lace curtains, colorful ethnic blankets, shades, grills; a rare balcony, many fire escapes, open windows, shut. Nostalgic doorways, a few plants—dead ferns wavering dry stalks.

Those guys who assemble here; we've all come from different lives. High universities of learning. Prison-industrial complex. The streets. The Vietnam war; war in the Middle East. Me trans-queer, from a queer mega ghetto, which is a very elite cross-section of the universe.

We all went thru a lot together—trans—he thought back to TARC, in the heart of the awful slummy Tenderloin, Kitty Kastro's Tranny support groups; jail bar entrance opens into a large room with scattered decrepit furniture, mice scuttling across a worn linoleum floor. Bad food shipped over from a local church which feeds the homeless daily; above all the tall, under-fed trans women in high heel pumps, X-tra large hand-me-downs from a free box of a straight woman's life, full too of its hopes and shattered dreams; 2nd and 3rd hand dresses& skirts of tall, or oversized shop girls & himself, lonely in a crowd, one of the few trans guys who frequented these services— how we've come a long way up the hill in social progress, for instance this nicer venue.

> You should not be lonely comrade. For many others have gone down this long path before you.

AM Thursday; June 5
Evening Descends Upon The Poolhall is a mediocre picture.

Am still ironing out the kinks in the way my lighting is set up. Need a second tripod—or lampstand with high powered beams aimed from the left, the original one has been moved to the right—but this leaves dark shadows when painting canvas on the left side, as light is blocked by my hand, while painstakingly etch figures at bar of Poolroom.

Life's work not published. No publicity. No mentions. Nowhere.

Moments Stolen sounds like title of a romance novel—it could well refer to the artist who must steal/snatch increments of creative time away from necessary, survival jobs, who must carve out physical spaces in tiny SRO hotel rooms to do their work. Transman recalled when he continued composing his fine literature AUTUMN CHANGES on a desktop 2 one half feet square with room only for the typewriter itself and one sheet of paper besides it, in a hotel room no bigger then a slice of a regular room, which he shared with Jasmin, 2 parrots, & 2 cats.*
  *Ariel & Bijou, Benny—the orange cat; —and Mr. Mew, a grey.

Notes & evidence about this dehumanizing system, under which we labor: SSI Disability, Soc Sec; it discourages thrift, it encourages a pauper class. Can't have over $2,000 in the bank. My shrink says many of her caseload monitor their bank accounts religiously—if they dare be *one dollar* over $2,000 they can have *all* the money snatched out of their account—plus cut off of SSI. Promptly loosing health care. Which means if you have scrimped, saved, gone hungry, recycled aluminum cans out of the gutters to save a tiny nest egg for your protection against unforeseeables of the future—such as having to leave your housing, needing large rent-move-in deposit for a new place, moving expenses, etc, or ill health, and you have the allowed amount--$2,000 in savings, *and your SSI check comes in*—destined to go immediately out again to the rent—but in passing momentarily thru your account, it reflects $2,890, then you can be instantaneously cut off of your disability check, and your medical benefits!

If they are poor or not backed up by some institution or individual, the indigent artist must climb a nearly insurmountable hurdle into a niche of success, recognition, comfort. They are forced to labor for wages, thus cutting drastically into their time; they may not be able to afford or access scholarships, university programs; by geographical location they may be too far away to get hooked up into an arts circle, they must walk a precarious rocky road up to that carved out place in time, wherein their work is now seen by a public, appreciated, thus granting them funds; monies, which translate into time, supplies, rents, to accommodate their situation for the rest of their lives. This is what most of us strive for, as simultaneously struggling intellectually, emotionally, spiritually and physically to climb the pinnacle of our talents, our artistic expression.

Oh on my way after going to the Foundation Center today, on O'Farrell street, passed by St. Mortiz hotel; was looking into its drab interior thru a locked door, when an older man came up, turned his key in the lock—we chatted briefly; he informing me the rates were good--$200 per week. I told him, back in 1967, I had paid $13.50 per week there for a room. How times change! At those current prices my entire Soc Sec+ Disability checks would just cover this amount, with $5 remaining to spend per month! Renters rebate yearly, if saved and judiciously doled out; works out to an additional $37 per month, and my art—if I keep it going-- has come in a range of $75-$200 a month. Food giveaways provide the remainder, and government health care—minus the fee we now must pay in part for medications, thanks to the vile, heartless and cruel Republican party—which was entirely gratis to the semi-destitute senior poor before the plutocrats gained the White House 8-years ago, yes, Dear Children, all medicines were once absolutely free. This is my sorry financial statement!

This evidence is why people murmur about revolution—which means change. Change by peaceful means, --or violent. Babylon Falling bookstore, under its neon lights from the 15-foot high ceiling, where we had many conversations, ranging from highly charged politics, to gossip--- to great fun humor:

Red: Jasmin was disgraced by both sides of her family, her fathers father and mother both, her mothers side due to her father, Jasmin's grandfather, because back in those days, in the 1800rds, they had big families and the 6th or 7th child was pledged to the church—to be a priest or a nun; and her father was pledged to be a priest but he ran off with this woman—Jasmin's grandmother. And her fathers mother had disgraced *her* family in Madras, India, for running off with a man not chosen to be her husband, and of a different race. Likewise his Algerian father, who ran off with this woman not his race, and poor. And Jasmin herself was a disgrace by being a lesbian.

Donny (a certain older gentleman --anarchist --from Latvia): My family is full of disgrace, but it formed me well I think. It was a good example to me as a child when, my mother was thrown out of church by the minister for being drunk. It was at a christening. He smelled alcohol on her breath, and told her she had to leave. She cussed out that minister right and left. This was a great thing to me as a child, and at that moment the spirit of revolution was born inside me.

From behind the cashiers desk can be heard Sean's words to a parting associate:

Ultimate respect dawg, peace.

One artist after another arrives at the bookstore; it is a font of collective imagining; yesterday Emory Douglas, acrylics. Shaun Roberts & tall Alex, photography, film. Today Chris, C-3 baring electronic photos of his ill art—nurses, night nurses, hospitals, Tuberculosis patients all dying in his fine ink stroke illustrations on ghoulish green paper.

Oh, PS; just finished up the Kemperer Diary vol. 2, after a 2-month detour thru Russian politics; via Siljack.

This I know also, Dear Children, that we are created by a Creator. Goddess, God, Allah, Hashem, etc., its not simply a great intelligence & a biology which formed us out of the sweeping cosmos—we are created also by Love, an unending Love. This divine intelligence is not simply a mega genius to a proportion unimaginable by the human brain, It also is suffused with Love, is Love, gives Love freely.

A Very Short Dialogue:

Red: (To cat): Aren't you lucky to sleep on my bed cat, peoples beds are comfortable.

Cat: we cats make our own beds in the wilds. They are comfortable.

Red: Yes, in the wilds. Where you run free; *and you hunt birds for food*. Aw, that's terrible.

Cat: What do *you* eat person? What do you kill for food?

Red: Oh, yeah, well, yes, we kill animals for food.

Cat: *Small* animals?

Red: Yes some small animals, like chickens… rabbits.

Cat: Do you kill **cats** for food!?

Red: No! Cat! We love Cats!

Spirit of Truth: We are all comrades.

AM Saturday June 7
So, for 6 months now, he is where he wants to be; writing and painting—no longer the nagging regret of a talent wasted—for 40 years—funded, by a tiny grant (Social Security & SSI) decently housed (Saturday; smoke from mental patient in basement filtering up thru sub standard walls). (They want their lobby nice---but they don't want to take care of their tenants.)

29

Red was alive, active; according to Dr. Sam he was comparatively healthy: —*Many people younger then you have multiple physical problems.* So I create.

Now, waiting for some great thing to happen in my life.

What is most important—in order:

    1. *My Word.* -- Hashem.
    2. Your art.
    3. Love together and shared with the world.

As he adds his voice to the dis-empowered must take out time to dis some dirt:

There's an evil growing, seen among some lesbians, black people; and gay men—almost always effeminate ones-- an evil which is partially of their own making, and another part, societal induced upon them. Most definitely among effeminates. These snappish gay men-women, high drama drag queens, failed part-time transvestites, and evil tranny girls are comprised of hate. ---It is this specific type, to which I refer, not all of them, not even most, --who reflect badly upon their kind. Which goes to prove once again that it is not good for society as a whole to go along with, endorse, or maintain a structure, which harms some of its population. For this leads to a great hate, a Great Hate upon their victims part, which they carry perpetually, in a torch of infamy, unless somehow discovering the Great Heart to dispose of evil which comes their way—thereby learning to deflect it—and continue to try to be lovely gay men-women, drag queens and sweet tranny girls. The hate that brews continuously within the narrow breast of the evil ones feeds our community with a poisonous milk which spreads more hate out into the world; their tight loins give birth to vengeance, evil, anger, and rage in an unholy creation! People who pass by them barely avoid ice-cold dagger thrusts of their piquant tongues; innocent people who are treated meanly by them soon grow to hate anybody who looks like them! *I know God doesn't want me to hate. For S/He has told me so, thru a powerful dream which came to me just as I transitioned to being a Christian in the 1970's.* Thought old Transman bitterly. He had tried vigorously to dismiss the Hate from his heart and mind, but the abuses of the day heaped this upon him in great enough doses, that it was impossible to ignore.

PM Saturday June 7
One afternoon @ Bookstore he had recounted to the other young gentlemen there present, upon a caffeine-high—the following:

> Now I will tell classic story full of sadness, about a former web mistress, let's call her Alice, for anonymity's sake—although she is dead. Gratis, Alice had been my webmistress—coming over by bus to our small hotel room to work on our newly purloined Internet computer. We paid her with a dinner plus carfare both ways. Finding out later it was a hustle, as Alice secretly had obtained a buspass, and simply pocketed the change we gave her. We too were very poor. I realize now these cheap dinners were not worth the amount of work she did—that I could have shown her more love. Could have sacrificed more off my table to give to her --(Also thought she stole a box of teabags.)
>
> Alice also had taken upon herself the job of secretary to a TS/TG organization—in which she was soundly dis-sed (criticized & called-bad names) by several acid tongue members. Faithfully Alice answered my e-mail requests to do this job and that, concerning my site; and regularly we saw each other at the trans group, a TG/TS support group, which met at Pacific Center in Beserkley. One week Alice did not return my e-mail, then another week passed. She also missed the TG/TS support group meeting—which she had agreed to facilitate. The following week we met, no Alice, again. Afterwards, that evening, on the front porch of the lovely old Victorian center we stopped to chat, as usual:
>
> Red: Yuh know, Alice hasn't returned my e-mails, and she always does. And, she's not here at group the second week in a row. Maybe it's stupid, but I'm worried about her…
>
> Miscellaneous Trans Woman: Oh yes, I noticed the same thing! She promised to do my taxes for me—she does every year, but she hasn't called, like she said she would! I wouldn't have mentioned it, but now that you said something…

Another Trans Woman (hovering worriedly amid the others): Well I've been concerned about Alice too. Let's give her a call…. Does anybody know her phone number?

Red: I think her phone was disconnected.

1st TG Woman: Then maybe we should take a drive over there…

Now this was easy enough as some kind person would always give Alice and Red and a few other poor souls lifts to the doorway of their home, or to the subway station. (BART). Fairly soon a committee was appointed between 4 of the women who knew Alice well, and they arranged to go over to her house that very evening. What was recounted to Red later, was sad; it sent a chill pall over his heart. This is what they later found. —Approaching Alice's house in a very privileged, expensive area, they found, as usual, the front of it completely overgrown with untrimmed bushes. They picked their way up the stepping-stone path as many had seen Alice do before when they dropped her off ---after the group was over, after the fun, the sharing—to go home to that strangely dark, unkempt abode, her dress swirling away into the night mists modestly hidden by an expensive coat, chin to ankle length; revealing only her high heel pumps with a glimpse of hose, designer purse, hair in a bouffant; --and pushing aside boughs of low-hanging fir trees found the door. They knocked & rang the bell fifteen minutes, no one answered. Finally one of those large, muscular gals gave that front door a push—it opened—to the length of a burglar chain; there, sitting in a chair, leaned backwards against the door was Alice. She did not answer their greetings. Was deathly silent. Frantically the gals went around to the back of the house, searched the door, the windows, trying to figure out away to get in; and finally in desperation called the police. Shortly the blue uniformed officers arrived, the door was speedily broken down, and Alice was found dead. We tried to figure out what had happened. It pieced together as something like this. Alice had transitioned to female with absolutely no preparation nor gradual adjustment to the realities of harsh public opinion like do many trannys who begin their adolescent lives by going in drag upon occasion. No longer steady, bland John, to whom the neighborhood had been accustomed for 50 years but middle-aged Alice, emerging as a butterfly from its chrysalises, her sex change was observed with

32

horror by neighbors, relatives, and soon, after a lifetime of hard work in an office, she found herself strangely unemployable. Originally being raised to be a straight upper middle class white man—with all those ethics imposed upon men—of fortitude, of having to bare difficulties silently—Alice had not told anyone in the group of her financial straits. That the gas, electric and phone lines had been turned off from lack of payment. That her aged parents, now deceased, had not paid the property tax on the old family home for 10 years, during their terminal sickness, and the city was getting ready to acquire it—for back taxes, and she was being kicked out into the streets. Her stoicism even now as a transsexual woman attired in her deceased mothers frocks, (quite lovely) not indicating her true state of silent, desperate poverty went so far as to refuse to go down to the welfare department and at least get food stamps, for which she was well qualified, housed or not. Alice was starving, slowly, to death. She was under terrific stress. Those acid jabs at her from a few evil tongues at her new unpaid job as secretary in the TG organization did not help. At her age, her heart probably gave out. The preliminary autopsy did not suggest foul play---suicide---a second autopsy came back, also negative, and no more was heard of the matter. Her funereal was attended by a small church full of transsexuals-- seated on one side; & married male transvestites on the other; with a few straights, and a Transman or two scattered in between; who all stood up and personally gave testimony to Alice's intelligence, helpfulness, and altruistic views of humankind...

*

In his lonely rooms where the old Transman was busy scrambling up the jungle gym bars of his career—attempting to establish himself into posterity--he dwelled metaphysically, partially in daydreams:

> Will I be famous because of a cult of personality? Perhaps I will live a simple life—funded, housed, in habitat with a lover in a marriage, surrounded by friends & performing an occasional show.

And occasionally subsisted in memory of the fun times he'd had before, when he & the ex-wife were in show business:

> There was a time, we were doing theatre; I was a stage hand, and there was a closing scene when the hero/ine a male transvestite had

to be lifted up in a swing 40-feet above stage; this was done by counter weights—two ropes came down in the wings, one stage left, the other stage right, and 3 men pulled at each side. Well somebody wasn't at their post for this one performance, so suddenly the swing goes jolting up, up, up, into the air, with these two guys hanging onto their end of the rope for dear life, it runs out with the end of the rope disappearing about 10 feet in the air, because one guy is missing; so they shout 'Help!' Just as they were disappearing away, 15, 20 feet, rising rapidly up into the dusty loft of the theatre; Red leapt upon the fast unwinding rope which still dangled down, trailing from a coil on the floor; that made it stop, but didn't reverse the action, and this other guy jumps on the rope behind Red and down they all plummeted. Fell on to the worn old boards of the theatre; a heap of stagehands in a jumble of arms and legs. And here's the star, up there 40-feet in the air, kicking her high heels showing off her long, beautiful shaved male legs in fishnet stockings, her thick hammer secreted in her crotch—busting its fishnet seams--a tight bustier forming fleshy breasts on her male chest; & pretty lipstick, mascara face framed by lace just lip-sincing away, rocking on her swing like nothing unusual had happened.

More political discussion: Privately agreed with friend who had been a Hillary Clinton supporter, he'd be too demoralized; voting for Hillary and Obama if they were on the same ticket, Transman thought, that's the same as me! This friend states he might vote for McCain; so have a few others, I cannot! The Republicans will cut my SSI money!

A little brush with mortality last night. Blood pressure. Salt. After Carlos leaves town, and no more restaurant-dining, the salt intake drops.

Although great artists of the last 2 centuries are great reading source for me, cannot help to think, what they were doing through the wars, and revolutions, which transpired during their lifetimes. Stein, Picasso; were they speaking out? Protesting? Being arrested—like Dostoyifsky?

Dear Children; always consider the mental-factor. Not simply economics. The rich plutocratic man buys up all the houses on the block. A small house on the next block sells to an individual buyer.

34

"Why did we let that house slip thru our fingers?" Asks the rich plute. The above example illustrates the fault of the putting of everything into a political realm and not considering the psychological factor. When fighting the good fight every tactic and analysis and weapon must be used, —and not discredited as 'modern day bourgeoisie hocus pocus.' It is a fact that powerful people hate to see anyone else with power. The more they have the more they must take. The sign least sign of any one acquiring even the smallest amount of power worries them terribly—on the psychological level—and they go to draconian lengths to stamp that tiny power out. It is a beneficent and well –adjusted mind that can tolerate power in others.
--COMPASSION-2007.

The future is God's wild card to play. The future is totally God's, and no one knows it, unless it be revealed to them—by God.

This said in COMPASSION:

For so long I had a writers task, having been blessed with that vision and ability to start early—age ten or twelve, writing poetry, later novellas, and continuing on, now at age 64 so that after all this time I thought life would just keep going on like this, me simply putting my ideas, my great plots for justice down on paper. You should know that one of these days the time will come to put into action the sympathies which you have held for so long, those close to the heart. Those issues you've spoken impassionedly about, discussed & ruminated over in your small study groups, concerning those situations of injustice on earth which rankles your ire to such a fiery degree!

Russian revolutionaries of 1800rds. Who knows what those muthafuckas wuz thinken', as they fried meat in skillets w/grease dropping cigarette ashes on the floor, tipping up the vodka bottle to their lips; because they knew they didn't have long to live.

Sunday AM June 8
Interesting part about my history is that I led the queer life, exclusively; not the artist life, not the university circle; but the taverns, and 'certain' streets of homosexuals; lesbians, trans folk. All those cold nights in drafty bars. Evening Descends Upon the Poolhall

35

is done, and now I've begun one which is to feature two expressive figures, on a vertical canvas 30" x 24".

We must step on the framework of the Lord(ess)! The Lord holds the crossbeams, the rafters, the subfloors in place! Eternally! It is here we must walk and nowhere else.

Well as said, am fighting against time. Condo conversion of landlords greed evicting me out into some minuscule roach infested room not safe for me or pets, advancing older age; disabilities of physical mobility… Paint as my life depended upon it! Maybe can gain a foothold in the art world—enough to pay my way thru many seasons! Manic chain-smoker in basement pollutes the air on weekends, can't turn on fan in window, kitchen leaches second-hand smoke into itself from below! God save me!

Land management company sends plumber out to fix multiple leaks in bathroom; he does shoddy work—just fixes the bare essentials, the wall remains broken, tiles caved in, shoddy cheap workmanship, they don't care. I could take anyone to see these holes under the kitchen sink, the missing faceplate on wall sockets beside the stove, the holes under the toilet where the pipes feed into the wall. Smoke continues to leek into my kitchen like before—yet management company forbids us to place signs on door, mine to insure delivery of parcel services for my book shipments; --it might cheapen the property value! At halls end, the Chinese family have been forced to take down their gay red/gold good luck scroll they had hung—for over 10 years—at the property management company's office the stupid branch property manger won't answer 15 calls I place about these substandard blights plus the smoke—and the rents are driven up $300 per month to a new tenant. This is a rip-off, it is greed, it is probably illegal, but who can afford a lawyer. A revolution is called for. Hopefully not so desperate as the kind Billy Bradford performed in STAGE DOOR, *execution by firearms of these greedy parasites.*

People's first reaction to a problem is to ignore it, then repress it, and hope it will go away. Society has no listening ear to the people who act out, who create this problem, or, no heart nor desire to help change their situation. So the problem simmers and grows, and multiplies.

For so long, generation after generation back into archaic history, us transfolk were maligned, erased, and removed. But today there is far too many of us to ignore.

When I was at the height of my powers of creativity, my schedule was very simple. Painting a portion of the day—6 hours; writing another, 6-hours, a small bit of animal care, dog walking in the park, preparing a meal very simply, by boiling; fixing coffee in an aluminum drip coffee mug with the column in the middle—then going out for 2 hours to a gay bar every night of the week. Today my schedule is more complicated.

So we have all been racked and turned around tossed and pushed around this way and that.

If you are trans and knew it from day 2or 3, you have had a very disruptive life. Even if you didn't show this to the outside world. Most of us --90% illustrated our gender dysphoria from our primary years under age 5—and immediately caught hell from it by parents, siblings, the outside world. Those who hid their masculinity or femininity underwent the internal pressure this secret double life mandates. The straight people, they had a normal life.

It is quite common for small people to dream of power. & so, the old man did:

> Red Jordan Arobateau; I want to carve my name into art history! I see it nowhere.

Chair pulled up between two computers inside his closet; out in the main, studio room 5 lights blazing, aimed at canvass on makeshift easel; Wedding Day. Acrylic on canvas, 24"x 36". When he had selected it, in vain struggling to get a fresh, bigger canvas down from on top of loft, where it was by now wedged inbetween others, many boxes, canvass frames, rolls of canvas, and other miscellany, it was impossible to budge as now the largest canvas were trapped between this paraphernalia and the ceiling only 3 feet above; so he had settled for one of the pre-stretched more slender canvasses—purchased in anticipation of this great retuvia to his fine visual art nearly ten years

37

before; knowing it would hold two figures, (faces with expression) and would be slightly too cramped sideways to portray any intent, which as of yet he did not know what it was going to be, so the emerging Arms of the Temple, embracing the newlyweds must be suggested by their curvature in yellow, blue black and red line swatches. Wedding Day.

The Transman sat there battling cultural erasure throughout the long night into the early morning.

PM Monday June 9
Regarding your ex-wife Jasmin, what do you see? --Brokenness. Hurt. Pain. Is she drifting further away from me?

> Tips and fees:
> Waitresses (Back in the day 10%.) 15-20%
> Literary agents 20%
> Ho house 60/40% split. 60 to the house.
> Amazon They take 55%
> Art Galleries?

Saturday AM June 7
(Nothing reported.)

Wednesday AM June 11
As stated, my art is a stepchild. Spent an hour after setting up paints, canvas, working on Rondo edition of OBEDIENCE TO THE CALL OF ART, washing clothes in sink, calling bank about Bancroft funds, making list of what money orders for rent, inventory etc., need to be purchased---as can't leave too much money in bank or will be cut off of SSI check/medical coverage as previously documented. Now, closing file of OBEDIENCE and the canvas awaits. Is there any room left in the schedule to paint? Wedding Day is too flat. Needs depth, shading, arts expertise. It takes time!

AM Early (this means after midnight) Thursday June 12
Taking instruction from a street found-canvass, poorly done, nevertheless see shading under eyes, half of neck, under chin, etc. Fellow Peace was kind enough to rescue this for me from garbage can—finding two abandon; he kept one. He has also bought RETROSPECT and plans to buy a poster also. Sister Andrea purchased a RETROSPECT, and sat admiringly thumbing thru its

colorful glossy pages in a classic high femme lounging pose, dignified, elegant & refined, with her little Lady dog, Eartha Kitt faithfully at her side, either frolicking or safely within its lair inside her purse. Brother Eli also purchased RETROSPECT, to go with 2 posters he has already. Thanks for the support yuh all!

Must say undergoing very rough part of my life, isolated, not enough friends to fill the days but I continue to work. One thing is am dieting, and steadily losing weight, tho slowly; this may account for my lack of energy.

Having to rearrange his agenda so as to not be in my kitchen at night—smoke from downstairs troll—must hustle and bustle about in morning preparing dinner for that night—and this taxes Red's heart more then unusual. He did not like the extra burden of having to do shitwork in the morning! He need a relaxed schedule—get up morning with coffee and alarm clock, pull out painting gear, wash up, weigh himself see how much fraction of a pound have lost since the day before, put on painting clothes and grumble about slowly, circling the easel with wary looks, appropriating the muse with trepidation, contemplating the steep uphill climb of this mornings creation.

For my 2nd Retrospect, must do a thumbnail representation of all paintings in Number One—with an explanation of symbolism of each! People want to know! And all the new paintings in it will be full-sized with their appropriate descriptions, because it seems people are fascinated to understand this.

New found compatriots @ Babylon Falling; they are all young, sitting around bushy-tailed, eating hardily, drinking gallons of coffee & high energy drinks, full of hopes and ambitions, climbing up in their careers; they've seen disappointments before, but not constant disappointment, not like Transman had in his much longer life. Old Transman stopped a moment to consider the rest, those like him but several generations removed; his own unique history deep in poverty, struggling behind total segregation, lack of opportunity, lack of decent health care: then further back, a century and half ago, to slaves, his ancestors before him forbidden to read or write, the disappointment lasted from sun up over the slave fields to sun down again non-stop over their short lives.

Saturday AM June 14

A Being such as God is so suspicious to many women—if their sole knowledge of God is thru bible teachings—in which women are portrayed in an afterthought, as second class citizens, as slaves, to their husbands and under the rule of their sons and fathers and brothers. I have no doubt in my mind as to the divinity of the Holy Bible, Koran, Torah; it is handed down to humans thru human devices—and man is imperfect. God is Speaking and has always Touched all who call upon Her; but Her literate and recited Word are concretized in the technology of writing----and given in a patriarchal society, so naturally they have to be encoded in the mores & codes of the day; these superior tools have traditionally been appropriated by males, each skill and knowledge of them hoarded by males, and all others, women, slaves, outcasts, strangers, prisoners, kept from the knowledge of them. So man has written himself into the human book thru a slanted, and prejudicial viewpoint—harming all others who read it; worse, discouraging them from it entirely *and* from even believing in our Great Being Who gave these words from out of the heavens!

*

Life is better with art. Before you gaze at an empty wall. Nothing. Now you look at something beautiful, or interesting, some *thing!*

As time goes by your motivations for art may change, modify. Young, he might have said *I am working for fame and money*; older he might say, *I'm hoping to make some money at it, and forget the fame-- that is no longer relevant.* One thing which stays the same— the desire to create beauty, to have expression.

One big mistake the hos' make and so does Amerikkka Kapitalism— they value the individual by how much money they are worth. T was totally discounted thus, being a poor man, and still unsuccessful in his trade.

June 17

Struggling with the beast to copy my newly edited OBEDIENCE.

Just before the beginning of the Russian revolution—and after the freeing of the serfs, who still remained destitute—the countryside was

40

littered with revolutionists; students, middle, and upper class Russians who believed in, studied, talked about, and worked for—revolutionary change. Has our own country Amerika reached that saturation point yet?

Finally return to notes after 1-week absence—putting final touches on OBEDIENCE, the Rondo---to take to Bookstore. Was a hellish day today, up in morning, cigarette smoke from basement troll, couldn't paint because had to get out to send OBEDIENCE to Lulu Print-On-Demand @ bookstore, early, bright-eyed and bushy tailed; however Sean completely swamped in work again. Sat there meaningless for several hours—then onward to get my head shrunk up at Trans Center, having made no progress at all on OBEDIENCE. *I Will Bless.* Hashem said. Thought about this. Those who get blessings from the Most High are truly richly and abundantly blessed. Vollia! There in the street was a $1 bill, spread out flat, green, & white in the gutter. Took it into pocket. A few car lengths further on my walk, --another dollar! Spread out like the first! Thinking somebody lost their bus fare, continued on my way. THEN, in the bus stop gutter—more single dollar bills, folded in half! Quickly the Transman pocketed these, crumpling them in his fist, shoving the wad into his pocket while dragging the silver cart along with the other hand bouncing & jolting erratically—there, hot on the trail of the four singles are more singles, and, a pile of money; 3 fives, a twenty! Hastily he stomped on the twenty—just in case a stray gust of wind might sweep it away! MIRACLE! Pleased he went on to his shrink, money stuffed into his pockets. Here, his shrink, (after talking about it for some weeks) purchased The Blue Dog poster! Yeah! THEN, after Trans center, the now-jolly Transman proceeded up to Van Ness avenue, loaded with money, heading towards the office supply store to get long needed floppy desk crates. THERE! On the gutter—a single dollar bill stretched out flat---and near it A TEN DOLLAR BILL! This eleven dollars found in a completely different location then the first pile!

All in all the day Red found $50! Plus earned $20. ---He headed back to bookstore after having spent much on necessary items—there, in the same place that the money was found—a can of catfood! Mr. Fluffy's favorite brand! What a find!

Was not so lucky with OB's progress. Sean was busy until 8:15. At last minute he helped Red set up his file which the Transman hastily gave a look over—finding two dozen mistakes, his own two spell-checks had missed (one on each of his two computers)--- then log-on to Lulu. Miss Lulu was semi down for the evening—and he could not send it. Here the matter rests.

> Tomorrow is another day.
> --Scarlet O'Hara, Gone With The Wind, 1930's.

PS: I began to curse God to the heavens! How angry! All this waiting around the bookstore, then finally I get on, and the damn site is now malfunctioning! I caught my curse in midair! Had not Hashem blessed me with $70? Aw shit…. Transman thought… I should be happy. I'm thankful. Thankful Hashem. Bless you for your help!

Tomorrow is another day. A day in which to fulfill promise!

My father; a line of fine disgust etched onto his face in distaste for the job he was doing, daily, underpaid; tedious. My mother, her schizophrenic mad Mona Lisa smile; of cruelty, beauty, treacherousness. My own grin of unhappy mirth, using humor as a vent for sorrow—so much seemed funny then, and now, so much is funny, laugh so frequently; masking hurt, depredation.

It's a little depressing to hear about the musician who made a find—bought a bunch of old records and tapes for $10. It was all this great stuff you'll never hear or see again. Reel to reel tapes and old fashion records. And, the man walking thru Chinatown one night who came on a dumpster overflowing with big silver movie canisters. He opened one, it was an old Chinese art movie from the early days of cinema. Dumpster, tall as a person, two car lengths long; was filled to its top and overflowing with them—hundreds. The dumpster was outside an old abandon theatre that had shown these Chinese movies all during the 1950s, since the 1930s before television replaced movie houses and people stayed home instead of going out at night to a cold drafty motion picture palace full of strangers. The man went home got his car came back and hauled them all off to his basement—5 carloads full. The following night he went by the place again—the

42

dumpster was still there—and it was full again, of more movie canisters! Again he hauled them home. He went a 3rd night, there were a few more canisters. Then the dumpster was gone. It turned out the old theater had been owned by this ancient Chinese man, operated by him for 30-years, and he'd bought it from somebody else before him who'd had live shows with Chinese opera singers & actors as filler between the Chinese films. The man had kept all the old movies in these canisters in the storage rooms in the attic of the theater. And when he died, the place was taken over, cleaned out, gutted; to be remolded, and turned into a department store or a bank or some other mundane business. No longer films because the average person doesn't go out solely to a movie house for entertainment; this industry is no longer thriving. And all these priceless relics were just tossed out by the workmen. Again—good stuff you'll never see again. It is depressing to think about. Nothing is permanent. *These things that moss and earth corrupt...*

And so our records, our history to moss and earth return... *put not your fortune in these things...*

> Put your faith
> not in what moss and earth does corrupt.
> Go to where the days are kept.

Its all about our souls long voyage; The Path.... Well all my books have been about the long poverty of the soul. Each and every one, from the famous LUCY & MICKEY to the not known, but great HOW'S MARS? All of them. Women struggling in the streets; against poverty, cruelty, mafia thugs, and oppression. The indomitable human spirit wins; it shines thru.

*

If you have a friend who is a GLB or T they many not live as long as if they were straight. And thus, part of the norm, who have prospects far and beyond the ghetto walls. They have not had marriages, some not even friends.

> Poor people
> There is something for you

Did Damian Marley reference the poverty-queer with his fine song? We are a little-known minority. Nobody knows our name. For the rich gays have sold us out.

A Mercedes-Benz car baring a fascism-of-wealth insignia on its hood coolly slides by; puffs of diesel fuel toot out of its twin silver exhaust pipes. He lived in a neighborhood changing; going up, up, up,

2 brown United Parcel Service vans, side-by-side, mate in the street. Red lived between shipments of his books from the print-on-demand; so excited to unwrap his titles with their glorious Technicolor covers; breaking the monotony of his sex-charged life. He wondered briefly was one of those brown vans headed down to his place right now, baring a package; then his thoughts went right back to nervously ruminating about the yet downloaded OBEDIENCE.

Red participated in a dance to the omnipresent reggae beat, while hovering around Sean's cashier's desk. Sometimes Red had to remind himself *he's running a place of business*, when the young man, busy reordering new shipments of books & toys and political art stopped to ring up the occasional customer—while Red's latest book floppy disc burned a hole in his pocket in nervous worry.

His books—2 slim volumes sit, not known by name —packed within a sea of 3,500 in Sean's bookstore. His RETROSPECT face up on the display table; it's smaller, thinner then others of its genre—tho it was of the most original. It is times like this I'm very deeply & exceedingly glad that rock star from London threw his million dollars into the fire! Just because I had in my wallet only enough for two burritos —Food to last three more days plus ground beef in a bowl, cooked myself (by boiling) w/chopped onions, green pepper, a can of tomato paste.

Sun shines outside Babylon Falling. Its like being at a sidewalk café in NYC or Paris France (where I have not been myself but for many times in TV travels and imagination via intellectual books, Baldwin, Miller, Djuna Barnes).

Mexican Muralist; Rocheford; has just entered door of Babylon Falling via brown cardboard box disbarked from one of those brown

UPS vans. Red studied work of David Sigueiros, which he didn't recall having viewed before. Fascinated at inspired colors; muscular poses of the human form inspired by Dali, I'm sure. *Great!* Had he seen David Siqueiros in his peripheral helter-skelter art history education? Dreamily he gazed thru the window of the bookstore: *Observe the master brushstrokes of the sky blue & white swirls on light blue.*

This is a time am not sure what the revolutionary must do, ever more important to stay strong, to continue to form collations, to education people, to recruit, to educate, to go into the prisons with hope, to give analysis, form, and structure to the impossible miasma of the way things work and dissect what is happening now in which the average person is hopelessly ensnared, a giant evil net, which we can't get loose of from day one to our last gasp of breath. --& just to maintain; maybe even until the next generation.

Even if you are a sturdy strong revolutionary, but the system has tied your hands; so you feel you are doing nothing! Don't give out! Don't give in! Don't give up! So, I did not be serious about holding a regular job, tho I did. Chose art as a way to fight back against unfairness of the world & to avenge mothers state and fathers state & now my own. —Not to be a part of the shitwell of the common denominator---contributing to universal pain as does a criminal; to the status quo as does the ordinary person —but be as the extra ordinary person whose payment is sacrifice & going on & on in a long journey with no rewards.

So tomorrow comes---rises as a new building rises level by level in cement.

PM Thursday June 19
Nothing to report tho stuff has happened, am tired, sleeping too much I think—11 hours-- must be weather change from cold to hot swinging back to cold, then hot. Or is it my slow diet, which is actually reducing my fat.

AM Friday June 20
Suffering from book post-partum. OBEDIENCE has gone to print, global, —cost $130 for ISBN plus the account, which places the book in different bookstores via internet here & there, and two copies of it.

Sean vacates his vulture chair, Red slides into it for the duration. Surfing the Internet---Djuna Barnes holding court @ Patchin Place, Greenwich Village for 42 years; solitary, with her whisky bottle & old photographs of the European days; a recluse. *Hashem, let my life be better then hers.*

Red entertained himself with another dance, in-place, himself ensconced in the vulture chair, stretched out over Sean's cashiers desk to peer intently at computer, rocking is body back & forth; just then a customer comes over, book in hand, the youthful proprietor must switch back from stocking inventory to discuss titles & hopefully ring up customer; Red adroitly moves aside, hesitates by the window seat, adjudging wither/not to stay, & walks out the door—goes outdoors to wait while Sean reels them in like a big fish—not wanting to put the kybosh on the tran$action. Day haze in sun.

Large city metropolis; birds of seaport on all roofs. The higher ramparts jut up to the sky. Sky light blue w/cirrus swirls of white clouds.

EREEK! EREEK! Cry the seagulls here in the inner city. They give inspiration—just as if us grimy populous was at a sandy beach at oceans edge, at civilizations beginning! Wind sweeping thru & whizzing traffic-- all together-- a symphony, which imitates crashing of physical water waves. Sun-run day.

Red standing in front of Babylon Falling like the watchman of the watchtower; reading VK as evening descends; soon will be too dark to see text & will go inside. He casts his eyes up from time to time where shades of night are falling over uneven rows of 5[th,] 6th story apartment buildings. Recalled 50 years ago, how he wildly relished the days last minutes of play at baseball in the alley; sun descending; their childhood shrieks of fun, the thrill of competition, the feel/sound that came from the knock of a softball against his wooden bat at twilight—must be home for dinner—A Tomboy's Life.

All evening long Red hung out here, getting bits of information he could not get elsewhere. Quickly & for free. Computer skills; the idea for the POD *fine arts* publishing.

Night. Late. Sit here behind closed bookstore grill; wait for proprietor to close shop—totalize on computer the receipts for the day; gaze at them, groan & complain:

Totally unacceptable!

*

All these last paintings I feel to be mediocre & not up to the stellar heights of The Arab with his/her translucent, transcendent expression. Waiting to see how Raiment Of Love progresses. This is the last of these latest 5. That particular one sandwiched in time between now, and my last big efforts back in that era of painting frenzy 1968-1970. Must push my limits!

I would just go as far as I can—running.

An artist, whose life matures, may become many things. Because their now every-day-business was once a hot bursting of creation—:

> Bobby Dylan—became a businessman of his own music creations.
> Jimi Hendrix—died young.
> Janis Joplin—died young.
> Shakespeare *was* a business & he knew it; kept writing to employ the actors of the theater he owned. Wrote fast making more & more plays, straight-out quill on parchment, making no mistakes, nor changes.

Stare at my painting easel, bare, no canvass on it, the paint tube cabinet not pulled out in middle of floor to resume working. Stagnate.

Some of you may be interested in how I got to selling my stuff, making copies of it, de facto becoming my own 'publisher.' I began by being so much of an outsider—my creations, quantities of originals addition after addition adding up in my room, not going anywhere, no recognition, not hooked up at a university department, or into a small publishing circle, so due to my outcast, black sheep, apartheid status decided must take matters into my own hands; and imitate the forms and means I saw—beginning with the poetic which is known to me now as the 'chapbook' with titles such as Train From Overbrook. A Child's Herstory Of Birth.

47

Those of the church/synagogue will criticize—*you need the discipline of regular attendance, of prayer, of torah.* I have the regular discipline of art. It is up to me to stay in touch with Hashem and be inspired. To touch the mantle of Jesus and be saved—out of my blues, depression, or defeatism, and get encouragement for today and for the future journey. I must continue!

I feel randy... I'll paint a picture! ---Wild Whores In The Night! In black, jet black, velvet; voluptuous woman, her back arched in estrus; breasts jutting forward swollen in lust; eyes closed ecstatically with flaming blue-black hair blowing back-- as would be a horseback rider at a gallop, red lips parted; she moans in rampant pleasure—the suitor, a satyr, also in black quite narrow physique; lean hipped, lean from so much copulation --plunging forward at the hips, his teeth gritted, eyes squinted with determination—he stands close, but not yet touching the whore—these are the central characters, others abound in sin suggested in the dark night sensuous sin backdrop! SSSSTTTT! GRRRRRRR!!!

Well, I think me, who knows so little about how to achieve happiness—and who wants it so much—have found a method to protect myself from the emotional disruptions—of cataclysmic intensity which are bound to come along in the stream of life. To have 5 solid basis instead of only one; like many people do, -- their one tenuous thread to the remainder of humanity, too easily severed, leaving them dead on earth suffering within eternal blues. Here are the other 4 solid positions:

> To have a lover/marriage, being of course the first.
> To have a career which gives one pleasure.
> To have a circle of friends.
> To have an altruistic interest or project in which one is involved with cohorts.
> To have God. God Eternal.

Well there is the five! Lets go over this with refined points—a career which gives one pleasure and is successful, and brings one acclaim-wither this be large or small, but certainly not semi-hidden away from public knowledge as is my art career as of now.

The surreal statement, which is the power behind the more or less mundane bride/groom of Wedding Day, is the spiritual embrace of the Temple behind the couple, in which sits the bluebird of happiness!

Woke this morning 6:30am—smell of cigarette smoke In My Studio! Had turned on fan too early & caught the dregs of the foul troll puffing away before he goes to work!

Hot out, again smoke, no friends call. Ennui. Struggle to do my work. Am fighting bears; ravenous bears!

So there is art everywhere in this town; Michelangelo's statuary, naked, hand on hip posing in a 3rd story apartment window. Infernal art college students and their projects, which will come to nothing. Many foreign students here are using this college in order to get a 4-year degree and pad their resume thus enabling them to officially work in the states & get green card; maybe emigrate in future. They will not employ art ever again in their lives! What a racket the owner of the college has! Charge them exorbitant rent, thus slowly buying up prime realestate in her name! She is a rent mogul in disguise, and far from being an art-loving art college authority. She is a connoisseur of quick realestate acquirements.

Sean is busily ruminating over a contract consisting of 25 draconian points; which signs over rights to your art perpetually, exclusively, and non-transferable to his store! It says such hideous stuff such as; *Artist agrees not to do anything with his or her own content.* **Retch! Ugh! Glog!**

Patience! Says Hashem. Wait! It will come to you. Wait *–like a pot simmers.*

The proprietor & customer are speaking of ----, a prolific author.

Me? Queries Transman from his nook

Proprietor: Not you—(to customer. & pointing to Red)--- He's got a shit load of books too.

Customer: Does he?

49

Red: Does he have more then me?

Sean: No. (To customer, pointing at Red) He's got 80-books.

Customer: 80!

Red: (Lame voice of Transman from his window seat): Titles! Not just books; it includes poetry collections & plays!

Red stood outside Babylon Falling, book under his arm. Low rows, like brown crags, buildings are creeping over the earth. The last songbird in this decaying city is warbling.

Oh God help us, or I don't know what we'll do!

Hashem says to keep on.

145.
PS, this is stupid! This stupid Journal has only one huge chapter since the beginning of the book! Chapter markings have become an afterthought with the advent of actual diary-like *dates!*

Yes your art interferes w/your social life—painted to the last minute, got to Trans Center, my peeps just gone. The food was eaten, the movie over. —Glad I worked, infinitely more—also missed my peoples. This all because of ennui: couldn't get up in the morning until twelve which pushed my schedule back.

The hot sunny empty days of summer stretches out, older now, when I was young I worked just a bit then went outdoors to hang out in the village with the gay kids. Made friends easily. Just fell into it.

SF inhabitants walk about in the dazzling sun; unaccustomed heat. See an old dike standing in front of the Seniors residence in her trousers, small shouldered men's shirt, bobbed hair, boots. Her life like my own. I remember the girls of the outlaw lesbian bars; she spread her thighs for her—to do what ever she could do. She went down—the sweet liquor smelling pretty lipsticked party girl mouth on her pussy in the backstreet hotel that rented to whores, hypes, criminals, and queers.

Long dark chocolate transgirl, lean limbed, she towers in high heel pumps, 6'5: high girlish voice singing in the outer rooms, somewhat unpleasant; obviously feels she's blessed with the tone and training enough to sing in public non-stop 45 minutes. Was relieved when she left.

As I walked I noticed in my linnear eye the glass pane of bus kiosk met the slanted sidewalk, which tapered into the end—in a word perspective. Lines meeting in perspective. Now here's the tie-in; at Babylon Falling:

> Red: Aw shit! Something told me to bring my coffee today goddamn it!
>
> Proprietor: Why make a big deal about it big guy! Come on.
>
> Red: Yea, I should be more positive
>
> Proprietor: Perspective my friend, not negative…

It confirms what the Spirit showed me yesterday.

It is true, I must be positive! See life from not such a me-centered *perspective!* See reality. In fact this heightened outburst in response to a minor incident, this exaggerated extremity is part of post-traumatic syndrome (PTS)—as a child no matter how minor, every abusive incident is the End Of The World. For as indeed a child whose mother turned into a raging hurricane of rage—it was.

I must try to look at things differently. First off, how very fortunate I am! Despite all these hardships!

So much to be grateful for, --- I am creating. I am allowed to have the tools. Despite my gender, my race, my status in life.

Well guess the important thing to remember Stay Positive! Put everything in perspective! Manage to get thru the worse days—the loneliest times, chin up, knowing in the future, only days ahead, hours head, lays fun! Fun, friendship, food, & merriment!

Met another artist today @ Scott's dressmaking shop; Anna Seven commented that his Oyster Eaters is like Van Gough's Potato Eaters. Both agreed they never heard of an artist who features—*blurred paintings*—on their website! Red/Anna agree that Van Gogh and each of them would have been friends.

Everytime walk down the street see a scaffold squatting on the sidewalk before him, struck up beside some apartment building where improvements are being made.

More towering erections crowd the poor out of this city. Daily upon his routes, dragging his silver cart full of books/art's prints for sale, on his way food-shopping, to Trans Center, & Bookstore, Red passed by these sites. He'd see the extra gauge rebar interwoven; twisted into columns of concrete pilings, its thin cement skin, on the exterior—only 8" wide. Strong, tall, one inch in diameter thick rebar: smaller gauge one-quarter rebar, twisted around and around, uniting them. Plywood frames set up, then poured full of cement. The 2" by 4" framing; and 1" thick CDX panels. One day, a newly dug hole. Stop to gaze down into the bottom of a construction pit—big open space; criss-crossed with a cement cat-walk. Fresh smell of lumber bracing. Clank/bang of corrugated iron sheets. Poured cement columns squared off in boards. Ladders. Machinery. Pipes. Wires. Scaffold walkways made of a bare board platform slung between pilings, stretched out over space.

Chet Helms fonky art gallery, replaced. Bookstores gone—but another beauty salon! —7 of them in 5 blocks of this street! Where the fine old Masters once held court from dusty tomes of yesteryear, now hear high lilting voice of the queens in their beauty parlor.

Will I too be lost?

Vainly the old man struggled with his art! It alone would save him! He might earn enough to secure permanent housing, monies to attend him when reaching an ancient age. Right now he struggled, as do all, with despair…. Ennui… tired depression.

52

The empty chair beside the easel; the closed cabinet full of paints in tubes; beckons.

*

UP IN HEAVEN

Cat emerges from the fantastically beautiful green lush jungle of Gods Great Garden of Eden baring a fish in its mouth, approaches a human friend.

Cat: I've caught you a fish. Will you cook my fish Red?

Red: Yes cat.

Red cooks fish in olive oil, butter, & herbs; with lemon; lets it simmer in a skillet. The sole fish turns into a pan of fish.

Red: Fish for all.

In heaven where one cooks a fish –all have fish.

So everybody ate their fish, savoring it & everybody had 1 large fish on their plate and when they were done eating this if they wanted more, their single fish turned into 3 fish & each has all they need, three fish or one, miraculous, God had set it up so all had enough, yet none was left over & so there was no waste. Always enough. Never any waste.

ON EARTH:

Worker in orange jumpsuit: This is 10-3; picked up a bunch of homeless debris; would like you to come by & pick it up before somebody busts it open.

*

Today outside the bookstore sunny rays beat down over constant breeze—is like being on the beach; lounging in a metropolitan Riviera.

3 blue-uniformed officers from the Coroner's Department; in white plastic gloves drag a deceased person's corpse in a pink plastic body

53

bag downstairs; bang, bang, bang, the corpse hits the steps; see the imprint of a human foot at the end of the bag. They turn the cadaver, lifting it now, onto a stretcher there is a full side view, bloated gut, expands the sack. More. Arms fold into place. The imprint of a head.

Mutters on this street; fragments of conversations about the death: 'poor Miss X; she didn't exercise, doctor told her to; blood clots...' etc. *She's at peace.* Transman thought, looking upwards at the blue white sky of the windy day. *A great peace.*

Slender Seniors' backs bent by the soil in his distant homeland in South America, pass by on streets of this Del Norte city, leaning on a cane... You got your head down, but you keep moving. Shuffling.

Slowly a line of shade creeps across the street; dark hits first upon the sidewalk on the far side of the block, then licks out over cars @ the curb; soon it will eat up the sunny asphalt, before it slowly devours the sidewalk upon which he stood; then darkness & cold falls.

> We have so much loved one another and do love one another.
> --VK

Hashem—bless all that I care for immediately. I keep them under my jurisdiction, & my love.

Well, I'll be honest—Kemperer's situation was worse then mine! Even despite that he had a faithful wife at his side thru thick & thin— hounded by the Gestapo during their every waking hour & in their fitful dreams.

146.
A quote spoken to trans man at the TS Clinic by Daisy, a trans woman, pretty; very passable Latina, who works in the straight world; stealth:

> Are we going to die here? We see each other every time; one day one of us won't be here.

Sex-worker girls sat hatching plots to make mo' money and do less work. The girls are in rare form tonight—Marylyn in particular who sings in falsetto.

All the good looken' women come out tonight—for the clinic. Andrea with her marvelous, fluffy, tiny, dog; pitch-black, curly fur, Eartha Kitt. Haut bourgeoisie.

Red had seen the evolution of queer in America. His peoples climb upward out of the shit of this world—to success. He now saw them holding pristine power in a safer, cleaner castle. After first having known the criminal underworld gay bar life, not so fine con artists, fences, strong-armed goons. The ever-present jukebox, red, blue, lime green & gold radiating an expansive solid air along with its tunes. An air tainted by corruption. Alleged Mafia connections. Organized crime, blood in pools on the bare wood floor. Gay, suicidal dikes & fags revolving from one nightclub to the next in their drunken boats, navigating bright lights along the strip of bar galaxies. Killing spirit, killing precious time in jail of apartheid created by 'normal' civilization, the 'proper & right clean society' which rules over us freaks who must scuttle around in the shadows. What passed off as fun, —was only excitement. It is so difficult. So, so, hard. Being the odd man out.

David Steinberg's Divas 2008 book release party @ Good Vibrations on Polk Strassa:

The small crowd of aficionados circulated around the 4 walls, gazing at David's fine work; pausing to nosh at a refreshment table—here Transman took his stand, dining vigorously and for free; a small plate clutched in one hand, fingers of the other plucking morsels. From time to time he'd join the ever growing throng to circulate, revisiting the Stars he knew. Viewing photos on the walls, here is a one: a Diva sitting in an obviously bar chair, in a cramped back stage dressing room between rows of hanging costumes; legs spread, a run in her stockings; glistening chain around her neck; her own hair (or a wig) bouffanted up and hanging long to her shoulders; a showgirl. Voices drone in background of the queer unconscious—you can just hear them; one impassioned:

Do you know how to work the system? — You lie! Girl! Tell them lies! Tell them what they want to hear! Get what you want!

Red gazed at them all and knew many. Alexis, Melanie, Daisy, Monika—who is dated 2006-- who died 6 months ago—not of HIV.

A sister, black; large scrotum and penis under a fishnet panty hose; see her in the back rooms, the cold rooms, the gender dysphonic hideaways—for those of our kind; moments before we see the light of day. Hang in there, sister! Brother!

Alejandra, Yvette; the beautiful bartender from Jezebel's club; my eyes return to Monika. Pleasant-mannered Monika. During her bottle-blond hair phase. Monika, her eyes glisten, looking out of her portrait; sad smile on her face until the last… Coy gaze, her hand on her shoulder.

Monika was always nice to me. Big red lips planted a soft kiss on my cheek every time we bumped into each other in the street; pretty Hispanic face; what a flirt! —In her better days. Was so shocked to see her turn up at Tom Waddell clinic suddenly so emaciated…when they get that thin, they've not much longer on this earth…. Monika's picture is off at the end in a corner—marking it as premier, muy importante—yet remote, most easy to miss. Other beautiful divas attend this event, in real life! Sashying into David's show fast, perfume-scented, atop high, high heels; decked out in fine dresses, furs, --- they catch sight of Monika, dying, in the corner, quickly avert their eyes---pretending they did not see! Or, that they have seen— nothing of consequence. Yet the observant can observe a drop of water well in her eye—threatening to ruin the mascara on her cheeks. And she walks on past, *runs past*—how many of them know but do not confess their own secret fates, the disease now circulating thru their own bodies; they avoid Monika's tender eyes, they postpone fate a few more years…

After having hobnobbed to the full of his capabilities, amid luminaries—Joni B, founder of Good Vibrations, Michael Rosen, another master photog—of kink, trans; demimondes to which we are accustom; he would depart. And finally, Teresa Sparks, trans gal who is liaison to the police department. Quite a trans success story! She

56

comments on how the Tenderloin is slowly being compressed; the hype, druggie, wino, insane, population is dwelling in what has become a containment area for them, as corridor after corridor is gentrified with sweeping changes. Upon saying goodbye to many glamorous divas who he knew, old Transman made his way out.

Cold wind now blows thru the once summer air. Outside; retrospective of the common economics, which slashes thru all classes, which impacts us all—sooner or later; -- a humanbeing bent all the way in half, his upper body stuck inside a garbage can on wheels.

147.
There are people in art world who have pushed their way to the top—relentlessly, thru cash, people they know, people they maneuver themselves into the position of meeting—these are not necessarily great nor even that good painters, only standard, with a few odd quirks or tricks which by which they can pass themselves off as creative. While as others of far greater, deeper ranging performance, languish by the wayside, totally unknown. Transman believed himself to be one of these, as he laboriously went about his studio routine. Thinking of titled, privileged lives… And then, like some of those Divas of the night before, staring out of the walls of the gallery he had led a life of a harried criminal.

First day, with resumption (after 40 years) of using a double pallet. It works well—now must scurry off to art supply to purchase second housing box, so as to enable use of same dabs of orange, blue, red, white, green acrylics following day—they dry so quick!

Red's eyes cast about studio, in search for a shim to even out expanded pallets to be level with each other; found two DVD plastic boxes makes up the exact increment needed. One of these was a recording of a once-friend of yore. A very unappreciated, lesbian musician/songwriter/ singer.

The lesbian life can be brutal, cruel and a dead end. The violence perpetuated first and foremost—by the hateful normal society and threat of violence from straights maybe instigated thru wagging tongues of heterosexual women, but in force usually carried out by male bullies fists. The firings, kicked off of jobs when 'aberration' is discovered. This was the apartheid status of the lesbian. All this is internalized. Each lesbian women, fragmented and jarred shell-shocked, retreats into her own small private space, working, laboring for (on some petty job) a room of ones own. Community is tenuous; often lesbians don't reach out to support or encourage others. The lesbian artist, writer, is often dead. –Career wise. Unpublished by her sisters, her works not hung in galleries. She may abandon the quest and stop altogether. Some die, hanged in closets, but usually just eating themselves into fat oblivion, or drinking & smoking to an early grave thru cancer, heart ailments, and related disease. Most often, abuse is from self; lesbian becoming used-up alcoholics. The violence secondary—much of this from other lesbians, their own oppression put upon them, turned inward—to attack their own small community, their sisters. This particular artist I believed suffered the cruelty of isolation and being ignored, unsupported by her own lesbian contemporaries. I wish her well. Whatever happened to her? What ever happened to a slew of other artists? Whose names I remember, but do not see anywhere anymore? They have been so cheated! So subsequently they are angry, frustrated and defeated by the poor quality of their lives. Wherever she is, I want her to have peace, love & empowerment, and a community to which she can belong.

Don't know if my transitional status will help me gain recognition in the art world—that's not why I did it! Most of us seek only to correct a mistake, which has been haunting us since age 3 or 4—as documented earlier in my Semi Autobiography AUTUMN CHANGES. ---To stand as a visible man among other male artists, does this enforce my position? To be privy to the conversations in inner circles of other men? Have I begun doing more things that a female would not? I have no idea, none of this might be true; regardless, I am one of the queer artists who has continued—putting my art above every other thing—and this in obedience to the Call God, the Most High, has given me, tho, unlike others wrapped up in religion have, in the past, dedicated their work exclusively, ever after their conversion to God, to mundane religious icons, repeating over and over, thus ignoring the more subtle gifts Hashem has given to us, like exploration, probing new horizons, pushing boundaries & frontiers of many topics, means of statement, ideas! Which to the public are much, much more of an enticement, then an analysis, a study for students in art classes going round the galleries on teacher student tours, outings, etc; and in the long run are vital to the Service of Higher Things.

148.
Am writing these Notes for JOURNEY while going back and forth from easel besides the windows to computer in closet —(about ten steps) to type them down as each thought become apparent—often arriving in closet with latex gloves still on hands, maybe a paintbrush hastily shoved into mouth, holding it with clenched teeth for the duration of a depictive sentence or two.

I must use some of this for 2nd Retrospect.

I want to be great! I want to create beauty! Great beauty! Great meaning! —Statement! Statement of the art!

Statement might be quite simple, material—a statement of perspective, a geometric depth to the painting, a statement of vibrant color, a statement of beauty —or this, and a meaning within or under the apparent meaning.

Maybe that is the difference between a good, a regular work, and a masterpiece, one makes a statement, the other is simply a stylized or personalized photograph of reality… Not every painting will be a masterpiece.

In the hindsight of history, I would never, never paint over a picture —for it's too valuable. Because there are great pictures & mediocre ones, and if artist becomes known even their poor pictures will sell, and even the poor painting is saying something worth sharing—even if it is hung in a backroom where people seldom go. Artists paint over their own canvases because they be poor and want to save money not having to construct an all-new canvas out of expensive materials. They paint over what they might not judge to be up to par with their recent work. And other reasons—some, of dislike for what they have painted. Unless a work is absolutely *awful,* save it!

When I was young would take 3 weeks off, and not go job hunting after being fired; I always had to return to a job; but today am retired, never have to return to jobs. Have illimitless time now… Confluence of all resources at this juncture in my life; all I have to do is hang in there and keep working. Rent paid monthly by the government; supplies sit, ready. Space to work, connections in the outer world, have the time, also am validated by the fine posters of my work for sale, plus RETROSPECT, and my name & work going up on several new arts-sales Internet marketplaces; am inspired!

There are episodes when people are going to call you saying: "I know its early in the morning, and you said not to call, but just wanted to you know we're going out to the country, packed a picnic basket all your favorite friends are coming, so why don't you just put that paintbrush down and come with us! We can swing by and pick you up in an hour!" Now you don't go, you know if you put that paintbrush down, you may never pick it up again. If you break your schedule over & over it becomes a useless cause!

Expanded easel today. Need a 2nd pallet for mixing paints. Put the pure dabs from tubes onto the first pallet. Back in 1998, remember I used two separate treys full of paints each. Will expand pallet in tomorrows painting session. Cleaning off ½ inch thick sheet of glass, solid, sturdy, found on Fillmore Street—perfect size. Scraping it free of dried crusts of oil paints used for painting Student At Golden Pot briefly; as I have seen other artists Seen at Hunters Point Navel Shipyard Studios do this, but its too time consuming—rather then disposable paper pallets, for using this sheet of glass as a pallet requires extra labor—plus a good drenching of toxic turpentine. Instead will try to use this glass as a 'shelf' to hold pallet paper pad and water/turp & linseed oil.

Even as I write, am coughing because this poisonous cigarette smoke floats up thru the holes in wall, ceiling, or from God Knows Where. Realize that I should be glad, exceedingly glad and very grateful— that I have a studio, that the studio is here in the heart of SF, center of so many resources to myself (at least ten as aforementioned), that I can paint, that I have supplies, that there is time for me. So bear with closing windows, reopening at appropriate times to turn fan on; peering out of curtains to see if smoker is home/not home, smoking or not, etc., and make do, until a victory raises me into a better circumstance (or I drop dead!)

Am Sunday June 22

Older lady haunts Babylon Falling, raising Cane about her cause
celebre, a HOH Overseers Board to supervise the renegade individual
Home Owners Associations which proliferate the landscape—there is
a private board per condo housing development which can level
draconian demands upon small individual owners housed under their
corporate roofs. Show her RETROSPECT, she sees in Lost Dog
something I hadn't isolated mentally—enough to comment on-- 'the
dog looks so ethereal, innocent, whimsical, but look at the powerful
chest and front legs, muscular.' So everyone is free to see in my
works—in all art works on earth—what they wish, its always
interesting what others get out of it. Might add, that people,
commenting on my work of 40-years past see stuff I never noticed,
tho been looking at my canvases off and on depending on the state of
my housing and where the canvases were stored, all this time, but
missed those particulars.

Oh, regarding #2nd Retrospect—Statement: As Sean says, to have a
fixed explanation of what my paintings symbolize, is to close the door
to interpretation of others. So must say this is MY interpretation—
you may find other meanings. Thru time in showing my work have
encountered many other interpretations, adapting some of them for
myself. The most recent is, Sean's observation of the lecherous wink
in the right eye of The Pig (his favorite painting), which, tho it was
hanging on my walls of this hotel room and that, down thru time I had
not noticed in 40 years!

PM

I've got a story I want to tell you. It's about an elderly community
activist, a 'batty old lady'. She got her money by working. Being a
Civil Servant for years—as a community organizer. She is over 65,
I'd adjudged. Was instrumental back in 1986, in writing and
engineering the Rent Control Law---by which so many hundreds of
thousands of us now live in a modicum of safety paying low rents on
increasingly skyrocketing rental units—which we could not afford
otherwise.

While the two talk, outside the glass windows of the bookstore, one
after another they turn the corner, big fancy shiny new automobiles

61

costing maximum dollars, behind the wheel of each an upscale fancy rich younger plutocratic yuppie.

Do not think that the sight of that old lady in such distress didn't bother me. Tied up in memories of the past, caught up in the impossibility of the future.

Now she is trying to form this Committee to supervise HOH associations. She comments:

> Little Old Lady Activist: Wonder why is it so much more difficult to fight these people then it was back in the days when we established the rent board.

> Red: Because this is a much richer city then ever before you have the funded corporate people all against you.

> *

> There is no revolutionary art as yet. There are the elements of this art, there are hints and attempts at it, and, what is most important, there is the revolutionary (hu)man who is forming the new generation in his own image and who is more and more in need of this art. How long will it take for such art to reveal itself clearly? It is difficult even to guess, because the process is intangible and incalculable, and we are limited to guess work everywhere we try to time more tangible social progress.
> --Revolutionary Art. LITERATURE & REVOLUTION. Leon Trotsky, 1928.

149.

Tho I'd had worked in that media circa 1968-1970 with The Inspired Maid, and a bunch of others—all on masonite, wooden frame backed; after painting on 3 recent canvases I now begin to understand the properties of acrylic. What can do with it—what cannot. Overlays, transparencies. Negatives? Dries too fast, can't make a mistake for it cannot be cleanly wiped off. Oils are more suitable for the changing ideas forming for one who creates *as they paint.* The Positive, acrylic dries so fast! It's not messy! It's simple!

I want these pictures to come, want to fill my walls with them! That's why I keep on painting!

These are *observations* ---not for any one to say that I'm setting down instructions for the artist, no! This is not a manual of technique, these are remarks, comments! There is difference!

Well, Wedding Day has turned into something of a slightly magnificent painting... With its final touches in place.

Sometime the painting must be fine tuned by the *meaning* of it; it is the *meaning* of Wedding Day which caused me to go back and paint over the deeper yellow beside the Temple and turn it dark blue—color of the ominous spars of the city below and at top which overly engages the picture and brings it out of the mundane, flat, too cheery state into a deeper depth of a stronger statement. Some art must say *something.*

Double pallet is working well and very necessary; which remember I used—two separate treys full of paints each. Was this technique as far back as age 17, 20, back at dads house, setting up my thin-legged aluminum fold-up easel with smaller canvass, and several rickety TV dinner trey tables to paint in the small living room?

The artist will go before the firing squad convicted by the charge of egotism—supremely so-- and of stepping on others. People don't understand—you have a Call, and you must do this work Called for—it gives you no permission to misuse other people, however it must be clarified that your life is not an ordinary life, you aren't doing ordinary things; you are dedicated to this gift, it must be done. Often one blindly steps all over others in their single--minded pursuit. The artist must find a holistic place between taking care of self, health, being sociable enough to not become a hermit, one who is emotionally desperate, and/or addicted to drugs-alcohol instead of a living in balance with people—and yet to maintain the steam, the passion, the fire, the single-mindedness art calls for! The preoccupation! The dedication! However, being mindful, that after awhile once the brushes are soaking in turpentine and the paints put up for the day, and you go out, to be a human among humans, remembering your new found wisdom and do not completely bore the hell out of a spouse, friends, etc., in your non-stop talk about The Work! A balance is required—but to blend in too much, to give up too much of ones self to mundane things will result in a compromise of The Work—that cannot be done!

You will sponge on the largess of everybody around you until you are discovered and begin to make money with The Work

You will toot your own horn incessantly (call myself Master Artist because no one else is, and if I call myself this enough, afterwhile it will stick, stick into history) until the day comes that others toot it for you, and then you can retire back into the constant passion of art, while being sociable enough to not go quite mad within oneself.

Monday AM June 23
Peevish w/Jasmin. Feel blue, depressed somewhat, at my stupid personality which argues and demands and gets on peoples nerves.

Walk with Me Red; walk in the Light. The beautiful Light.

PM
RE: food fascists; a little ha ha, from a dear gentleman, member over 40-years @ Grace Cathedral; during one senior's lunch—in which slices of ham were doled out in the singular, one per person, under strict guard—coming thru the food line, after having received his solitary ham slice on a big bare white plate, the gentleman winked conspiratorially at one of the Deacon ladies (who is not a fascist) and whispered:

Mr. Churchill, now that the war is over hasn't the rationing stopped?

To which she calmly rolled her blue eyes, which twinkled in politely restrained mirth. Well I do miss Grace, the Commanders Bible Study, the folks, food dramas, will-I-finally-get-to-show-my-fine arts posters drama and all. Maybe will make it this week—especially as am running out of CASH!

*

Now I'm painting, nobody knows I am a writer. For years I wrote—nobody knew I was a painter.

64

One thing I learned from the demise of my group—its hard to get a witness. Its hard to get people who know the truth to come forth and tell it, in support of you. Nobody wants to take the time and nobody wants to risk themselves by being involved. There were people, who knew the truth about a certain individual in the group (that MTF who was the original cause of the whole uproar)---people who had witnessed her behavior also and had a great dislike for her; people who agreed with me in private but would not speak in public—at least 3 of them.

AM Tuesday June 24
Sometimes I wonder about myself and the society in which I'm directly in—trans/queer world; have always doubted, picked apart, and scorned much of the greater world; in reference to lack of friends, family, and stable community—to find happiness there in.

Wedding Day is progressed magnificently, am satisfied with it!

Now to finish touches on the other 4-acrylics, & back to the oil, Raiment, then will have 5 for Richard to photograph unless he decides on 7.

AM Tuesday July 8
If you've ever been down on the abject bottom of society you will be looking up, as if out of a deep pit, towards a faint lighted window exit and know, absolutely, from within the chilly bones of your being, that this situation is wrong; that this situation needs to be turned up-end, reversed; so that all of us down here clamoring and crawling over each other in mayhem, in the slime of the refuse pit would be suddenly sitting on top—out in the clean air, the free air, with food, with plenty, with peace, and the few ghouls; bloodsuckers who are our jail wardens, as their fortunes necessitate it, *they* would be cast down into this uttermost bottom.

My journey into revolutionary thoughts begins here, at the bottom of the pit. While struggling to have a life—me being a lonely soul who makes few friends, and none easily; a fine arts painter to the best of my abilities, and writer of a very good if not great, degree. I am recounting my life's journey as of the last age which began concurrent with my sex change—starting around 1998, in AUTUMN CHANGES, thru PASSAGE, and now the contiguous JOURNEY

65

with its many Rondos, (a group of 5 smaller chapbooks), deviations into tall tales, which enters now it's 4th Rondo in which I deal with the elements of painting rediscovered after 40 years in which slaving on the time-clock for pay lost in the maize of Kafkaesque bureaucracy; dizzy, cycling endlessly on a treadmill rat race of the kkkapitalist system in which I could not paint for lack of time, but only wrote, and between the pointers and observations of a fine arts are these *gestures* of a revolutionary, nascent, pacing in the pit down here in the bottom, in the flesh, in barely a crack of light from that far-off window to give me hope we might one day escape.

So you thought this book was going to be all about art, did you? It is not. It is all the things mentioned by the title, taken in; for the human construct is not just one simple definition any more then the greater universe, which surrounds them. Many artists have been revolutionaries down thru the ages. And many revolutionaries were of an artistic sensitivity—in fact of a *religious* sensitivity! It is recounted of the those pre-USSR Russian radicals, how many of them switched allegiance from the Church, to become terrorists, in an attempt to overthrow the Czar and his cruel mechanisms of petty bureaucrats, judges, soldier-enforcers, all the way down the chain of command. How they embraced revolution with the same passion they had once given themselves to Christ, and threw themselves into the struggle for the people in the fashion that as young women and men they had given themselves as the brides of the church.

This book too is about religion—especially the worlds much well noted one, Christianity, to which I belong, also referencing the Hebrew, from which Christ, the apostles, and Saint Mary, came—directly—on the shores of Galilee! These because am most familiar with them. —And all of them, seen thru a feminist lense!

I will paint revolutionary pictures. Holy pictures. To inspire faith, hope in the people—and enlarge by all possible means the window of Light, which stands before us all as a beacon!

Dear Children! If we cannot personally throw Molotov cocktails into the infernal machinery grinding us down; the cogs and wheels of this mechanism set up by the rich & powerful thru their lawyers, consultants, & soldier-guards to enslave us—at profit to themselves;

if I cannot restore a proper domicile for myself, and for you and every person—to wrest that one small unit, or tiny cottage out of the gargantuan corporations who have bought the titles to thousands of our homes---and to be able to give everyone a place on earth, with clean running water, safety, peace and quiet, and freedom of speech, then I will inspire all your children, and your children's children, and your ancient mothers and fathers—to pick up the paintbrush, to begin their individual words on paper, to do the dance, to sing the song, to recite, to orate, to agitate thru the arts. We will do Revolutionary Art!

Ha ha ha! What have you gotten yourselves into now Dear Children—thinking this was a mere coffee table book, a primer for recalcitrant painters to get started, and a comfort and diversion for seasoned ones taking break with coffee cup beside an easel, and paint brushes dipped in color... remember, you are painting the food for the masses who will stroll by to look... so *say something!*

Tell them something real!

Let me present my political stance. I personally think the unit I live in should be owned by myself—yet this entire building is in the grasp of a single owner, and is controlled by a corporation. This building has 33 units each having approximately 2.2 people for many have children, tho some are single dwellers; that's about 70 or more human lives living in this pen—all paying out cash to some single owner somewhere; these units, mine is one—rented to me for $1,015 monthly—taking my entire old age Social Security and disability pension—and still I must raise $130 from other sources to pay the remainder of it—are fast escalating in price, so that the Rent Control Law is the one safety net which keeps us here. An owner has control over my living quarters, and thus a majority part of my life. This is a social arrangement and it is a social construct, which is not fair. It is unjust, and must be changed. Revolution means change. We all hope this change can come peacefully.

Housing, food, access to clean water, medical care, education, jobs, and freedom---those freedoms, of speech, the press, religion, political choice. Are what each human citizen must have—each on earth, women, minorities within the majority of a nation, all. And humane rights regarding raising of children and the keeping of domestic animals. As well as respect for the environment. To behave in any other way is not a viable issue anymore. We must have change! WHEN? Those participant in ownership of the lands of others, and controllers of the wages of others—by a single owner or family rule over a massive factory in which thousands of other people work long hours—for a pay which is craftily constructed by the owners to give them just enough to live on, while stealing back the bulk of labor--which equals money, produced by the workers hands, to use this money for themselves, and to pay off the security guards, police and soldiers they use to quell riots, to break the heads of demonstrators who gather at the factory gate in protest of the inhuman treatment; these controllers must have all powers wrested from them; their iron, paid goon hammerlock upon the masses of people broken—so that true freedom can begin!

Before I slip into too much of a polemic let me say this—revolution is an idea whose time has come --today.

Don't forget Dear Children, all earth, and her universes are God's possession! They are created by God. We were created by God, and S/He will overturn this system when S/He is ready, and She is nearly ready, I'm sure! God will turn it over! She is sick and tired of this mess Her humans have gotten themselves into! She will make a way! Don't you want to be a part of that fine day? Well get up off your knees, and get ready for a revolution!

Was at a spiritual assembly of Leeza E., Life Coach and Healer. After a led meditation in Buddhist tradition, soft music with vibes, chimes, Leeza lectured about critical mass, and mass collective of the unconscious. I gathered that in an experiment performed by a female research scientist there were two groups of monkeys, each group was kept separate from another. Every monkey was given a sweet potato—which they dearly love—covered with sand and grit, so that it was impossible for them to eat with enjoyment. This went on several days, the puzzled monkeys turned over their gritty, dirty, sweet potatoes, quite upset at not being able to eat their favorite food. One day, one monkey had a brilliant idea. The monkey took her sweet potato to the water fountain washed it off—and it was clean! The monkey dined in relish upon the sweet pulp of the potato, grinning all the while! Enjoyment! The other monkeys saw the first one and soon

68

they had clustered around the water fountain washing off their sweet
potatoes too, and eating happily. From then on each time they
received their gritty sweet potato they took it straight to the fountain,
washed it off and ate it—problem resolved! Now here's the amazing
part—and the part about the collective mass unconscious. In the pen
of monkeys separated by location, out of earshot, sight, or smell of the
first monkey pen, they too began to receive their gritty sweet potato—
and, immediately they began washing off their potatoes themselves,
without having had any way to learn this behavior from the removed
group in which the single monkey had so painstakingly discovered it.
They had learned via a means, yet invisible to the scientific human
mind, undiscovered by research. —Repeated tests of this was done
by different teams all over the world, with monkeys, and with mice—
they too found that a kin group somehow was able to utilize the
brilliant discovery once it was made, by another one of their species.

Mine coincides with Leeza's theory, that today is a time of change—
and its headed our way—major transformation, with many prophets-
like myself—all speaking the same truth; as if this truth is slowly
winding up out of the mass unconscious of the whole human race--
that there must come an end to the barbaric practice of an individual
clawing ones way up the socio-economic ladder to become boss over
the others, fiefdom barons of factories, political bosses, controllers of
smaller human lives beneath them; but, just as the pharaohs were
overthrown; empires overrun, false kings and queens deposed,
beheaded, and a new order was set up, so a new world must come into
the making—one of free travel between all places, of superior infra
structures built up everywhere on earth to provide clean water, food,
and a house owned by oneself to all people, for education to include
all, women, girls, the poor, and that humankind must come into
holistic alignment with itself, the animals, the environment, and to do
so speedily!—Failure to do so will cause destruction so massive, so as
to be incalculable.

Oh, forgot to mention---it's AM Tuesday July 8--
Awoke sickly this morning. Oils doing me in? Well have finished
Raiment and begun a self portrait—my first—in oils, set it aside to
rest, and move back to less toxic acrylic.

150.

I have had to skip ahead as you will see by the dates, in order to present that previous drash.

After troubles and arguments @ bookstore with young owner-plus witnessing the shit he is going thru to work out some merchandize problems at store, Red felt like he had been drinking a stale pot of coffee all day—down to the dregs and again. And when he returned back to the privacy of his studio, the smell of stale cigarette butts burnt in an ashtray. He felt like coffee dregs, which have been warmed over—then left cold.

There's an old adage—you make your bed, you lie in it. People make their beds irrevocably, unchangeable. In an instant they spin the course of their life off in a different direction—sometimes for ill. The split-decision of an investor who makes a rash choice on the stockmarket—bankrupting his family. Red once was an attendant for a quadriplegic who, as a teen dived into shallow water, paralyzing himself from the neck down, for life. The regrets he told him — thinking back about that moment in time. The die cast. Harsh words, spoken once too many to a spouse —who deserts in the dead of the night. Regrets at what we shouldn't have done, what we should. If Red had been more attentive to $ money, took it to heart, clutching each penny as a miser—he would not have let material windfalls slip thru his hands, and would have more control over his living situation today. ---Also he was convinced, sadly, he would not have produced as much *art*. Dear God I want no more regrets—no more then I already have. Lead me in the proper path. May I follow Your wise teachings, and not ignore them. Keep my feet on The Path.

So I am piecing things together out of scrap. Wait for proprietor to find the time; setting in the window seat, book on lap, waiting to work online. It's so difficult! All but the creation—that part---that part which stops most would-be writers, most would-be painters—that part comes natural for me. Today, the bookstore owner is angry over his business. Red felt like an adjunct; some unnecessary particle adrift in the wrong whole. Stiff. Inadequate. Don't have the computer skills to enter my own work to the POD! In living flesh Transman himself illustrates, in flaming *Crimson*, the technological divide between lower class and those upper. Underprivileged.

From many sides I have heard this remark:

> Children know more about technology then adults. My 3 year old
> is doing her own website---I'm 50, and just learning how to log in.

*

> I still have not abandon my plans to re-assume being a fine arts oil
> painter, maybe I will paint pictures fit for the church:
> --DAUGHTERS OF COURAGE, A NEW ORDER OF JESUS CHRIST, 2007.

Can't believe I wrote those words so recently—and now, as of Jan 1st,
AM painting! And love it! tho finding time in AM's is difficult,
crammed between chores, left-over writing from night before,
sleeping too much, wanting to get out into the street and see people
maybe talk to some, and get some sun rays before its night.

Amazing thing happened—was sad because of something racial
which happened today, which I cannot mention—but it involves me
being a misplaced person. I wanted to cry, but cannot cleanse myself
this way, because men can't cry. Literally. Since my beginning
testosterone shots ten years ago almost to 4 months from now—not
been able to cry with the ease of my former dispensation. I needed an
outlet. I reached for LAMENTATIONS IN THE COOL OF THE
EVENING, which is very much a religious book. There I found stuff
of interest, and depth. This encouraged me—as if it were a
springboard, or stepping stone, or gateway—to reach for my bible.
First I gave that red-bound edition a mild cussing out—because of
being unable to find it due to the temporary mess of a project going
on my desks. Found it, opened it, --the page fell near Lamentations—
the book… Felt God(ess)/Jesus knew my thoughts and was right with
me on this. Then reopened it---the page fell on Jesus feeding the
multitude. I felt release upon witnessing this miracle —after 2,000
years. That there is a place and time when everybody will be fed, and
we will be fed, with boundless love, food, and all our needs—met.
Now we see in part, we walk in darkness—but there we'll see in full!
Now we see thru a glass darkly—but then, face to face.

I want to re-quote what God gave me, regarding this feeding of the
multitude---2000 years ago on the shores of Galilee—later, transposed
to our modern time & date.

Cat: I've caught you a fish. Will you cook my fish Red?

71

Red: Yes cat.

Red cooks fish in oil and vinegar, with lemon, in a skillet. The fish turns into a pan of fish.

Red: Fish for all.

In heaven where one cooks a fish –all have fish.

PM Wednesday June 25

Red had a very strong ego, at least for many aspects of life; and considered himself to be a master artist and writer—perhaps too high an estimate. He dwelled within this fantasy that he was by far the best artist, the most proficient of all others on the landscape, ranking himself among the Faulkner's, Hemmingway's; Van Gogh's and Picassos respectively of that bygone now-dead world. And his life operated on this assumption—of his greatness---yet undiscovered. But as a now-Christian/ Judaic, he had a very strong belief in the placement by God; that is, the supremacy of Gods decision *where to place him*—and if this meant in truth, after all the evidence of time was set down, that he wasn't so great an artist after all—if this was God's Will, then he would truly be happy with that decision, and content in the placement assigned to him, no matter how hard he might have labored under a superior assumption while driving forward constantly believing himself to be the very best; he would happily take the honorable mentions—was this God s doing. The Most High being first and foremost in his life. Thus, doing all he was capable of, would rest in the arms of the Eternal One, at peace with his achievements be they great or small.

AM Thursday June 26

Paint artist!

Stoop, bend, hoist; lift. Pick up my burden for the day's Journey…

Evening Descends On The Pool Hall is rough and somewhat decrepit, elucidative of decrepitude's—in it's haste; unevenness; and lapses back into amateurish techniques employed to cover the canvass background in green paint & it's draftsmanship fails—this coincidently illustrates a true nitty-gritty poolhall, which is can be in

72

fact very nasty, and decrepit, old, and poor; pooltable veldt dirtied by the grimey hands of its inhabitants. The rough green felt of the pooltable so worn by endless rows of poverty poolshooters in the tavern. It was not engineered thus! But it is an observation I make—in that these two elements do work together—by chance---nevertheless if its small, not-well formed characters don't seem well drawn, it is not the end of the world!

Another painting done—frozen in time. Poolhall—last touches.

I want to repeat that these are companion books—these of the JOURNEY series, which are art-specific. The lonely artist, unsung, not yet popular may find comfort in painting and reading bits and snippets of this in coffeeshops as they progress, or, right there beside their easel. I have created these these JOURNEY's along simultaneously with doing my paintings, going back and forth between painting /computer as before described.

PS, have just now gone back into the Lulu-to-publish file of this latest JOURNEY, renaming it, by adding ART, & it now reads, MY CONTINUING JOURNEY—INTO ART & REVOLUTIONARY THOUGHTS.

Homeless man lays on a bag full of crushed aluminum cans, snoring, stomach up, arms akimbo in the cold breezy twilight air. Past him homeward bound, Red tromped, stoically, pulling his silver cart; he had these thoughts:

> Maybe God will publish me soon; way overdue—*but right on time.*

151.
Women's rights must be written into every revolutionary movement, or they will not be there. Change must happen at various times in history; women seem to be an afterthought and if their interests are not specifically addressed, and this point hammered upon over and over, they will again become lost in the shuffle and wind up being dealt out of the bottom of the deck, having again the scraps, the oppression, the unfair share of the burden; the pain.

Mao's revolution freed women to attend school, to not be sold into marriage. The Middle East needs such a revolution, also India. When

Mahatma Gandhi led the road to freedom from British rule—did he forget about women? Who were being sold into marriage some as early as 11 years old; who were flinging themselves upon their husbands burning funeral pyre, because life in Indian patriarchal culture would be too impossible without a man to represent them?

Why is it always the women who suffer? ---For the troubles of everybody else? Men take out their frustrations on women. The world takes out its frustrations on women. Is it because women are the easiest targets, being the bottom line?

As reported by many, worldwide—the relationship to hatred of women and hatred of Gays.

The necessary secretiveness of the queer life works against us; in regards to lack of connection to a greater society into whose hands we often fall, as an end result when all our gay friends die off, or are lost somehow in the miasma of city life, of rural isolation, of life in general. At the end, all an oldtimer may have left is the big town around them—primarily straight, often homophobic. And into this thus cast, their secret isolates them, walled up within it like a prison of self within the city, fearful to disclose their true nature, knowing that by closer intimate contact they will be discovered. It is quite easy to die in this state—decomposing body to be discovered in horror by neighbors who did not really 'know the man/woman.' So sad.

PM
Being a woman, being a man is a many-layered thing, which occurs from the 3rd month of gestation—the first two months being devoted to becoming an embryo, which is human. Then there is growing up; overlaid thru the prism of gender, there is culture, siblings, peers, interactions on all levels combined with actual female or male hormones and biological changes sweeping over the body. This happens, --this growing into a woman or a man over 18-plus years. The transsexual is expected to master it in 6 months.

AM Friday June 27
RE: these vitriolic arguments w/proprietor & others in my life--people are like kegs of gasoline sitting. You say the wrong thing to the wrong person at the wrong time—there's an explosion. And time and grief shed to repair it—if it can be fixed at all.

The parents dream for their own future—becomes their children's reality. The adults struggled; fought the good fight; dreamed their ambitions, and in the advent of greater maturity, begin to question if their dreams will ever materialize; then spanning the arc into older age, seeing their lives slip away, eventually they abandon ever realizing their hope--- but like Moses wandering in the desert—passed the flame along to the next generation. This said, friend Sean called me on the phone late night to say, turn on the TV, there's a program about TG children. I nearly cried seeing young 8 years old, 11 years old, 16 years old FTM's/ MTF's all from homes with loving parents, who were understanding, and facilitating their children's transition! Well I had stated in AUTUMN CHANGES—my theory that it was going to be our generation who was a generation of dinosaurs— extinct. That the young up coming kids who arrive on the scene just as knowledge about us has spread to the intelligent and non-biased vanguard of parents, are going to reap all the benefits we struggled for. Parents not wanting their children to grow up to be freaks, will let them start hormones at 13 years old—and the male born women will have much less masculinization to wage battle against; female born men may grow taller, be more male-like, by circumventing female adolescence entirely. Both genders will be more passable— and catch less hell from their peers.

I see the changing world of trans…

Cross dressing since age 3, 4, all the mannerism of women /men after never changing but sticking to their story that they are indeed a boy (or a girl) so that afterwhile a thinking person has to step aside out of their dogma, their religion, their accustomed tradition and say to themselves, *there really is something different about these people….* And I was only a matter of time before the doctors, psychiatric and medical also agreed, transexuality is a physical and/or mental condition, which cannot be altered nor treated so as to return the person to the physical conformity of the gender assigned to their 'appropriate' genitalia. So we are trans. Many of us older trans grew up in a time before the scandal TV talk shows involving trannies having sex with their twin sisters fiancé in the closet then knocking down his trailer with a bulldozer in the trailer park in a fierce tranny adultery expose—most of us older ones were acting on our feelings in the 1940's and had never even seen a television set at all except at the Worlds Fair as a oddity; the TV didn't come into popular use until the mid –50's. Yes, we had seen the few, precious few others of our kind---the one lone transsexual boy in a 3,000 student body high school already kicked out, into the streets to be a prostitute in back alleys; his shirt tied like a blouse across his stomach accentuating pushed up flesh of his male chest, resembling a woman as desperately as he could; haunting the back streets after sunset, the worse parts of town where people don't care; the masculine woman in men's trousers, gruff, unsmiling, hat brim low over head desperately tried to be the gangsta man scurrying unsafely in the streets, between places of ill-repute, courting some 'funny lady' some blasé showgirl. These were our role models and the occasional banned book, the odd character appearing on a precious few Hollywood movies. Reality is, that, we were taught by an unseen interior teacher; we learned to be who we were thru an inner prompting.

The queer person has had a lot less than many people; it shapes you, it strengthens you, it crushes you, it kills you.

A lot of transsexuals are beginning to have gainful jobs, and as they get jobs, with it comes paid healthcare, so they are moving out of the public health system—thus disappearing from the Trans Sexual Health Clinic—you know the one dearie, the one over on Ivy, (Leche Wallsea Street), at the back of the Public Health building @ Civic Center. Tonight did not see the Transman as he sat on his throne up the hill @ Babylon Falling. Red had found a new place to be himself.

I would be boastful, foolish to say money means nothing to me. We are hooked by the shorthairs to civilization. We must have medicine—that's basic. It cannot be foraged for as can be food, or shelter. Modern medi-science has prolonged human life 3 times over what it was—and still pushing the outer limit.

It's going to be hard to have a revolution—major change in our nation and in the world, because every citizen now is tied into this system by their heartstrings—literally. Change certainly won't come down from the White House, where in rules either of two very similar parties, Democratic and Republican, as both parties have been bought, sold,

collaborated with, blackmailed, lobbied, and gotten-into-bed-with
each other so many times there is no hope of any purity; and, each
presidential candidate is mandated to be a millionaire—by
practicality. Change is going to have to come from some new
direction.

There's people who want to live their life. There are people who just
assume the living of life, but their goal also is to *acquire*. Anything
they acquire more then what they directly need is stolen from
someone else. —Someone else's house, someone else's chance at
business ownership, money out of someone else's paycheck in order
to pad their own paycheck.

Have just come form a brief brush with politics-----District 3
Supervisor candidate David Chu, this position recommended to him
by 2nd term incumbent Aaron Peskin who must step down according
to the 2-term limit; and there-in spoke with organizer Miss Daisy and
others, including some small business owners. Miss Daisy spoke of
the disfranchised, small apartment renters, who David Chu supports.
And NOT the big corporations who would do away with rent control,
---who would acquire more and more units unto themselves and
whose fondest wish would be to sign leases with tenants who are
completely dead—making no demands whatsoever, making no wear
and tear in the normal course of every day living on their rental units
at all, yet paying exorbitant rent in perpetuity, with never a complaint.
These are the acquirers. And we are against them! Returned to
studio, surreptitiously leaving political flyers in the lobby, and
returned to my overpriced, way under-serviced unit with its ceiling
dripping bathroom, decay and holes in wall behind toilet, holes in
wall behind sink in kitchen and noxious fumes of troll chain-cigarette
smokier in the basement. C'la vie.

No matter how fine and clean and good & made-equal each human
soul is; there is a still an important place in the human spectrum for
the virtuoso. The special one. Hands calloused rough and ignorant
can't play the fine violin—only awful sounds will come out of it, and
soon they grow frustrated—throwing the instrument away in disgust.
A waste of the fine instrument; a height of beauty unreached. Both

77

are important—the beautiful soul, and, the not so beautiful one who is able to produce beauty from the talents of their hands.

Was very sick momentarily—but God healed me along with rest and drinking water & vinegar.

> I will not forget those who have dedicated themselves to Me.
> --Jesus Christ to the Prophet.

Time may come in the life of a person, when they begin to make careful measures to preserve what they have taken for granted in the past. Suddenly the profligate may be found in a health food shop, dieting, exercising, and being mindful of their health. The gad-about-town mother may finally fly home to her brood, partially grown by now, and take careful steps—patient steps—to re-acquaint herself to them, and to demonstrate the love to them she hadn't had time to show before. And the artist—having once flung manuscripts around here and there, and the painter, stacking their canvases atop each other in an elements-damaged storage, heedlessly, may now begin to take a mature view as to the longevity of their work. And Red had now, for the first time in memory, made a proper niche for his artwork in his possession—an elevated space on top of a bookshelf, with proper dividers, leaning canvas after canvas between them, with sheets of cardboard between to protect the most frail. (Earlier works chipping & flaking.)

I moved around a lot and took the stuff everywhere, and stashed it anywhere convenient--- not always hanging on walls. When it all went into the strange locker, they were crammed together, shoved down in-between a file cabinet and the cement unit partition—taking a few feet space of width. They were wrapped in plastic, or bare; covered with dust, set in rooms near moisture, and carried with me like a wild gypsy might cart around as an afterthought rare artifacts he/she has not stopped to appreciate, pushed by external pressures necessitating them going from town to town, sometimes in a mad hurry; holding on to them as valuables, yet not treating them very well.

AM Sunday June 29
All paintings evenly standing in rows! Beneath them a fireproof box of art & text discs.

Not feeling well, melancholic—people commented on this.

Building fronts, locked doors, sightless windows. This world is a cold & lonely place; to make friends & keep them is a really most important.

Tranny days and tranny nights.

So many are no where; drowning in the world; a silent cry self-stifled by a pillow held to their mouths; those who have worked so hard on their craft. All is lost but in that they are archived in the minds of a few ancients who remember.

AM Monday June 30
He swept the kitchen floor with the broom; opened the refrigerator door and swept out the lowest shelf—the white metal refrigerator bottom ---with the broom, of all its accumulated crap. Then mopped the kitchen floor with bleach. Cleaning.

Thing about an artist is, well, some people are going to say *'you're no good.'* Or, *'you don't really want to hear what I think about your work'* etc, well, you get depressed you go in and hide under the covers—a day, a week—soon art reasserts itself again, and once again you are at easel, piano, barre, writing, drawing—whatever your medium, this time you are more selective about to who you show your work. If you keep at it long enough you will have modeled your own niche, curated your own collection, constructed your body of statement, that no one else has, no one can take this away. Keep at it!

The Sacrifice Of Art!

AM Thursday July 3
Mr. Emory Douglass @ Babylon Falling speaks of crime/drugs in the ghetto—and how this is condoned by police and politicians in power above the masses-- which Transman himself had always believed. That it is an issue of out-of-sight,-out-of-mind. Of *containment.* The Powers That Be are terrified of the idea of social change, of revolution, of black people seeking restitution for 400 years of slavery—and would rather their ethical beliefs give way, and stand back to allow drugs overrunning and murdering that community;

repeat offenders in and out of jail over a life time; drug families and crime families and powerful ghetto gangs---as long as they are contained in one place, in *their* place --the ghetto.

God did not intend the human race to simply sit around reading torah/bible all day and not till the field, raise children, write books, or adventure out across the seven seas to visit foreign lands in wonder. So, another day, noon arrives, Transman stood again at his easel, painting in oils. Placing finishing touches on Raiment. — 24" x 36".

The feel of poison of the oil paints gives my flesh goosebumps, will finish Raiment, then back to acrylic—maybe.

Feel like I'm working in a factory—toxic fumes, cigarette smoke down basement wafting up, oil paints, leads, turpentine, oxides, oozing into my pores up here. Busily grinding away inside the toxic machine shop of artistic production.

The meaning or statement of Raiment came to Red in 2008—not 1998, when the work originated, with that Colored face, oddly tilted. Didn't know what that was going to be nor had he worked on it long enough (only a few hours over a few days—if that) for him to know at all.

PM Friday, July 4
Art is tied to motion; walking, dancing between application on canvas, and the step-back for perspective. Shake body in delight! Not so the sedentary writer @ desk, fingers glued to a keyboard!

I did not have the training, so working on my own, over a long period of time, developed solutions which were not correct—but individual-- adding to my style.

Works like Pollack who I love, is a balance, a composition, a beauty—it is not a graphic statement on the earth-level, such as Raiment Of Love, upon analysis, in which is portrayed the duel conflict of human nature—love (symbolized by the valentine shaped heart thru which the black evil head of the snake (serpent-wisdom!) appears bringing its pain, truth and ultimate vindication. Pollack and other totally abstract artists have a 'higher statement'--one of form,

80

and vibration—such as 'outerspace' music may be to the listener's ear. My stuff has the aforementioned symbolism, then some of my work is just fun stuff baring little symbolism—like the Oyster Eater.

So not every artistic statement is made of the earth-bound material an observant observer can understand!

Well, here is title for #2nd Art/Text book. -- Statement Of The Art 2nd RETROSPECT. It is written for the sheer love of art, to convey a message out to the public—the greater world---and further, as an encouragement to myself.

I keep inspiring myself.

AM Saturday July 5
Time! Time! Will take it out of one thing to give to another! Overran time w/birds perched on each shoulder editing and setting up CONTINUING JOURNEY which was neglected during the Great Rondo (OBEDIENCE) Finishing Up; and the time, tho shorter, taken   to finish oils—Raiment--, so postpone taking package to Post Office – Google, with RETROSPECT for Amzon order. Want to get to Bookstore by a decent hour—it closes at 7 today.

Trying to paint w/toxic oils, need ventilation, downstairs troll lights up another cancer stick—waft into my kitchen –thru the walls—and into my open window beside easel, must close window; thus no ventilation. That subterranean unit was added on for extra profit— cramming existent tenants more and more in a crowded space---all for money sake. And this is minor as to what involves the indigent peoples of the world, crammed into stick/board favlas on the side of sliding hills of debris; the polar bears on melting icecaps.

Again must add I hate this money system; oppose it, am against it. We should not have money—God did not invent it, it is not of God; nor for the ultimate good of humankind, nor animal kind, nor of earth—but causing its destruction.

They use the courts to legalize their profiteering. They use their intelligence not for betterment of humankind, but for cunning in more effective methods to exploit people and the soil & seas. They use

81

their brawn to overpower the weak and bring the old and sick into subjugation—stacking up beds full of living dead in nursing homes to reap revenue; stocking the brothels of Babylon by selling female flesh, drug running and strong arming—yet it is all legal! —The way they connive to do it!

And to remind you that those deceivers who call *us* the outlaws are themselves the burglars, thieves, crooks and thugs of the highest degree--.

When he finally made his way to the Bookstore, was just in time to hear the young man casually tell a customer about his upcoming show:

> There'll be a DJ, drinks, premiere my teeshirt line… a book burnen'
> --Sean Babylon Falling Bookstore, re: his upcoming show.

AM Sunday July 6
Its hard, its hard, now, being older, to find the energy—to write and paint both; I love both, have expertise of both; there are things you can stay with painting, and not with writing and visa versa, must do both!

It seems like just yesterday I left my room in my dads house, and began to go out into the streets and bars—of queerdom; artistdom; soon I ventured the earth—or as far as young Red was interested to go—East coast, then West. Moved maybe 30-times? Into as many housing situations in my life. Now am fixing up studio--throwing away more junk, condensing, simplifying. Would be quite happy to live out the remainder of my days in a better place, albeit this size, would do—especially if it were a place I could not be moved from— as in *ownership!* A space of one's own.

A quick note maybe good for artists struggling with depression— when I was young, 16, 17, so depressed, having been abused as a child in my mothers house—now that I was free, living with dad, did some writing, and often pulled my paint-splotched TV treys, oily pigment smeared case of tubes and portable aluminum easel and a canvas board—or actual canvas--- out into the living room in front of the TV to paint, but most often didn't. Without energy. Sat at desk awhile, wrote poetic lines over & over, reworking them on an electric Smith Corona typewriter. Then back to lay on bed in a grey

82

depression; ennui, boredom; slightly insane. Teenage Red had
clipped out a magazine photograph, of a woman artist standing in
front of a super-large canvas 8 feet by 10 on a scaffold --impressively
large; it was a mind-stretching idea to a 16-year old, especially to
someone coming from a more conventional vision of smaller
canvases. On her painting table was an array of huge paint tubes.
The sight filled him with such beauty; so compelling—tho it was just
a glossy magazine print, cold, intangible; Red could almost smell and
feel those tubes of paint! Up to that time he'd been painting with the
smallest, thus cheapest tubes— tiny ones about half inch in diameter
(0.34 fluid oz.) ---and had also purchased a few slightly bigger (1.4
fluid oz), which to him was big. Red had seen the complete giant
tubes, (6.8 fl ounce) but always ignored them, since they were more
expensive—also, so advanced! The teen held onto this scrap of paper,
taking it out of his desk drawer to drink from it as one does from a
water-well. Knowing; expecting, one day he would paint and write,
free, the fetters taking off his mind and from his heart.

Paint!

A biographer must say, Red lived his life like a wild animal—his first
60 years or so—it was not a torah-based life, nor a bible based one—
not a Ten Commandments kind of life. But now he knew. Now he
got a glimpse of the final picture, the end would someday come for
him, as it does for all creatures; he felt he must try to live a grounded
life, in a more humanly holy way. And if he did, his life would go
better after that.

1967:
Red remembered preparing a sequence of 5, 6, or 7, canvases in
advance—trip to lumberyard via bus, caring large quantities of wood
to the amazement of bus passangers--return with wood to saw by hand
with an old fashion non-electric saw, making canvas stretchers, which
were often uneven, and can be seen still on the back of The Howl, and
Madman, stretch pre-primed canvas over these, using the old fashion
canvas pliers with tacks & hammer. So now, his studio today-fast
forward 40 years, had a growing accumulation of found stretchers
recently canvassed off of a giant roll gifted from windfall money; and
other found canvases gessoed over, or waiting to be stripped of
worthless canvas and redone. He had found two excellent ceiling

83

light housings—box frames-- built of wood, in the hallway of the apartment building which now were converted to stretcher-frames, having their maintained their original square shape plus addition of 4 strength-baring angel irons 1 inch each, at each corner; now one was canvassed over with conveniently saved scrap after cutting a bigger piece off the large roll, and the other awaited the same. His studio was growing!

Little jars of pigment… Etcetera, minutia—this is not the writing of great prose, poetry, or drama, but details ad nauseum. One might comment (a stupid book reviewer's acid pen for criticism; jabs of the poison quill) that *sure, if it was Van Goghs minutia it would be interesting!* However I remind these critics (who are usually worthless drains on the public largess for mind preoccupying dreck)—*that time also will make it very interesting*, even if the Transman did not become a major player on the artfield of gigantic proportions such as those names of masters ensconced in all the art books in all the museums in all the big cities of all of Babylon… time. Muthafuckas will want to read this, 100, 200, 1,000 years later! Pouring over each sentence raptly! Wouldn't you want to read how the cave artists of the Paleolithic Age, 40,000 years ago chewed up pigment then spat it out over their hands held against the cave wall to create the interesting hand-prints we see—which have survived all this time? Enough Said!

PS one might not hesitate to make a bet that Red was too busy writing about art to fully immerse himself into that genre totally, so as to produce, produce, produce paintings! One square, one rectangle, one giantsize, one small, a plethora of canvas, ---hundreds of canvases, in an outpouring unprecedented— but one might also observe, thru history how many masters have also outpoured themselves into the fine art of painting exclusively and after their initial creative genius burst, settled into a comfortable niche and continuously produced 30 years of stuff nobody likes—as critiques accuse Pablo Picasso in his later years, of being stuck inside his continual masturbations of colorful abstract/cubist works, after a brilliant youth spent in magnificently executed physiques of his pink & turquoise periods.

PM

Some individuals by their placement in time are great; a Vermeer, whose paintings are still available—whereas other painter's have been lost, dropped thru the portholes of time & decay. A professorial-trained Victor Kemperer living thru the war years of 1943-1945 in Nazi Germany's diary will be lifted into greater interest then a john doe, living during a peaceful time in a peaceful place.* Example Gratis: Prepared breakfast for Eva and myself—disturbed by Nazi Gestapo at the door in their infernal inspections! Must hide food immediately—we could be sent off to the concentration camps for having non-ration bacon! Or, Prepared breakfast for Jane and myself—disturbed by a neighbor kids trick or treating for Halloween a day early! Must hide food immediately—we could be eaten out of house & home by these children!

Who can anticipate what makes for great art!

PM Tuesday, July 8
Nothing. Am busy wrapping up chapters already written, stretching canvasses on found frames.

AM Wednesday, July 9
Cat asleep on bed, little hind paws stretched out, front paws cradling two of his toys, the catnip mouse, and a ball. He had pulled them back to his spot from here & there over the bed covers; he slumbers peacefully. Hot out, interior still cool, both fans going—in studio room, and in narrow kitchen; just gessoed over a bare canvas cloth/stretcher assemblage—found in warehouse of artists studios. Typing up some more JOURNEY to take up to Trans Space and Xerox up –gratis--the Bancroft's de facto copy, and my own. Timeframe set to begin painting in acrylic at 12:00, then, out by 2; march over to bookstore; from then to get my head shrunk at the Center.

AM
PS, have just now gone back into the Lulu-to-publish file of this latest JOURNEY, renaming it, by adding a religion genre, to contain those thoughts which also burst from me; so it now reads, MY CONTINUING JOURNEY—INTO ART, SPIRITUAL & REVOLUTIONARY THOUGHTS.

The ever-adjusting times vying between my painting slot and my writing keep changing like a cat changes its sleeping place—and it's driving me crazy! One month the cat sleeps at the foot of your bed—

suddenly the cat is gone! Search high and low for cat (in the middle of the night) oh! Here is cat, over on a towel forgotten on a table. Next night, no cat on bed, go immediately to table—there is cat! Cat has changed her-his sleeping spot. For weeks I got up and painted, came home, wrote at night. But the leftover stuff of writing at night spilled over into next morning, which is cramping my painting time! However at first did not paint on weekends, and now am painting anytime I choose, --all 7 days if possible—and am painting a lot longer on days when more urgent errands of a practical nature aren't pressing me. So, as you see it is not steady, a regimen---which I like, the security of it, and am all over the clock, all over the week, all over the month helter-skelter.

And don't paint at night, because can't open windows with fan due to toxic troll in basement, voluminous clouds of poison. Almost 1pm finally peel on latex gloves to get to work—one hour left to paint only! Oooh, PS, would love to have some joy and happiness in my life—of a social nature, or recognition, or a companion… and not simply the little happiness one finds as a solitary traveler.

AM July 10, Thursday
Self Portrait #2 Writer-Painter, Acrylics; 16" x 20".

The wonderful, wonderful thing about painting is that we are free to use imagination--- paint anything we want! Important, is technological mastery of the human body; hands, faces; the animals, birds, trees—to render an accurate conveyance of what it is-- but now, from this place to launch on into surrealism, imagery, impressionism in all fanciful designs!

Paint treys put away, the space gives way to the books; oils in a corner, acrylics in another—of the sealed kitchen; the desk emerges, the words, the paper! Text!… I keep inspiring myself…

AM Monday July 7
Two gentle THUDS, 10 seconds apart, of the green parrot alighting on Red's shoulder, then the white parrot; a bigger thud—as she is more ounces big then him.

Am Friday July 11

This Rondo is a journey into politics, art—and religion. Well now to the spiritual part of it: the landlord of the house is coming home—and after the terrible mess we've made of this earth, our home—after the selfish, lustful, violent hateful things we've done to our human race, to the planet, to Gods creation, its best that we, the inhabitants of this house be found running around frantically trying to get our house back in order; bumping into each other, running into cross paths—not any more with desire for self, to hoard, to take, to cheat, to aggrandize self—but in order to clean up this house, to repair, to fix, to build it back up—quickly, because the landlord is almost here! The most satisfying thing S/He can find, the thing which may give Her/Him pause not to punish us—even if we are rebuilding it with mistakes—is that we are all finally cooperating, all working together, all building side by side—with only one common interest—the interest of the home, each other, the animals and plants. This and this only may deflect Gods coming wrath.

Sunday AM July 13
So—a line of tortured slaves in chains, shackled together—neck-to-neck, hand-to-hand, foot-to-foot---we dance across the horizon of our lives like a surrealistic motion picture.

Let me talk one more time---about justice; a universal, overarching justice must come—the galaxies must turn into such a place that position us into alignment with the good of each common human being and each nation—in equality! I am troubled (living right on the poverty line) here in a nation of so much plenty knowing that my comparative abundance comes from the economic subjugation of much of the underdeveloped world. We are a tyranny, a global oppressor. We are one of the mighty giants who vie amongst themselves for power and more power. We have clean drinking water, available food, housing, medical needs met, educational outlets; respect for gender & sexual preference in increasingly growing percentile of our nation. —Even if it is eating meals left over by some rich tourist on the tops of garbage cans and wearing cast off-clothes (& have well-furnished my house with the cast-off excess of Babylonia which is left by the side of the road)—it remains that I'm still here; have not been forced to move from my place—by *law!* I have freedom of speech, freedom of writing words. I am comparatively free, but not you, not you here and there over the globe. I'm eating your meals out of your plate, -- you here, and there across the world, --- under financial leverage and lack of a world democracy. With unequal input from all human beings.

152.
There's people walking around pompously, amid much fanfare, who say, "I'm Vincent Van Gogh, I'm El Greco, I'm Pablo Picasso—and they aren't. They paint, they're good, but their Bill Walker, they're Alice Smith. Their pictures may sell for $300, $400; people appreciate them because they want real art on their walls—painted by an individual—not mass-produced crap. If those paintings last long enough and there's enough of them---they may sell for thousands several hundred years from now in 2200, ---but they will never sell for multi-millions. Placement of the art. This is another thing, which is important. Where you place yourself, where others place your work. What you aim to be in the beginning. What capability you have to fulfill even part of that aim—this will place your art.

Am thinking about green file cabinet which housed my forgotten novels 11 years when I relished in economic work; (job), a new budding relationship (w/Jasmin,) a nailing, lifting, digging, carrying, building, work in the backyard of my house which was my playground; on Lyon avenue in sunny Oaktown. This green cabinet is now history, lugged down into the basement of my building for recycling. What am I getting ready to do?

If you are crossing a great highway at night, for safety you look for oncoming headlights down the road. And, behind that, you peer intently for the dark shapes of any vehicles coming, *which don't have their lights on.* So, in life, one must be ever vigilant for what is apparent—*and to be tuned into to what is not.* Well… regarding this flurry of throwing out stuff, economizing space, etc., is God getting me ready to make some great, unexpected move?

AM Sunday July 13
When I said I wasn't sure about this Obama, and in fact I didn't like him anymore—for so prematurely coming into the playing field, a newcomer nobody really knew, and seize the election from the not-so popular, but proven Hillary Clinton. Now after he has blithely endorsed on 3 counts the Fiza bill on the floor of the US Senate, the

red flags are raised for every thinking person, and it has begun to confirm my dislike of him. Is he a puppet, put up upon the world stage by greater forces then we know?

As before noted, my 'loft' in kitchen is overcrowded—crammed so could not extract the larger canvases; so am building a mini loft beside bed, adjacent to bookcase, atop which canvases finished, and primed canvases, pristine, sit stacked—to the ceiling, each, vertical, in its niche. To complete this project, fortuitously purloined a stick of wood—perfect size of crossbeam. Incidentally in keeping with the helicitlac laws and commandments of the Most High, did analyze the situation—the beam seemed to be abandoned, the door was locked, the job done for the night. The workmen undoubtedly neglected to throw this last piece out that evening. Next day vowed to ask permission if I saw anyone—sure enough two workmen. I asked; "do you have any spare lumber you're throwing away?" Got a fine leg for the loft, one almost perfect 2"x 4"x 8-footer; borrowed their Phillips head screwdriver, removed 20 little screws, will pry nails out tomorrow… Will begin project. Oh, for the shelf of it got 3 small boards Sean let me get out of his bookstore *bathroom*, and substituting them for the larger one-piece plywood board under my bed, which gives a firmness to mattress; have most of the stuff I need to set up the project. Screws and bolts all found in tool kit—minus one nut; will undoubtedly stumble upon this at some time. The project can now be set up! Can't completely use it until its finished, but can use it at one end. Will be completely finished when I find one more cross beam and one more leg, —or two more shorter pieces of wood which can sister together to create the necessary length for either piece. The shorter pieces naturally, are easier to find.

Why do I keep on hustling? Struggling so hard, depriving self, —in order to keep a house? Well, there's the cute little feet of Mr. Fluffy peeking out from under the covers. Two irritable parrots perched together side by side in their shitty cage… a forest of found & saved plants… the books… the art works peering down off the walls, like undiscovered Mona Lisa's'….

Never before in my life have I had the luxury to be able to come and go into my house, to work to live, all funded by monies which arrive to me monthly. Not having to go outside and spend 6 to 9 hours working for someone else in exchange for pay in order to keep roof & board. All because of the work of a ragged tribe of activists half-century ago, marching thru main-streets of America their banners uplifted, who institutionalized the Social Security program in our nation! I have made good use of my time—very.

*

I think Adolph Hitler was partially insane. That is, insane enough to imagine, and execute the horror he visited on all of Europe, yet not insane enough to be shunned, avoided and discounted from the beginning. Borderline insane is a term I've heard people in the psychiatric profession use, to refer to those individuals who are sane enough to function in society, worse, sane enough so that they will never question their own state of mind, nor the validity of their behavior, --yet divorced from the human reality enough to be problematic in every one of their relationships, their work place and in their communities. –While never questioning themselves, that most of this destructiveness might be their own fault!

This said I feel it's a nightmare entered into my life—about 1 year ago---when this mental patient, chain-smoker has moved into the basement substandard unit. He goes out into the courtyard and screams up at the other tenants. He called the building inspectors over & over about violations of all kinds concerning this building, before his stupid mistake of calling the building inspectors about the garbage chutes—and has forced all 90-plus tenants currently to have to walk down flights of stairs, or take unreliable elevator down to the basement to dump their garbage, rather then simply carry it thru the hall of their floor and throw it into the chute. I'm sure the manager and owners regret ever having been convinced of his worthiness as a tenant—and brought this super troublemaker into the building by law of lease. Well I'm getting a big dose of his unhealthy cigarette smoke—which never happened the first 6 years of my tenancy before he moved in. Again, feel I'm going to be forced to move out of my place---never a home for me! Like we had to run from my witch-mother 40 years ago one day when she was out on a window-shopping spree. So I'll have to pull up my slim stakes and move once more? Only God must provide an answer, and a place. If it was not for this shit would simply work on dwelling here as long as possible under rent control, until forced out by an Ellis Act for condo

90

conversion which would put the residents of all 33 units out into the street, or by me becoming rich and moving up. I might come unglued form this place any minute! Never a home. *The foxes have their dens, but I have nowhere on earth.* --Didn't a famous religious figure say that once? Well, God will have to work this out! I don't have all the pieces of the puzzle in my hands! Yes, I might come unglued form this place any minute!

> When you start travelen' all over you see the same corrupt shit happening everywhere, it brings you to a higher state of enlightenment.

> Yeah, I know it's the end of the world n' shit… Babylon falling… Empire in flames… But part of me is wondering if there's some way I can squeeze a condo out of this apocalypse…
> --Red in Conversation w/unknown patron @ Babylon Falling.

AM Monday July 14

The work begins. Time to call Richard & photograph next 5 paintings for 2nd RETROSPECT—first 3rd of it. He will also take one of Jasmin's excellent watercolor's, which I have been encouraging her to do—to take her talent more seriously. Will build 2nd loft, paint on 2nd Self Portrait, write, begin to close up this first-fifth * (This has become a triad only.) of the next Rondo; this book, raise my voice, eat, drink coffee, enjoy, live.

I'm going to put some kind of meaning into my works, deeper color, stronger line, more depth—more meaning! If there isn't enough depth to the picture—then will work it, try to bring its meaning thru.

Another mini-loft set up to hold excess of bare canvases and new paintings; the Arobateau painting Machine is gearing up!

I am resurrecting my dead art out of the pits. Drawing it up out of the depths of inspiration.

God I hate my position so much 2nd hand cigarette smoke making me sick. Bronchitis, actually ill and must take medication for 3 days— ugly mental patient in basement non-stop cigarette smoking. He has no friends, no life, so when not away at work is locked in there, smoking himself to death. Frequently goes out into courtyard and rants in loud obnoxious voice at other tenants. The greedy landlords stuffed him into that spare, deficient unit to gouge more money out of this building—how do they regret it! He's caused them thousands & thousands of dollars damage. May cause tenants to move out as well.

> Since then my depression has gotten steadily worse, exacerbated by physical things—I am tortured by my teeth, I am hampered by my foot, which refuses to heal, I am worried about my very palpable heart, I am depressed by the chaos in our domestic affairs, to which there is no solution, and which harness me to domestic chores, I am tormented by my eternal tiredness. The principal calamity, nevertheless, is that no one is interested in me professionally. I hear nothing from X! Nothing from Y!
> --Victor Klemperer; THE DIARY OF; 1945-1955.

I have put this excerpt in my own Journal because it has been my personal refrain for so long. —Being ignored by all the literary galaxy from straight to gay.

So, I continue to write! I must tell all, as I dish all the dirt--least I be damned in some circle of hell along with the Sodomites, & Pharisees.

PM Monday July 14
Money and living up under the money system is destroying the planet, and we need to get up out from under it. It will take the teeth right out of your mouth.* It will kill off your first born child. It will destroy your life—if you let it. *Red's financial status necessitated health care, which was sub standard. Had to go to a low cost, cut-rate, hack saw dental clinic, because of it he lost teeth.

AM Early Tuesday July 14
> I was sold
> Down the river
> From my little old shack
> Kiss goodbye to San Francisco

> Won't be coming back.
> All of my life I got caught up
> In the rat race.
> Will any good come of it?
> Only that people can say I tried.

> Woe Amerikkka;
> What a disgrace.

153.

Often I had no one to talk to so I learned to talk to myself.

The heterosexual world is a huge, overwhelming world. Transman
had found these new people--- rather then be lonely, miserable in his
retirement as are so many seniors—where he spent much time, seated,
sunning himself in the window seat while the people came and went.
He'd get up every so often and run off to do his errands, and, to visit a
very fabulous, secret, and *special* place. Well, after talking to straight
people @ the bookstore all day, you stand before the elegant
burnished wood door w/golden fixtures; you open the door to Trans—
a glimpse of a very unique sort. Déclassé girls, and high-power, diva
girls, alike. Sparse amount of boys—we are passable and thus out in
the regular world, working.

I was not really born a man and you were born a man—we are not the
either one, we are a new thing— I can't figure it out and either can
you, but we are a new thing and we are as old as time. People don't
realize but its more then spirit, more then mind—we are governed by
biology to a great degree. First trimester of a woman's pregnancy the
human embryo begins being informed what gender it will become &
then is infused by small doses of testosterone. And when the signal
gets confused, that's where we all start—before the beginning.

Whatta life I've had! Whew! Old Transman thought… God, Jasmin
& me had a lot of adventures. Adventures in being evicted; in
running out of gas on the bay bridge (twice!)

Don't forget, Dear Children, we are tried in the furnace of adversary.

AM Thursday July 17,
Car alarm stuck beeped on & on as he went down the block, the
honking of the horn imprinted on his mind long after it had stopped.

A reminder Dear Children--- there is an evil, a Satan-----your torah,
koran, and bible studies inform you of this name Satan-- it is only a
reference point---this fallen angel in one scripture, this minor player
in another, depending on how far back in time one translates and
compares verses. It is a handle for humans to grasp. For there is

93

indeed a deep evil, deep as the root of God—but not quite. We must be ever-vigilant not to commit those sins the devil loves (and the devil loves all sin) so that he doesn't get a grip on us! I have sinned—sinned as an outgrowth of my abused/tormented childhood; sinned out of ignorance; and sinned, full-knowing, and by my own informed decision; and the Lord done whupped me. Done kicked my butt, done reached down and whupped me with my own cane—so that my soul shines.

My goal; to go as far up on this earth as a human can go.

Oh, don't pick up pennies anymore. But did stoop down to pick up a nickel... When will I win the genius award & be rich? When will I be able to tell others:

> Guess what comrades, I bought a condo! I've joined the
> Amerikkkan fascist mainstream middle class! The idiots gave me a
> new credit card—after I disgraced myself with the last batch of
> them. (Said shyly, looking down at feet) Aw, n' it's my birthday!

The Shaun's. (Mr. Snarley & Mr. Oto et al) were taking 3 weeks off to go to Jamaica. Red gazed forlornly at the bookstore's shuttered front. Thinking of The S down on beach in Jamaica—privilege—the world is for straights; more places they can go. —Then also thought of other queers, affluent and upper end, who would swap ENDA---to have rights written for them, homosexuals, and cut us transsexuals out of our human rights. Decimating the queer body politic by cutting out trannys, along with other arms of our own queer family. –Such as disempowered blacks, & Native Americans. But I'm happy & proud of what God has made me. A little Red, exact duplicate of the Great One; God's big enough to have formed all kinds of humans for Her/Him to love; we are all tiny images of Her Being repeated in perfection.

The old man briefly thought to himself:

> When will I say—so ends the saga of Babylon Falling?

And too, myself, will I soon be singing this song, along with other ex-San Franciscans made homeless by the great moneyed machinery of fascist housing acquisition?

I was sold
Down the river
From my little old shack
Kiss goodbye to San Francisco.

Won't be coming back.

Red Jordan Arobateau
July 21, 2008
2:30 AM Pacific Standard Time
San Francisco, CA
USA

MY CONTINUING JOURNEY—
INTO SPIRITUAL & REVOLUTIONARY THOUGHTS

Volume 12.

You should know that one of these days the time will come to put into action the sympathies which you have held for so long, those close to the heart. Those issues you've spoken impassionedly about, discussed & ruminated over in your small study groups, concerning those situations of injustice on earth which rankles your ire to such a fiery degree!
-- COMPASSION

154.

Sunday PM July 20, 2008

Once again I enter the magic of the church. —Closer to the heart of God!

Red slid into the deep mahogany pew of a thousand seatings @ Grace Cathedral. Soon a clatter behind him, sound of a body taking its place in the row; a peevish exhalation of air—unmistakably that of a gay man.

The great toned organ struck up; Transman could almost hear Christmas bells suggested in the rich choral arrangements; human voice singing words of good cheer, *we wish you a merry Christmas...*

I would do good works. —Works of great generosity & goodness.

The organ music booms. The Liberace-like candelabras stand flaming; the choral arrangement is a brook, running... down hundreds of feet distance along the immense grey stone rock carved corridors. Out of the inner sanctum of sanctorum bursts forth the verger carrying the verge; leading the white robed flock of deacons, priests; the choir; a cleric, Crucifix uplifted. The processional melts down the center aisle headed towards the choir loft; the bible incased in dazzling pure silver lattice-work upheld by a stalwart sister deacon; the smooth procession moves forward...

One among them---a too thin young stick of a person, prematurely white hair—built of a sparse physicality---- blinded, taps with a cane, frail young ankles.

Red: God! Why have you created some so afflicted? Such suffering?

Holy Spirit: What is important to God!

God: What is important to you, human? ----That they be whole, jump about on the earth, conquer society—or that *they be closer to Me!?*

So, this life, soon to be snuffed out, is important to God—even to be born for this suffering?

98

> I hold them closer. Says God.

Red went to church & instantaneously was re-converted all over again. Words of extreme positivity drained into his ears, were liquid gold.

To my left I saw five black snakes, long, thick—one of which I had painted in Raiment of Love; transposed in black stripes of the holy garment.

> Have faith. Turn to Me says God. This thing issues from you of you, pulsing evil; this issues out of a human heart; these snakes are many; fear, lust, greed, hate… have faith in the Lord says the Spirit.

Vengeance—revenge is one. The knife buried in a prayer book in the first act, which will be taken back out by the end of the chapter. Conniving machanizations for gain.

> Tho your sins are as crimson, they will be as white as snow. PS-- Soon God will give you one of your great joys—which in heaven are without number.

Some cannot be criticized—for even a mild discipline put upon one who is come to this arena already scared, damaged, is far too weighty; where as an ordinary person will receive instruction, a mild discipline, and use it at their discretion—this weak one will react violently & then any good will have been contravened; they will go off seemingly unaffected by any training—but seething with resentment---- meanwhile, as well, they have a self-remedy for your unwanted correction, a counter revision of their own argumentative intent—they will use your instruction against you, will hold it to strike back at you at some better time and opportunity for themselves.

These people are not necessarily evil, but are those who dwell very near the breaking point; their center laying over a great chasm of despair—so that any tampering nearly destroys them and they must strike back in hate, as a means of self-preservation. ----Their statement, a dereliction to their former self? —One greatly broken, debauched, criminal in fact—the wrappings and old shed-off clothing of an evil self which they have valiantly been able to struggle out of, over many years of trials…

Is this myself to who I refer? ME and all my hates, blackened crusts of evil for the feast and glory of gleeful demons which find harbor inside my breast; which lodge there...

All around him the immense 800'rd strong congregation stirs. Many persons are preparing to come to their moment of truth. Double-file, to either side, they march up from the pews; approach the communion table.

> The Blood of Christ.
> The Cup of Salvation.

Seemed so long since I heard those words. All around me, the white robbed ministering clergy, holding golden chalices of the Blood, plates of bread, the Host.

PM Thursday July 24

Transman was in a very strange position—tho not one unfamiliar to him-- upon his knees, his ass in the air, --no he was not receiving a sexual pounding in his front hole via doggie style from a handsome bio, or transsexual man, -- while visions and expectations of the mans hard dick sent thrills of excitement thru his supine body, -- no, his face was on the ground, hands clasped! Red was praying! Rather beseeching, or isn't that the true way we should pray—heartfelt, dramatic; prayer rising up from the gut, from the soul! Anyway, he was asking God to set straight his crooked paths of hatred, vengeance, resentment –maybe even to cast him into the outermost night-eternal circle of fiery damnation in hell—rather then its alternative—*which was to hurt God.* To have wounded our God which the very thought of it drove him crazy as well—so much that he could hardly bare the idea and believed to do his time in hell would be a preferable; alternative to that of injuring God—however Hashem (God) had swiftly (as a kick in the butt) reveled to him that *Both* were painful to Her/Himself—for if Red went straight to the bottom pit of hell, then a little part of God also would be there, in hell, which was as painful if not more so, then to clutch Red to his breast in fierce, Divine Love— while kicking his ass repeatedly, for being so full of sin—either way God was hurt, Red was hurt, so the best solution was, after all, to obey the commandments set down 3,000 ago in the torah—and to forgive his horrible enemies—even the hideous basement troll, even the skinny food fascist, even the vile France-candle-lighting pseudo

100

nun-like member of that long-ago church society! To forgive! & To forgive even each one of the backstabbers who had kicked him out of his own hard-worked for group over a year ago! Forgive—and to bless them! *Yes!* (See instructions given by Saints Francis, Thomas, and others; and the Buddhists* ((given to him by a small Witch in her Boundaries Are Beautiful workshop @ Trans Space)) instructions already set down in time by saints and gurus of old!

So, he had to do this. That was all there was to it. But chicken shit as he was, and lily-livered, Red simply flung himself prostrate down on the hardwood floor of his studio and begged God to just take over the whole mess –hedging on actually forgiveness—however did find himself spitting this out, thru clenched teeth:

> Bless them God, bless the members of my group... Bless the food fascist, bless them, bless them, and now let me move on past this!

Even as the stench of dead cigarettes smoldering in a overfilled ashtray rose out of the basement rooms, assailing his nose, and he knew he was being poisoned to death; even as his half empty belly due to the continual exclusionary tactics and eternal presence of the monitoring fascists was causing him to starve to death as well; and even if the rejection, and lack of true friendship showed him by a few of the ill members of the church society, and by the erstwhile members of his own co-opted group were causing him to die lonely, broke and painful in his twilight days—in utter isolation--- *even despite all this:*

I forgive!

AM Monday July 21
See why lonely people go to church 5 days a week, even 5 times a day. There people are friendly—the Greeters greet you. The deacons, the priests know their job, and stop to have a word with all. ---But its an institutionalized friendship, not the deep seated familial care you need. So that you are not really connected. If you wake up in the middle of the night, there's still nobody you can call on—but an institutionalized hotline for suicide prevention in which a paid/volunteer staff attendant will try to talk you back up out of the misery of deathly despair.

155.
So I continue my Journal JOURNEY with its 12th book, 4th Rondo
(inclusive of the 1st Rondo in PASSAGE, which was also a journal),
in which you readers will find out about my loves & the ordering of
my life.

As you know I am not a socialist, but as it is the finest analysis of the
present corrupt, archaic, dying, poisonous, and planet-destroying
system—advanced kapitalism-- we must discuss it. Point by point.
And so this 12th JOURNEY will broach that subject from time to
time.

And remind you this is a issue so poignant to my heart because of all
the suffering I have had to endure on this planet; IE: Its very difficult
being a small person on the margins & you will emotionally hate &
loathe the big people---for they take up too much space, and for their
greed.

PM Monday July 21
In this city, affluent, ever-changing population—there is a fact, so
funny, he looked around his studio:
> Now all is ready just need 3 more small cupboards, 2 drawers high,
> small, to replace hideous milk cartons (one under fan in studio; one,
> larger, --wider-- to hold 3 cartons beside easel; one at end of kitchen
> under another one holding not-yet bound books, one in entrance
> way to replace faulty, sagging also found plastic one which holds
> sox, piss rags & washrags).

Eyeing his walk-in-closet wherein sat The Beast—*redjordan*—
positioned next to its sister, (inherited from Dalora during one of their
acquisition frenzies of advanced consumerism & materialism), the old
man added:
> and a computer chair—then this backless swivel one can go back in
> kitchen under table—to be pulled out from time to time during a
> quick meal.

Then, eying the plants pots beside the window & parrots, seeing 3
empty soil-filled pots:
> and 3 large plants for the 3 remaining pre prepared pots, and two
> small ones for small pots on window ledge....

And to think he would go 'shopping' outside on the city streets among Empires cast-offs and find literally all of what he asked for. Some genuinely nice furniture. Free.

> The dog had sinned — greatly — in the Master/Mistresses absence. She/he felt so bad he/she hid under the bed with only her/his tail showing, but when the Master/Mistress returned the dog, wanting to be near his-her Beloved, came slinking out from under the bed went up to the Master/ Mistress and promptly threw up at his-her feet. There lay the forbidden junk the dog had stealthily eaten. — Gold, silver, palaces, fine cars, jewelry; unimaginable wealth. There was all the sinful booty of the world the greedy dog had devoured. The Master lovingly patted the remorseful dog, whereupon the dog licked the Masters hand, and slept soundly on the Master's bed all night, relieved and in joy.
> --A short tail by Red.

His financial status: drained my last bank account dry. Waiting for renters rebate of $345. As well, maturing of CD in bank--$1,750 plus $40 bucks, then must remove this from bank before SSI grabs it for potentially going over the $2,000 limit one can have (so much for thrift or an attempt to save even on frugal monies); submit this fine crap to Bancroft, wait for those funds. & all book, poster, & art-book sales in-between. Oh, still have $14 in food vouchers from a Trans Space, Federal Health Department survey....

> LA is a boutique city. NYC is a boutique city — you see what happened to that... San Francisco has become a boutique city... Chicago isn't a boutique city. And it's a big city. SF, this is a boutique city.
> ---Jason, real estate agent, a handsome blond man.

The dollar is the bottom line. Everywhere you go, that's it.

> San Francisco has become a playground for the rich. It helps to be rich, but wealthy is better.
> --Gina, Social Worker @ Grace

Rich is bad enough, but that this is their playground! A toy! A trivial pastime! And us, all of us poor trying to survive!

The old Transguy thought: I am going to write a book. I'm going to call it "City Of Privilege."

Socialism 101: They amass the riches of earth for their own private use. Hooray for that Rock Star who burnt up all that money in London. Piled 1 million dollars in hundred dollar bills into a furnace & set it on fire. Topping that, Saint-like, a very obscenely wealthy shah in India burnt up all *his* money---then threw *himself* into the fire!

> Put your faith
> not in what moss and earth does corrupt.
> Go to where the days are kept.
> --MY CONTINUING JOURNEY

Tuesday AM July 22
Painting today after weeks' absence due to building. --As one can see I've become somewhat of a carpenter—and continuing to be a scavenger.

Pink feet.

--His notes read in the sketch-drawing book he no longer used for its intended purpose, drawing, but to hold notations, random sketch-snippets done on miscellaneous sheets of paper; preferring to draw now exclusively in color, on canvas. ---Pink feet now appeared on the self-portrait.

I will continue this running commentary on my works in progress in which to portray my creative process.

A voluminous purple is needed to complete the left chest of Self-Portrait balancing the billowing blue side at right.

Hour & a-half painting; Self-Portrait emerging into near-completion.

In regards to the signature on my paintings, I do remember dating a few of them 30 years back, but all 11 in RETROSPECT are unsigned. Of these, several, on their original stretcher bars, in the back or on the side, bare a date, or address written in ink, which locates me in time. Am making a point these days to engineer in my initial (A.) and date

104

('08, etc.) onto each work done—tho nearly slipped up & forgot on several pieces.

Signed on to a second arts painting web-sale gallery today! Now must fill it! Other artists have dozens and & dozens, hundreds of paintings! Equal to the amount of books I have authored... I have so few in my possession—18 now, or 19. And the other 20, lost? No more then 30 out floating in the ethers either as carbon molecules—long since destroyed; ground into pulp probably, or if fortunate, to come into the hands of someone who could at least appreciate their structure as valuable material supplies, thus gessoed, then painted over...

Desire and aim for a long life—to do more work! To gain the long eluded happiness (outside of that 16 & 1/2 years I was with Jasmin). Well, have said previously, my art was a stepchild to the writing. Now, working as much as a bit of depressing lethargy and necessary chore-schedule allows. Will I measure the last days of my life in how many paintings I can accomplish?

AM
I wish to speak more about my style of painting—which is not commercial art. When I begin a painting most often it is with no idea in mind as to what am going to say—only that its highly charged; a feeling. I'm going to *express* Myself. *Extend* myself in vibrant colors, motion, depth—perspective, meaning, & by statement; defining this in symbolism & thru all the above-mentioned facets. Why I'm standing here before the easel today, is to imagine & paint. To visualize & execute my inspiration into material form, and simultaneously push the limits, to discover on canvass.

When I look at the art around me here in downtown San Francisco, some of it very, very good, I think---Artist! You must continue! Only you can do your work! No matter if the others are better! Do your art! Are they better at being what you represent? NO! Time will tell who will last, who becomes important, who has technique but no soul, who has an eye-catching quality but no compelling inner force to hold the viewer.

156.

> Assimilation is a lie; it is spiritual erasure.
> --Lani Ka'ahuman

> They tried to assimilate me, but it didn't take.
> --Red Jordan Arobateau

Would never have thought after all these years the wellspring of art would burn out-- & it has not, after 64 years; am still pumping out a gush of red blue green yellow orange paintings and words! Words!

Sold a The Blue Dog at church today--$20. Thankew. Buyer commented on Lost Dog, "Look at those big ears the dog has! With those ears he could fly home! He wouldn't be lost for long!" Later said, "with those big ears he could hear his masters voice and not be lost for long!" It is interesting what different people see in each painting.

PM Friday Shabbat, July/Matot 25
That weeks Torah portion, the Rabbi's thoughts were about journey; what a welcome drash to return to after almost 6 month absence from Temple being as he'd been working on JOURNEY all these many months, in fact years, of his lifetime. Journey. And at oneg met still another fellow traveler going on the Jewish Journey who was not a Jew born, but a Catholic in fact. *Journey.*

> We come into the world clean and we will leave the world the same
> way. In between is our journey-
> --Rabbi Larry Raphael @ Sherith Israel

Took the motzie & kiddish after service. So this makes the 3rd time this week have partaken in bread and cup; —fortunately Sherith Israel provides *grape juice* as well as wine! Haglopian—fruit of the vine. Let those with ears hear! --You clergy up there on the hill!!!! So this is a holy week, and it's keeping me from a grey depression or a blue fonk as my main support system, the bookstore, is closed for 2.5 weeks. Pray for the upliftance of my soul, as it drags very near the bottom; and the prayer or is it the One who answers all prayer, did lift me up some, so that a smile soon cracked my face.

PM –noon, Saturday, July 26

Took down the letters of Vincent van Gogh today. It sat on the rich brown mahogany desk top; (a salvaged bureau) a pocket book, blue yellow cover, with all the letters between two brothers—the genius painter and the art dealer Theo. ... Untenantable madness! Vile atrocity! Reading the editorial notes to Vincent's Letters we see that only one translation was ever made and that in 1927, and nothing has been done to reprint them since then! Except this book published; Athenaeum, 1963 to 1987, in a series of 12 editions! Madness! Insanity! That the fine literary outpourings of this great artistic master not get broader exposure?

Oh, as you have seen Dear Readers, it is occasioned by force of flow of ideas to cut and paste some of these daily JOURNEY entries out of place—i.e. the entry for Sunday PM July 20, 2008; and the one for PM Thursday July 24, which flowed together in a single thought---tho were written down at different times.

God has given me a vision---a red stain in the cup of Self Portrait—it is Blood! The Blood of the Lamb! Making it a Communion Chalice! A fleck of blood to be added in the corner of Red's mouth, the cat's mouth, & a tiny speck in each of the birds beaks! Holy Communion/ Self Portrait, acrylic on canvas 16" x 20", soon to be finished!

I realize I want to push boundaries. Further development of facial expression, the hands; --- of depth, and perspective, twisting into the painting, twisting the viewer's eye into infinity, by suggestion. By mid-year I realize I have settled, laid down the brush with a quickly finished picture without pushing further techniques; so thus have many complete paintings, 7 so far—because I wanted to have a storehouse of them—to begin my art again—and now am approaching 20; those other 25 long ago lost etc., so when I had a statement, I finished off the touches of color as needed here & there, and let it go at that—without pushing forward, as is seen in The Arab, which expression was achieved, if my memory serves me, by many repeated washings off with turpentine and redoing until vollia, a few strokes in a 4-minute interval—and then I had it! Captured! And not to be disturbed! Must push further in subsequent paintings, and not settle. Will acrylics work for this—erasure and beginning over? Well there's those oils every 3 months have pledged myself to do.

In quite a randy mood, the Transman sat legs spread, sprawled out in a painting chair (having carried the little cat to bed and covered him up with his blue blankie—thus liberating the second painting chair which the cat had commandeered, and had been meowing piteously upon—while eying the trey full of paint tubes, as if making up his mind to pounce upon them). Transman sat; gazing at Holy Communion/Self Portrait, deep in contemplation, wither or not to paint in the suggested dicks, or suggestion of dicks—sticks, lines— etc., on the 3 derby-hat wearing males dancing in a diagonal sequence from the paintings left flank. To paint them in will raise a questioning eye, and might eliminate them from showing in some places. I.e. children/young adult classroom education, religious classes, women's studies groups. And he did indeed want this painting to be one for everybody to enjoy. The dilemma—satisfy his urge—to paint in those dicks, or, to let them remain hinted at, by the positioning of the 3 male figures. While he thought, the following came to his mind, pressured up into his conscious because of so much undue stress; and of course he wrote it down:

> The Countessa de Nies was a very wealthy woman. She required 3 men to satisfy her—sequentially-- every evening. Alas, the Countessa de Nies was a lesbian. This sexual pedeciello made it quite awkward for any lesbian lover—to lay in bed waiting for the Countessa to return to her side, alerted by a flurry of skirts carrying the aroma of sex, and barefeet padding; swiftly back down the hall of the palatial Masion de Lago in Southern France—from her encounter with her l'arangemont. Although muffled by several rooms distance from the moaning & groaning ecstasy of the Countessa, as she was mounted in sequence by each of 3 stalwart, handsome & muscular males who rode her to orgasm, her lesbian lover's imagination was far worse, imagining all kinds of vile & unspeakable perversions; inadequacies on her own part; defilements of a criminal nature; fears the Countessa was laughing at her behind her back with her 3 paramours, etc., so it can be seen that these relationships—true relationships of the heart—did not last long. For jealously gained the upper hand each and every time.

> The Countessa—whom shall be further referred to as de Nies, for simplicity sake—being very very wealthy, soon devised an answer so she could restore peace to her life. Sex for 45 minutes nightly, compared to the other 23 hours spent in the pleasant and loving companionship of a lesbian lover. The 45 minutes of lust was

threatening the peace and well-being of any lasting, loving relationship! Each and every time, a lesbian lover soon disappeared into the night—after robbing the Countessa blind. This was the remedy the clever de Nies devised:

One afternoon, while seated with her lesbian lover, across the lavish banquette table, upon which was prepared an extravagant breakfast repast, de Nies calmly proclaimed that in the future she was going to entertain her lover with a dancing girl---a mysterious courtesan schooled in the art of bellydance, & erotic acts; --- this, for her lovers entertainment and enticement while she, de Nies was 'down the hall attending to business matters' (the male studs of course were in her pay, thus it was not a lie…). The lover was to allow herself to become aroused—but not so much so that she approached too near to this dancer, nor attempt to take away the veil from her face…. That way 'you will be ready for me, when I return from my business affairs, to romance you…'De Nies secretly hired a bellydancer, Fatima of Egypt, whom she chose after careful scanning files of several local theatric modeling agencies, for one of their Stars whose face, build, & mannerisms closely resembled her own. It was by suggestion and intimation that the lover soon believed this was de Nies herself who was her source of new nightly entertainment!

So this was the state of play—de Nies believing her lover was fooled into thinking that this bellydancer, Fatima, was actually *herself*, the Countessa in disguise---when in fact it was only a substitute, while she was still down the hall being pleasured in her fantasy-come-true tryst.

Thus for months, the lover was pleasantly enwrapped in a false dream—that de Nies had given up her adulterous liaisons, and was now standing before her, shimmering in diaphanous veils of a bellydancer!

De Nies was pleased with herself—her current lesbian lover, *this one*, whom she hoped would finally become her life partner was a diminutive, high femme, very passive in bed and easily convinced of everything! De Nies assured herself all was well, and thus relived mentally, thrust herself wholeheartedly to her adulterous physical debaucheries without a care. Now, one day, de Nies was shocked to find a large sum of money had been extracted from one of her accounts—immediately suspecting her lover, who, having intimate living arrangements with de Nies, was in easy reach of her personal documents. Robbery wasn't the Countessa's concern, no, being so extravagantly super wealthy, from a fortune built on Empires of the old world, and inherited many times over; no, the fact that the lover may be preparing to leave her saddened de Nies much more; in fact terrifically, and she felt the bottom fall out of her world, --again. Coincidently, that very evening she was in for a second surprise—she arrived down the hall to her theatre of sexual engagement, to find that one of her male studs had fled the stable! What reason? She asked the other two, pissed; -- they were by now all compatriots and might know—she was informed, 'he got a better offer.' *What better offer!* De Nies was indigent, and pondered this grim news as she absent-mindedly parted her garments and flopped down on the bed of sin, over which, vulture like, her remaing 2 highly-paid studs, naked, erect, hovered, jockeying for position, waiting to perform. *I don't know if I can 'make it' with only 2 of them... oh the help these days....* De Nies moaned, selfishly, to herself. Unpleasantly pre-occupied. But in the moments following, all of them were in for another surprise! Suddenly the chamber door burst open, there appeared a strange man, quite a looker, short in stature—had the 3rd stud been replaced? But by whom? And at whose bequest? —This extremely handsome, small man, immediately knocked the other two aside mounted her himself, and passionately began to romance her, sucking her breasts, fingering her twat; administering teasing love bites to her aristocratic neck, and wet kisses all over her not quite alabaster, yes suspiciously tan skin—(a permanent tan); shocked, she succumbed to his bold & experienced advance, savoring it! The other two studs stood by uncertain what to do. De Niece succumbed; lay under this stranger, submitting herself totally to his masterful control; warily eying his cock as he slowly ran his hand sensuously up and down it's hard, thick shaft, stroking a beefy, superhard erection. He continued stroking himself from time to time as he continued to squeeze, tease, lick & suck each inch of her erotic body. And then, when she could bare no more, inserted himself with gusto into her pussy and began humping vigorously, with a debauched leer on his face, as if enjoying it immensely; and then, still another shock! He kept going and going! His cock stayed hard! His cock did not peter out! What a cock for such a small man! What hot, fully loaded cock action! As

110

he thrust into her de Nies felt her whole body rise on fire, as if surmounting the highest pinnacle of Mt. Everest! He was making her cum! Only one man it had taken! Exploding in passion she flailed about like a beached whale, deliciously navigating the orgasmic waves. Satiated she lay back and fell asleep. The gentle prodding of the other 2 studs soon awakened her. ---They knew she must return, post haste, to the bed of her beloved girlfriend. Now, when the weary, satisfied de Nies, bedraggled, came into her master bedroom, her lover was just emerging from the shower with a guilty look...

For many months de Nies was a pleasantly awed participant in the intrusive 4-way, and did not bother to look for a replacement for her third stud—so happy was she. The fact that monies kept disappearing from her accounts did not trouble her the least—as these monies were constantly replaced by the ill-gotten financial leverage won by her patriarchal grandfather 150 years ago, as he had indulged in the black slave trade in Africa, plus cotton, sugar & tobacco, in the Caribbean Islands, plus opium in China.

One night, however, a clue as to this mysterious re arrangement of the set was given. De Nies's twin brother, the flagrantly gay Count de Nies—Nepthfu de Nies-- (De Nephew for short) had come into town after a lengthy sojourn in Florence Italy, at University where he majored in tongues--- of different sorts. One evening after night on the town with dear old queenish friends, over breakfast de Nepthfu revealed to the two lesbian lovers:

> Darlings, what a lovely evening we had last night— Alice, de Nies, the two of you *really* should accompany me, we attended the opera, Alchina—the Stuttgart Version, tee hee--- had a sumptuous repast at Restorante Toujours Lamoure, and there were graced by the most sensuous, and astounding performer, bellydancer Fatima of Egypt!

At these words, The Countessa dropped her spoon of gelato!
> What! What name did you say brother Nepthfu! *What* bellydancer?

> Why Fatima of Egypt sister!

Arrguhh! How could Fatima have been entertaining in town when she was suppose to be performing in my bedroom—while I was down the hall

111

getting laid! However, in the fashion of the upper classes she shoved this matter aside, regained her aplomb—and made light conversation until the meal was accomplished. Filing the information away into her brain, she vowed to contact Fatima as soon as possible!

Ironically, the whole sad charade was soon revealed… It happened like this…. One afternoon, while de Nies was in her office, a call, registering on the answering machine, came in from a distraught Fatima:

> Madame, you have paid me to be away from your house these past 7 months, generously leaving me to my own affairs, with reassurance as to your continual financial support, for whatever reason I'm sure is none of my concern. —According to the terms of your last communication I'm on a paid leave—you said so in your kind letter, but now I find my check—most generous—was not in the mail as expected! And, MY ROOM RENT'S DUE!

So! Fatima of Egypt had *not been* entertaining her lesbian lover in their bedroom! Well Hell! After hiring a private detective, the Countessa de Nies discovered the truth; it was her high femme lover, --Alice, a gentle and feminine creature, who had stolen the money, and used it to pay off Fatima of Egypt, and the Countessa's 3rd male stud. Alice, a trifle fancy-free; a bit of an airhead when it came to financial matters; had simply allowed to slip her mind, the monthly mailing out of Fatima's stipend! YES! It was her own high femme lady, who had revealed a complete personality turn-around, revealing an alter ego heretofore not seen, and had become hard, cold and masterful as she had fucked the unknowing Countessa every night for 7 months! Yes! It had been Alice! Who, leering, stroking her perfectly outfitted penis; was at last culminating a long suppressed fantasy, as she lay atop her butch Countessa stroking into her pussy with great relish; a sexist leer in her eye! *The truth was out!* **The Countessa de Nies had been topped by her femme!**

157.
Saturday 5PM July 26th. Notes from Trans Boycott of Enda dinner @ swank hotel downtown SF:

Union Square Park. Am surrounded by a swirl & flurry of queer people. SF has the army—we activists are at still another rally for our rights!

After all our singularity—the fairy male swishing down avenues to the threat of his life, of arrest by hater cops; the dike woman assaulted by hater gangs, we transgenders of the 1950's, 1960's; we 'first gays'—obvious to the public---who ignited the gay civil rights movement from the beginning---us, the real freaks, the obvious queens and studs, us clearly queer—we are being cut out of the legislation pending in the White House on Capitol Hill, Washington DC, to give civil rights to what? -- A symbolic victory for GLB's alone; leaving suffering for us left-out T's.

Young queers scurry everywhere. This boy, a bit short... That girl— a little too angular... We are assembled *across the street* from the swank hotel wherein is meeting a Testimonial Dinner for all the gay bigwigs of America who have tried to jam this discriminatory bill down the throats of middle America. —Leaving us out of it!

Of course there was always those of us living fabulous lives,
— Liberace is a stellar example. Marlene Dietrich. Ann Bancroft.

> You think I don't see
> You think I don't know
> --God

This protest, this picket, this boycott, is called The Left Out Party. And there is no food. 5 symbolic tables stand, covered with white tablecloths but without silverware, in a traffic zone of Powell Street. No one will sit at them. No posh waiters carrying bountiful treys of delicious food will serve them. We are the poor, the riff raff. This blocked-off car lane with tables covered in fancy linen is a symbolic. Part of the protest; & has been roped off by police barricade due to order of the City Permits Board... It helps to have some queers elected to the City Permits Board Dear Children. Don't forget your lessons of a political nature.

Passerby's, tourists, throng in the street; those staring, snap photographs; what messages of shock and hate will they carry back to the inner homeland. La Scandle! Queers carrying picket signs boycotting a fancy hotel—with more queers in tuxedo's & evening gowns inside dining high on the hog! Yes, Alice, this *is* a queer city!

113

Golden saxophone plays! Old Transman heart swelled with pride &
his spirit soared! Better then spending a lonely Saturday with nothing
to do but work! **We are the people 2!** A chant goes up:

> One, we are the people two.
> Three, we are just four all genders.
> One, we are the people two!
> Three, we are just four all genders.

Our picket line is a gigantic oval, walking up and down, back and
forth in front of this upscale hotel. A worried boss has stepped out of
the golden doorways of the entrance, a heavy; swarthy, black hair;
tough guy decked in fine suit, glittering jeweled watch & rings; he
walked down 3 cement steps, and stands there; with grim face surveys
the chanting queers on his doorstep.

A crowd of tourists armed with little silver cameras snap snap snap
away at one end of the picket line. Here a silly plute, middle class,
white young girl sits on a flowerpot polluting the air with a cigarillo,
pretending not to notice all the queers picketing her hotel!

Fellow conspirator, queer poet, author performer we see each other:

> Well---here we are…. Again.
> --Tommi Avicolli Mecca

He and two other Italians will be outstanding this evening. The
second, queer City Hall supervisor, Tom Amminao. The third,
Figueroa, Mayor of Los Angeles—more about that later.

Well here I am out in the streets protesting--- Transman Robert
Haland; an emissary from Mark Leno's office, straight man Arron
Peskin, many other politicos attend who hard fought for political
offices here. Denise d'Anne; who got the endorsement of labor but
still missed the supervisors seat, is out; old pal Stephanie Ann, former
high ranking Civil Service West Coast Supervisor who boldly
transitioned on the job, snaps a picture with a 3-D camera, state of the
art. Queers crossdressed in the most gaudy display, such as silk
dresses w/moustaches, high heels sequins… yuh know the saying
Dearie "come to San Francisco--- they put a picket sign in your
hand." A base drum, a slide trombone, saxophones! The band starts!

A tour bus circles this block full of clean cut white Americana middle class; inside a young clean cut sporty queer—stealth---lad peers out at us freaks outside; marvel at the wonderland which is here! He discovers himself to have arrived in queer paradise—in living Technicolor!

2 blasts from way past: young man wears a tight torso tee-shirt, black, sequin sparkling which reads—E.A.T. T.H.E. R.I.C.H.—does he know who first coined that phrase? It was from a song by the same name, first written & preformed by Blackberry, a handsome, gay, African American man, singer and song writer, activist. And, meeting a young white dike named Jasper—Transman had to inform her, did she know her name in African American community of the 1950's and earlier was slang for a lesbian? That one could hear this slang, derogatory phrase used as late as the 1960's and, maybe in some demographical areas, rural, it may still be used; to which information she looked quite surprised.

Well-refreshing sights; –living art of San Francisco; almost naked woman—breasts incased in sheer translucent plastic bags—each of her breasts in a separate pink shopping bag; parceled off like meat; she wears a pink diaper. She stumbles in high heels thru the crowd. So nice! We've all taken over their neighborhood, so this afternoon it's not so tourist dominated—a pack of wild queers rejoicing! Assembled together...

Brings a tear to my eye—feeling old and left behind. How could it be that I am sad, after this event? Could it be that my day has come and past, and I barely had a chance then—as a criminalized queer, and being so old no longer have a chance now?

The boycott won a victory. It registered our great discontent into the American ear. Small irritating details they might have wanted to ignore, such as trans lives--.002 % of the human population. Oh, Keynote Speaker for this gala event, mayor of Los Angels canceled. —This is the 3rd Italian, he is pro-labor, and labor sided with the picketers. It was a picket line and he would not cross it.

158.

You know, you see...

Us Transsexuals carry a very heavy burden; anything can be expected of us, any reaction; any bold words—or rude acts.

I don't think in the entire gay, lesbian, transsexual, community are you going to find a tongue that is not acid! This is the life we have led—one of apartheid, discontent, disfranchise, and violation; it brings about a state of perpetual sorrow—deeply internalized—which all of us feel if we can still feel; plus, second, this HATE we have digested since our early days is acted out in the theater of our limited worlds; *against each other Mary!* --In taverns, bathhouses, restaurants, parties and streets whenever we as a people gather together-dising each other, dishing the dirt! So, it is a way of life--- this negative thinking--- and a lifestyle alien to many straights, ay least those of whom have had happier circumstances.

As the result of his abused childhood (6-7 years of torture) & later fright by being an obvious queer in a cruel straight world of violence against him, foreboding for his youth T was defensive and diagnosed with PTSD (Post Traumatic Stress Disorder)--- which involves actual shrinkage of the brain, a permanent state for which there is no cure.

Proof is out—in color scientific imaging; damage due to Post Traumatic Stress Disorder. A lot of medical information is learned during wars. All those injured soldiers to be examined; as their bodies pile up in the wards of military hospitals, so do the documents. All those surgeries, trial drugs groundbreaking medical techniques worked out on those soldier boys during wartime. PTSD patient lose 5-10% of their gray matter, yet more neuron damage. Doctors can see this on an x-ray screen! Transman's mental disorder!

This accounts for his frequent outrageous outbursts at offenses which would be considered slight by others who are mentally healthy—some of these 'offenses' not even existent, but miss-interpreted by the ever-vigilant Transman. And confirms itself again, in his previous substance abuse.

> You have a condition. —I forgive.
> --Hashem

Dear Readers, I give you this minutia, these details because:

---owing in part to the power of attraction exerted in our time by the artistic personality as such—a power of attraction extending to every available private and intimate detail of an artist's thought and conduct—

--Regarding Vincent Van Gus letters to brother Theo, introduction by Mark Roskill

159.

Walls crumbling, here is the site I used for the destroyed church Transman Starvax & his family in the wilds visit in my Si-Fi trilogy. No Trespassing sign posted; pigeons, grey/white, w/pink feet, roost on the exterior ledges; this church; 3 stories high, made of grey stone with belfry whose windows long ago were broken out by vandals throwing rocks, standing gaping, un-boarded; 2 human bodies, cocooned in blankets & sleeping bag, make their home each at separate entrances of this church on the corner. They zipped up their coverings against oncoming night; disappeared from human society; wrapped up in their perpetual defense against the world.

> God sees your church fallen into disrepair.
> God sees your people fallen in disrepair.

11 AM Sunday, July 27

3rd day back in church. They laid it on thick. Massive pipe organ plays chords of Oh My Soul. For it is the soul we deal with... This is forgotten in the daily world of interactions & bargins and material survival.

Transman had a vision, of a paradise-like futuristic world. It will be a beautiful place—inclusive of all, encompassing many city blocks, holding as many tribes as the are—under its beautiful tensile strength metal exo-skeletal dome, where, together, we'll bow down to the Eternal. All will take communion simultaneously—in their various traditions. Use all-inclusive language, non-sexist, none to be left out. Worshiping the Eternal, by Her many different names that human tongues give.

Then Transman had a revelation—about himself, and his placement on the true divine scale of human living. He must shed his pride, his vanity—in the light of Greater Things. Somewhat in the nature of:

> Building proud towers that shall not reach to heaven
> —Anglican hymn

So thinking within this knowledge, along the lines of his favorite subject, this wisdom was given to his mind:

> I would say that this art is of God. I am just its workman; neither of heaven, or of hell. … Stuck somewhere inbetween—in ordinary time—not saint, not completely a sinner. Dear God be my strength & my shield, and my deliverance.
> --RJA @ Grace –2008

Wow that was hot! --That service. —The service! Old Transman sat, in contemplation; both feet in his still-new tan construction boots planted firmly on the granite stone cathedral floor.

2-African Anglican sisters wearing religious headscarves, downstairs @ hospitality—(which is the Christian oneg)-- speaking how a baby was born in their country to a mixed race marriage. The husband became an American citizen and left Africa—his baby, born before he became a citizen now has no nationality. An innocent baby! Nowhere!

It was one of those services that you want to save your program, which he did, and later that night, at home, consulting the scripture chapter & verse therein—(old Transman did know his way around the bible)—turned swiftly to Romans, he began to read:

> Likewise, the Spirit also helps our infirmities; for we know now what we should pray for as we ought; but the Spirit itself makes intercession for us with groanings which cannot be uttered.
> And he that searches the hearts knows what is in the mind of the Spirit because he makes intercession for the saints according to the will of God.
> And we know that all things work together for good to them that love God, to them who are called according to his purpose
> For whom he did foreknow, he also did predestine to be conformed to the image of his Son, that he might be the firstborn among many children's.
> Moreover whom he did predestine, them he also called; and whom he called, them he also justified; and whom he justified, them he also glorified.

What shall we then say to these things? If God be for us, who can be
against us?
He that spared not is own son but delivered him up for us all, how shall he
not with him also freely give us all things?
Who shall lay any thing to the charge of God's elect: It is God that justifies.
Who is he that condemns? It is Christ that died, yes rather, that is risen
again, who is even at the right hand of God who also makes intercession for
us.
Who shall separate us from the love of Christ? Shall tribulation or distress,
or persecution, or famine, or nakedness, or peril, or sword?
As it is written. For thy sake we are killed all the day long; we are
accounted as sheep for the slaughter.
Nay, in all these things we are more then conquerors through Christ that
loved us.
For I am persuaded, that neither death nor life, nor angels, nor
principalities, nor powers, nor things present, nor things to come;
Nor height nor depth, nor any other creature, shall be able to separate us
from the love of God, which is in Christ Jesus our Lord.
--Romans 8: 26-39

It is bad—being an adjunct to the normal world—not placed—not at
the center of things, your work not being recognized professionally-
being held up under a spotlight of observation and added to the
storehouse of human knowledge.

> I must I paint 10 more years! Attain the age of my grandmother &
> mother--72! Then, surpass the age of my uncle—84—and in this last
> quarter I would have joy in my life? I might preach; repeat Gods
> Word to people! I must preach & teach—everything that God has
> taught me.
> Red's Great Revelation beside fountain @ Grace Cathedral pavilion, SF

I have entered into the exciting new world of the fine arts online---
where different people exhibit their wares, globally. This is indeed
the day of the Little Artist—who can now, via the Internet, sell their
own books, their own artwork direct to the public without the
intervention of a Publisher, an Art Gallery Dealer—some might call
them deadly, discriminatory; *Gatekeepers.*

Am Monday July 28
30"x 26". Acrylic on canvas; Hunger For God emerges. Transman
had always loved music, the nightclubs; discos of the 60's and 70's
had seen him shaking his bootie, partying down—over 2 decades
worth of dancing from 10 pm until closing at 2, so now he fairly

danced around the canvas jittering in place after having applied some of his master brushstrokes. In 'Hunger', it is God who hungers for Her-His people! See the red Tongue extended, the surreal parted golden /crimson Lips! It is God Who calls forth—baring a handful of chalices, crucifix's, Hebrew stars, menorahs, Om symbols, the Crescent moon, the Women's crescent/moon; for the people to take their pick, and thus enter upon the Royal Road, The Path, The Journey to greet the Most High—this being in all dignity of the individual—no matter how poor, nor smelly their clothes; no matter how blackened their heart with evil done, nor how crimson their soul with stains of sin and shame; in all reverence on the part of the person, awestruck at The Eternals Great Majesty, and reverence of sincerity on the part of Hashem upon extending His/Herself back to the human race. This great Allah, This God with us.

*

The world don't care about yo' art. It cares about yo' dollar signs! If yo' don't got no dollar signs, the world don't care about you! If they discover yo' art can bring dollar signs—then they love you!

160.
Tell the priest he can go suck my dick—thought Transman & saw the rage he felt, the anger; hate! & cast it up to God Almighty & lifted up his eyes, which traveled up along the grey rock walls, 6, 7, 8 stories high grey stone in the magnificent interior; gazing past stained glass windows depicting 5 duplicate saints in crimson robes & gold halos past a winged angel baring a child in its arms hung off a cornice in a corner over the choir loft at about 3rd story.

That's what I'm here for, says God.

God how I hate these goddamn churches! God how I hate their goddamn views! Transman Red realized then, how angry he felt, so full of rage, so hurt. After he left, behind him, in the niche besides portraiture of the Virgin Mary and a bronze crucifix, two Candles burnt bright, single white tapers in their beds of sand; in the cool interior of the grey stone monumental cathedral; evidence of where the old man had cast up his prayers.

I know mental illness—says the Lord.

120

Human beings have evolved thru the apes, who rose thru the mammals who came out of the fishes of the sea. More hairless, having lost our scales 22 million years ago---our fur 100,000 thousand years past. Now humans, clothed in raiment of our own making perambulate around Grace cathedral; clambering all over, curious; talking quietly among themselves, pointing at things--holy icons, paintings, bronze plaques; snap photographs with their cameras. Navigate dim corridors and adjunct chapels, all contained within the Mothership; curious, many not Christian, not spiritual, sightseers doing the whorls of the labyrinth, marveling at the sermon---we are Spirit children! Follow the great Teacher, seek the Eternal! The Creator of all Creation!

PM

> Brother Peace has no pretensions—he has sat on the sidewalks of
> dozen cities of the world.
> --RJA about fellow Transman Peace

Sometimes I think in terms of leaving something behind me after departing this world. Many do not think in this scope. If they do art, its casual & given away free as the wind; to friends, and it goes unrecorded. Like a poster on a billboard set up for the month which wind and rain will degrade, and which will soon be taken down. A talent, basically underdeveloped. Others devote their lives to it, using brushes, tubes of pigment; applying paint to canvas so it means something. To be the later, one must have a *reason*. A *cause* for this excessive dedication, this effort which pushes them over the top— cements them into the record book, carries them over the finish line of those artists known & those obscure & those not present at all.

My cause has been, originally as a teenager, when first taking art up, thinking about and assuming the burden on myself, to be as great as the masters—Picasso, Rembrandt, Van Gogh; and those of writing— Faulkner, Hemingway, TS Eliot. I assumed this was my task in life! Certainly nobody told me this! It worried my parents, me not having 'concrete scholastic goals'. Nor a gameplan for survival in the adult world, soon approaching.

Here is one who took himself very seriously; who held the position of artist in high esteem, and worked at the job daily, lived the part, --as if

121

he were getting a regular salary for it, which, at the time, 1885, he certainly was not:

> You must understand properly my conception of art. In order to grasp the essence one must work long and hard. What I want and aim at is confoundedly difficult, and yet I do not think I aim too high.

> I want to make drawings that *touch* some people. "Sorrow" is a small beginning; perhaps such small landscapes as the "Meerdervoort Avenue," the "Rijswijk Meadows," the "Fish–Drying Barn," are also a small beginning. In those there is at least something directly from my own heart.
> --Letters Of Vincent Van Gogh; Atheneum, 1987

AM early Thursday July 31

Here is another piece of minutia, which is very, very important about my process—I took myself seriously. I looked at my work as a professional. No matter my shoes were run over, my clothes rumpled; that I had no coins for a cup of coffee—I was a beggar, a freeloader— worse, my verse was misspelled and the first novel editions crudely stapled together; I looked at it as very serous stuff. Stuff worthy of being saved. Of taking great pains to preserve, duplicate and distribute—and had great pride when it was first archived in various libraries, especially the Bancroft. An example, currently two artists I know are engaged in blogging. A great deal of effort must go into this. My Journal is —a culmination of a life time of creative writing projects chiefly novels, novellas, short stories, a lot of poetry, and a few plays—having paid those dues, am writing a series of journals; I'd imagine its somewhat like a blog. But I get paid for my Journals, and contain them in a book-fashion.

Photographers, poets, painters, dancers, actresses; I have known them—they did not take themselves seriously. Their *craft,* their art— I should say; not necessarily taking *yourself* seriously—but your *gift,* which comes from God. ... In fact it might be the wrong thing to take *yourself* too seriously... Where are these people today? What has become of their talents? You got to push yourself to the limit!

Am now surrounded by paintings, canvasses, scaffolds, supplies— ceiling-tall; will eat, sleep, drink, *be* fine arts.

PM Thursday July 31

Every human organism wants to have their own child-- it's a built in biological response. It's this societal stuff superimposed which forces us to ask, is this feasible? Do I have time? Can we afford it? That many of us can't have or raise children is a modern day construct, a fact of encroaching civilization whose walls have gone up like a maize, which the laboratory white rats must learn to navigate, the passage ways, dead ends, traps and lairs growing more & more complex. It's' a truth that the highest birthrates are in the least developed nations.

PM

Nothing. (No painting.) Busy preparing Notes for Lulu Print-On-Demand master copy. Some prelim set-up for 2nd Retrospect, STATEMENT OF THE ART.

AM July 29, Tuesday.

Have 'date?' —arrange to meet African-American sista' @ art museum, we became acquainted at the bookstore. After this must hightail it back to Trans Space to Xerox what I now have of MY CONTINUING JOURNEY INTO SPIRITUAL & REVOLUTIONARY THOUGHTS (JOURNEY 12), speak with fellow trans brothers Peace, Luke, and watch movie about pregnant Transmen, while *eating!* Fun!

Hunger For God continued:

Meanwhile, back in his studio, the idea emerged. A hand now open; once closed. The closed hand in blue, delineation; red for the open hand. Transman made the necessary corrections. —Quickly sketching in the closed fist again, superimposed upon the open one— which had once been imposed upon the closed fist first, in the beginning---he stepped back and surveyed the fruits of his work. He cried; bowing his head, thanking Hashem, the Eternal—for the suggestion was there!

The old prostitute has rejected the Most High before, in her youth, but now she accepts. She reaches out for the Eternal.

Old Transman's eyes grew moist, he began speaking in tongues:

So that the people may see, so that the people may see!

123

--was the interpretation. This is what the people shall see in 'Hunger,' the old prostitute, arrayed in a low-cut red & purple striped dress unabashedly showing expanse flesh of her bare chest, large breasted, arrayed in a fine, gaudy red/purple striped dress & matching headgear. Her old face, toothless, upturned. Her hand clenched, now opens ---portrayed center foremost in red & light blue clenched in a fist, then open, fingers extended. The Light shines down, licking around her, also inclined towards another small figure canvas left (by A., -- signature). The light travels up becoming a tongue into Gods large mouth here above a platter, which holds a Menorah (symbolizing the 12 Hebrew tribes) the Buddhist Om symbol, a crucifix, the Islamic, & others. Hunger For God; Acrylic on canvass (found stretchers) 26" x 30".

PM Tuesday July 29

Must speak, anonymously, of a serious thing, which I witnessed today—and my intent is not to harm any individual by gossip, but make an important statement. We trans, we queers we marginalized humanbeings must speak from time to time on the fragility of our existence. The first incident involves myself—as I hyped up on coffee all morning painting Hunger For God, and did not eat—mostly for dietary reasons-- all but a few bites of meat & some cod-liver oil, plus many cups of strong coffee with milk, and worked hard. The body if not fed kicks into adrenalin mode, in which the person speeds up—maybe from olden times of our evolutionary past; giving a burst of energy wherein to forage enough food to stay alive; or run away from wild beasts-- anyway, when I got to Trans Center some strange men were about, evidently queers, but they seemed so straight --thus 'invaders' in a transsexual space; that I felt challenged, and my adrenalin and hate/defensive mode kicked into overdrive. Suddenly I felt breathless, and realized my center was gone, almost gasping for breath, as if my heart couldn't keep pace! I felt I would pass out if my body ratcheted up its hyper state one more notch. Felt sick. Saved by sitting still, in place, in front of the computer, and, half hour later, for the FTM movie night, saved by the food which came; ate pizza, and lounged there, doing little, eyes dully focused on the TV screen; which restored me somewhat but not back to normal. Body awareness. Reality check. On the background of this physical shock, there appeared a fellow Transman—a popular figure around town who shall remain nameless. The last I'd heard he was well housed, active in community organizing, and prosperous. Today he seemed blank, and his body shook rhythmically at times, as if from side affects of powerful medication—psyche drugs. He told us he was sheltered in a halfway house—not the excellent situation he'd had just a few years previously. This robust-hearted man was strangely still--- like myself. Did some great disaster befall him? Did he loose his habitat? Or did a lover betray him? Friends deeply wound him? What happened to this man? How fragile we are! How fragile is our transworld. The movie portrayed trans folk amid the joys and terrors we endure. Seeing love, fun—and suffering alike up on the TV screen spoke to my heart.

> There's certain things we're born with that cannot be changed.
> -----Transparent, movie.

Come home smell cigarette smoke. Cannot help but think that this second-hand smoke is increasing my heart rate—along with my already extant problems of high blood pressure.

I feel so completely physically trapped by my situation. Chain-smoker in the basement. Can't move from here because the rents have gone up, up and completely outstripped my ability to pay and hundreds of thousands of us poor who can't hope to make that kind of money—while the newcomers can.

Can't open window to air my place out until the troll goes to sleep or leaves, for fear he will open up his door emit a blast of poison air out form his cramped room layered by cigarette smoke and clouds of noxious fumes rise up to my window and get sucked into my exhaust fan. Living was not like this for the first 7 years of my tenancy— before they stuck in that deficient unit in down in the basement to gouge more money from the building, and before this idiot tricked them and moved in.

PM Wednesday July 30
Dread facing the problematic situation in his humble studio, he loitered at the Burrito Shop, read discarded newspapers. Felt like a lost little kid again, unable to go home, wasting time, until dad got there—and it was safe.

Burrito shop. Reading account in newspaper—young man from the nation of Laos making the Olympics; he worked all his residency here in America at various minimum wage jobs and practiced his skill—badminton—gave his everything and made the grade. A feat to be proud of. Though he was in school, did not study much, nor go for a degree, nor at $6.50 per hour did he earn enough money to send home, only to support himself—he made a lifetime dream come to pass, of becoming an Olympiad. Few others have done this thru history. He belongs to a very unique circle.

PM Thursday July 31
This time it is a white youth who goes crazy-on the subway (BART)---singing black rap music; tall, skinny, a mass of dreads woven out of his straight white folks hair; he sings & dances making jittering hostile movements down the aisle of the BART car, more hostility then artistry. He is another dumb soldier in an enemy war. Tall, 6'6". Very thin. *"If I don't bring smile to your face, I ain't doin' my job"*, he chants; in reality most everyone has a worried look; he grabs his moment of hostile attention & intrusion, getting no appreciation.

The sun beats down in West Oakland; the lots of rusted machinery; see the many grey cement overpasses twisting; serpentine-----under which we once parked our van.

Regarding my statements about overthrowing the rich in retaliation for their domination of U$ poor and global poor: If I'm ever rich & famous people might ask *would you take back your words?* I'd say, how can I take back now, what I wrote then? If you had asked me then I'd have said Hell No! I won't recant what I'm saying; — because I was suffering! I was at the end of my rope! Today I'm a different person—it's not the same feeling; the tether is longer, the pain has subsided.

> Sean says he feels more & more these days that he's living in a cage, like someone who thinks they're free all this time and suddenly realizes they are just on the end of a long leash. Or someone who ventures out and one day comes upon the fringe of their actual territory, and feels the charge of the electric fence, and then realize to their sorrow they're actually inside a penitentiary.

That old hotel that saved us from having to live in our van, declared a landmark, was thus preserved from being torn down by City Re-

126

development—which spells black removal, cultural genocide--- that old hotel positioned between 2 blue metal glistening steel glass high rise government buildings; must go by it one day & see how its doing.

Black young men—driving by—angry because they've been sold out by their do-nothing jive petty-criminal fathers; sold out by white Amerikkka & her prostitute politicians; shoeshine lackey bootlicker city & work program officials. The ghetto once was a big place; it went on for miles and miles. Now it can be found here & there, unfortunate spots inside a re-built, gentrified white city. This makes the blacks who should have inherited it mad, but its too late now.

> One last look, lets examine the words of Fredric Douglass, ex-slave:
> Fellow-citizens! I will not enlarge further on your national inconsistencies. The existence of slavery in this country brands your republicanism as a sham, your humanity as a base pretense, and your Christianity as a lie. It destroys your moral power abroad: it corrupts your politicians at home. It saps the foundation of religion; it makes your name a hissing and a bye-word to a mocking earth. It is the antagonistic force in your government, the only thing that seriously disturbs and endangers your Union. It fetters your progress; it is the enemy of improvement; the deadly foe of education; it fosters pride; it breeds insolence; it promotes vie; it shelters crime; it is a curse to the earth that supports it; and yet you cling to it as if were the sheet anchor of all your hopes.
>
> Oh! be warned! Be warned! A horrible reptile is coiled up in your nation's bosom; the venomous creature is nursing at the tender breast of your youthful republic; for the love of God, tear away and fling from you the hideous monster, and let the weight of twenty millions crush and destroy it forever!
> --Frederic Douglass; 1700

PM Friday August 1
Back in SF. The tourists arrive; speaking French, Farsi, British, German, Russian; and, all Asian dialects, particular the ever-present Chinese.

PERMIT TO BUILD; 80' high building, 25 units—condos. This notice posted on storefronts, telephone poles. Immediately pasted up next to it is the wail of a neighboring tenant's concern that the heavy earth-moving machines will damage the foundation of their old brick & mortar buildings; and, when the building is finished, permanently

127

block the light. Prices going up up up, and so the real-estate acquisitions. Spoke to a young white lady from a good family back in Baltimore. She knows money—associates with it. Went 3 semesters to that Hydra-headed Art College which proliferates in downtown SF, taking gargantuan bites out of available housing stock; reconverting old theaters, churches, other businesses, into college dormitories to house its global-affluent student children. So there is money pouring into this place. The money magnet skims over earth, catching the scent of money, attracting money to come here. If you are poor you can't even get into this country. If you are poor you can't afford to live here—inside *housing* that is.

We are here, on the Pacific North West... I realize I may never leave this shore---to venture over the sea to Europe, to Asia; may never leave this shore until I go up to be with God in paradise.

The biggest trip you'll take-- & the shortest; straight to heaven.

161.
Your art, is an entrustment from the Most High –must protect it.

The secret realized to me now, is having all this extra time. After a fair amount of guilt all thru 1970, 1980, 1990, as over & over made plans to begin, but could not jump-start art, having to go to a job—monopolizing 8-hours per day, 6 in work and 2 in transit. ---Work to survive. Now, the only deadlines are self-imposed. I am free.

Am now surrounded by paintings, canvases, supplies—ceiling tall, will eat, sleep, drink, BE fine arts paintings. Re-assumption of my career.

AM early Saturday August 2
Am so glad have opened up the doors of fine arts paintings once again, it has added a whole new dimension to my life! Gives a new direction. My writing had seemed to die---selling fewer books, but more art prints. It's a whole new world—am now registered on 3 on-line art galleries to display & or to sell my work; and one writers website. Can't stress this so much again, how something one does, or something happens in their life, opens up so many wonderful doors, you get to that fork in the road, you make a life change.

Writer, painter, dancer, poet, —you must create as if your work is already famous, of world renown; & that each thing you did was very important.

A lot of art is predicated by what the artist/the viewer think art is or can be. For some its pastoral landscape, truly representational. For others, portraiture, which is photographically identical to the subject. For artists like me it's the inner imagination taken out of my head & soul and put down on canvass. The Illustration Of My Thoughts.

Later Saturday

> Only with Christ and God!
> Only with all the goodness in heaven!

Money all but gone, back to a life of stealing, begging, picking up stray coins on the street and recycling aluminum cans. Must return to the life of a scavenger. Of going off in all directions pulling my silver cart to join the food hunters in snaky lines outside free food banks/give-aways across the city, wasting precious time & most of the food must set aside from out of my box and given to others, as it is too fattening, too empty caloric garbage. Maybe will get sales @ Babylon Falling—have earned several hundred dollars there, divided between books and posters. The proprietor is due to matt my posters and sell them there in the store set in the rack with Emory Douglas, David Young & other's works. Each $20 is a big lift to my budget— each sale makes me happy—for it feeds me for 3 days!

The bible has installed itself in the vacant niche—at arms length— which had been constructed in the course of his most recent throwing- away of junk and rearranging, condensing what it necessary to keep. A niche; which had remained mysteriously empty, awaiting his realization for its purpose no doubt. Reach to it for sustenance—of a spiritual kind—yet the *he's* glare out at him, soon after digesting the scripture phrases, and are discouraging, because this is a document written for men, by men, tho its inspiration comes from the sexless Spirit; from God, who is neither female nor male, so what has been originally intended for the human race has been co-opted by the male half of the genome, and thus subjugates women, cuts them out, suppresses their role, their worth, their very validity and makes them

129

prime targets for abasement in the law as well as on this physical plane, --a plane where a male can damage & dominate most females of most species in hand to hand combat.—(reducing the equation to its most base element). However women do outlive men and die less in result of war, so some of them still will be around to tell how things really were, how war truly is, stripped of its allusion, its pomp & glory—to the dashed out brains and blown apart bloody torsos with no arms or legs—or heads, of which hundreds of thousands come back in body bags-- to the ears who will hear. I am a male; was genetically designed to be such, it is believed, but a few random signals went astray while I was still in the embryo and thus upon my emergence into the world out of mothers womb I joined the ranks of those transsexual, transgender—a queer world, and led a painful life. I am a man am designed thus by clothing, action, and desire; however I still have a feminist outlook politically, so the 'he's' which glare out from any torah or bible serve to cut me off from the very meaning of the thing. The thing, which is God Herself!

God arrayed in all Her glory! Big, all-knowing. Sad for Her lost children.

In Daughters of Courage Prince Valiant, a butch dike self-styled minister of her flock* de-sexed the bible by S'ing; that was to put a big red S in front of all the *he's,* turning them into *she's.* And many of us must do the same in our conversation when imparting the words from this Good Book to others, and in our own private thoughts. *the flock of about 5 or 6 which met in their residence hotel on Telegraph Avenue in Downtown Oakland—in fiction!

PM Saturday evening August 2
Bad News! Had a nice trip courtesy of Adela's Fast Pass—3 days grace-- went to GLBT center, cyber center, then on to Safeway. Originally this was the cheapest big grocery store in town, beating out Calla Foods. Well Mary, those prices have gone UP! No such thing as a bargain! And many affluent customers, dressed in leisure wear & sandals as if on a life-long vacation, go flip flop down the aisle; one sees them just pick those expensive items right up without a care, tossing them nonchalantly into their basket. Whereas the budget-conscious shopper carefully examines the cost before deciding wither or not to take the item. Can see this store has forgotten the poor, and re-designed itself to reap big bucks these rich gays and gentrified

condo owners have to spend, who will not flinch at a price tag of gross inflation.

Must say, that over the long years of my conversion (from atheism at age 33 or 34) I know the bible is a gateway to the divine, to spiritual illumination, the key to find Jesus, to find God—but as itself, is a dull, dry document. A repetitious work. And that read without this 'turning of the key', without the divine touch coming thru —it would be meaningless. And so can see how some can read it and not be moved at all. I don't know what miracle occurs while assembling together to study torah, or in bible study (often the same thing) that one suddenly feels their heart uplifted as if by Angels, and a golden glow falls over the room—even if there are no windows to let in mornings light--- this is what happens to me in religious study, but before I believed it did not. From time to time needing upliftance I must pick up the holy book and open it, or my life would be depressed, sad, and lonely. Often too I start in reading Paul or somebody and think to myself *I don't give a damn about Paul,* then thumb thru thru armies besieging armies of various nations, these cultural struggles and not be moved, till finally come to the gospels-- Jesus healing various diseases, but still nothing. But by then maybe the Spirit of the Most High sees my searching and touches me, for somehow, my spirit has been encouraged —and I have done that what I was set out to do, rescue myself from the pits of depression.

Other times I read more deeply into scriptures, and as a blue/white clea-moving brook, the water of Spirit comes charging into my heart quickly, and each word of scripture carries full weight and meaning— not as before, the dull dry verses I read only days past. What is the miracle here? I won't attempt to explain it, but must say, it happens each and ever time I consult the Good Book!

To Find List:
1. Swivel chair with a back, which goes up higher for office to replace low backless one, which will return to kitchen under table.

2. Small two-drawer cabinet to replace crappy sagging plastic one to hold sox & piss rags.

3. Big cardboard boxes—huge-- to cut out the top and bottom making one full size sheet to use as separators to go in-between stacked paintings.

Well--another rejection! Gay man posts flyers at our queer venues announcing he's doing a documentary about Polk Street, and like a fool, I answer it. Of course after phone interview he says *it will not work to have me in it*. Wouldn't that be nice, a photo of me, and some written stuff—good for publicity. But as this man says, *its primarily for gay men and trans women*. So where the hell are Transmen? And where the hell are butch dikes? I was cordial to this guy as he rejected moi, because as I said, *Well, I don't like it, but it is your thing*. And it certainly is not his responsibility to include me in the friggen' study! This is the problem tho, all these studies concern the flamboyant gay male scene, and the scandalous demimonde of sex-working trans women working the lipstick off their big mouths sucking dicks in car dates; but us dull, hiding-under-rocks butch dikes, and non-offensive passing Transman don't make the grade ever! Well here is one Transman who is gonna scream about it Mary! PS., fuck your non-inclusive ads at trans spaces! Keep 'em to yourself you prejudiced creeps!

For a lifetime, the idea was impossible; because of money, because of attachment's, because of their job… they went on as their ordinary selves—very feminine males, or very mannish women… but once they see they can transition, this why they switch so fast---no one believes they had it in them! Without wasting a moment, in a *snap* of the fingers! Seize the moment! What was always in their hearts. They transition to men. They begin to morph into ladies. Trans-sexuality.

Sunday AM August 3
Notes concerning the underground:
> I know you don't like to talk about evil, Dear Children—but you must not be deceived about this. There is an underworld and it takes prisoners. It takes prisoners & holds them over a lifetime.

Sunday, Service @ Grace, Transman sat, now in a rear pew, as he had before, almost 2 years ago, when he'd first ventured in. As if hesitant to extend himself so freely, interjecting his presence into the very front rows as he had just 6 months prior in the white hot heat frenzy of his re-church discovery, before that too went sour, and he fell away, especially as being re-employed to do Gods new calling, his painting. As the organ played a magnificent corral, he had these thoughts:

> The body of Christ needs a great reviving. Every several generations turnover & over—a new order must take place beside the old.
> --Words of the Most High to the Prophet. (Concerning Daughters Of Courage?)

That mornings service progressed as usual, with him having a wonderful feeling, as he gazed up at the grey arching supports of the mighty cathedral, that he was a baby elephant underneath his immense protective Mother Elephant (God) who was watching over him with great Love. Then it was time for the Blood & the Body, which occasioned those sitters in the back pews to move forward up the center aisle. He entered the long, marble paved aisle at which end, against a stone wall above the multitude stood the Cross: paused a moment; bowed to the Cross-- pledging service to Jesus, then walked up to receive his absolution thru the elements. He ate. He drank—symbolically.

Rising from the communion rail as old Transman tottered back to his pew; he glimpsed the tortured body of one of God's frail ones, a very young child, strapped into a wheelchair. *Everything I have I give to her, to heal her!* He thought. It hurt him so bad to see her frail, thin, body twisted. *Everything I have, I give.*

> --Those who do not feel these emotions; how could their hearts be so cold?

As he marched back to take his seat, he argued thus: God it's horrible what You do to Your children!… Whoops… it s not You who does this evil---Then an entirely new thought occurred to him, which never before had; *Christ teach me how to curse.*

Yes, because he must curse the one who is actually at the root of all this pain and suffering on the planet!

So that's how it all came about. His instruction about the underworld. We all have heard the scripture *Lord teach us how to pray*—but how to curse? That's new. When he was young, and an atheist, he often cursed God, holding this Entity to blame for the terrible state of the

133

earth. So now he must learn to curse the Evil One—instead of putting all the blame on God---who only moments before he'd felt was his Mother Elephant, magnificently protecting him and loving him as Her little one.

By the way the best curse of all against the Evil One is to proclaim total love and allegiance to God!

Oh, these are a few scriptures of this day:
> Sometimes dreams are wiser than waking.
> --Nicholas black Elk, Native American mystic; 1863-1950

> The mysterious nature of dreams and the truth they might reveal has always been a part of the Jewish, Christian, Muslim, and Freudian traditions as well. Today's verse from Psalm 17, 'summon me by night'—asks for God's complete possession of our mind, imagination and will both day and night.
> -- Meditation on the Word.

> You have proven my heart; You have visited me in the night; You have tried me, and shall find nothing. --
> --Show Your marvelous loving kindness, oh You who saves by Your right hand them which put their trust in You from those that rise up against them.
> Keep me as the apple of Your eye, hide me under the shadow of Your wings.
> Psalms 17, Vs 3, 7, 8.

I never thought that I might be considered armament for the Lord. — Not all my high words of great artistry, but because of my life. Being so poor etc, and being an example of the class divide in our nation.

If my words have stirred any one of you, or my fine paintings struck a note, you must realize the suffering that went into it---and the ten thousand other people like me more worse off, right in this country. Suffering within the venom in the bosom of our nation. Individuals who have retained their decency, and not fallen down into drugs and crime---but who are completely destitute having no money nor hope and are desperately floundering to stay attached to a city or town with its resources so they can survive—for if they loose this habitat and are forced to move away, they can no longer access food banks, churches, synagogues, charitable help, educational outposts such as universities, city colleges, with free computers, libraries, not to mention health clinics, and general hospital for acute care; the list is endless.

> Dear God make my feet like hinds feet; make my heart, a lions heart.
> --Red @ church.

After Services it's down California hill to the Supermarket. – (Whereas after synagogue, Shabbat Friday night, its trudging back up California hill, again to supermarket). Transman trudged back & forth down the aisles of meats, vegetables, produce, cans, cheese, sausages, searching for bargains. Finding none he settled for a $2.69 poor boy sandwich. Would dine on the meat in it, and then for a later meal, finish off the bread, dipped in olive oil. He spied eggs on his way out the final lane towards the check-out counter. The tortured kind of mal-used birds, mass-produced, maimed, penned, & brutally slaughtered.

No eggs! Not for me! No more pain for the animals!

162.
So, going into it's 2nd year, he had bonded with the bookstore somewhat---- Transman sat near the cash register, and was happy when customer came over holding stuff and the proprietor made a sale: *He sells a book—feel like I've sold a book.* And there's politics:

> The rich rulers make sure everybody in this system gets something out of it. Too many people are too comfortable—to do anything.
> ---Sean, Proprietor

> They are bedazzled—by money! Dollar signs in their eyes! I'll find a million dollars; I'll get bags of money! I'm gonna beat everybody else at the game. So they never give thought to how the system really works, much have any idea how to change it, so you don't really need a million dollars to live like a decent human being.
> --General Conversation

AM Monday August 4
Oh their gonna hate that... Was the first word out of Transman's lips upon stepping back to gaze at final touches to Hunger For God, brush in hand, his painting clothes mussed; this morning (2pm 'noon') cup

135

of coffee steaming; staring at the religious symbols; 7 of them, all signifying The Almighty... *The old prostitute in red/purple looks like a witch... The women's symbol... Islamic... Christian... Hebrew... Buddhist... all these symbols... and the title...and a witch... Aw shit!*

The Light licks down over the prostitute, embracing her neck, and touches down the back of the Arabic/black boy as well; whose gaze has been fixed on the nude figures frolicking in the greenery mid-canvas... Incidentally, least their be no doubt of Creator's Love, the Light of Hashem has made a proper collar around the old prostitutes low-cut dress.

Old Transman thought, goaning as he now stooping to pick up a dropped paintbrush; *Aw shit! Pain! Aw Mother of Jesus! I don't know what happened Lord, I was just living my life—all of a sudden I got old....*

PM
The old man thought about old age and dying. He had led a life of little harm, and reassured himself about heaven tho the whole proposition was very uncertain!

Early AM Tuesday August 5
Cash reprieve from pretend-cousin Angelo—thank God! $25 check in the mail from Madison, WI. AND Jasmin advanced me $175 to cover rent check, which will pay back to her when Renter's Rebate arrives. What a blessing. A Bingo Morning. Dined well that evening. The day for Transman consisted of visiting the Foundation Center and doing a casual look for grants—to the extent of his uneducated limits. Had to walk down 6 flights of stairs due to stuck elevator! *Bless God*, he thought; *that I wasn't trapped IN the elevator when it stalled!* After a long, tiring hike up/down hills, old Transman slipped an envelope with his *full* Social Security/SSI check—*plus $130 extra*--- into a gaping, evil, ravenous slot at the infernal property management company's office—which nearly chewed off his fingers in its great haste to devour mo' green money. Then on to the TL, where at its fringes on the downhill slope from a rapidly gentrifying area avec Yuppies, & potted ferns—was a Chinese market, very cheap. Got bunches of spinach, & cilantro, 1 huge yellow onion & $7.00 worth of ground beef—total price $9.70! Much cheaper then any big name supermarkets. Oh went in Trans Center—got Xerox,

gratis, for this book, and had a free dinner, Nicole cooking, fabulously as usual; baked pork slices, w/potatoes, mushrooms & celery. A delicious feast. Brother Peace was there, and the office manager Luke, a very nice young, tranny man who purchased RETROSPECT not long ago, and other stuff. The Center is planning an outing to SOMA, specifically to view the Frieda Kahlo exhibit.

> God excelled when it came to making cats & dogs.
> Dogs come from the well-spring of life.
> Are an integral part of humankind.

Why do I give my allegiance over to God? —Because the alternative is so horrible. Because I want to be able to champion the weak.

> Earth would be so much better
> if we all acted together
>   as a loving tribe.
> No more lonely moments.
> No more un-fed ones.

Did some work on 2nd RETROSPECT, which should be laid out like the 1st. Except for the inclusion of symbolism explanations, beginning with 6 thumbnail-size paintings from 1st book. And explaining all new ones.

Tuesday AM August 5
His pen flew over the page in a torrent of unedited thoughts. The old mans Journal JOURNEY continues:

Strange to see Ho's Bath laying on her side, up in storage loft.

PS, The Arab was the only painting I ever tried to transport by removing from its stretchers and rolling up the canvas---as was told professionals could do. Well its got a mass of wrinkles due to this, and I believe sustained more damage that way. Who knows? Well, cannot purchase it an exact fit stretcher bar set-up—my original hand made wooden frame was an odd size.

Worked on "Hunger" this morning---and had vision for a new work the other day, yellow/green stripes forming two hands, one large, one small, in perspective. Now am waiting for:

137

1. Richard to call and say the photo files of my 5 paintings are done.
2. Find a way to pick paintings & discs up from Richard.
3. Renters Rebate check to arrive; must buy:
   a. Stretcher bars to re-stretch The Arab.
   b. Fire safe box to hold eflusuiama of painting discs.
   c. Pay Jasmin back for rent advance.
   d. Take discs to Sean for Internet stuff, & to the infernal Korporate Kapatilist Kinkos to make posters & postcards to sell.

I thank Sean S. Richard P. & D. Jasmin, plus others for doing work for me, for enabling me, feeding & coffee-ing me (& loaning me money) for they've helped me on my journey—which is not easy.

> My greatest victories
> I count as loss,
> when I behold
> the wondrous Cross.
> --Standard hymn

PM Wednesday August 6
Bad health today and yesterday—feel all my strength gone, exhausted. Heart? Over exerted self, carrying those five 8' 2" x 4"'s up hill and frantic building. Now pay for it. Overdose of coffee—and continual conjuring up stress-issues out of my worrying mind. Am resting more.

It's just a 5-brush day, touch ups on painting. —Usually have 15 brushes or so laying in box with their bristles next to the appropriate dab of color, green blue, red, silver orange... or mixed shades.

PM Wednesday, August 6
Many times Transman had been forced to take his fine literature collection back to the used bookstores from which he'd eclectically purchased them at $2,3, $5 apiece—to trade back for food/rent monies. TS Eliot, Faulkner, Djuna Barnes, Kathy Acker, Shakespere, et al. However one genre of books he'd managed to hang on to—his fine arts books. En toto these consisted of:
O'Keefe & Steglitz
The Success & Failures of Picasso
Gaugiun, Quest For Paradise
El Greco
Van Gogh, Paintings & Drawings

European Master Paintings From Swiss Collections
Georgia O'Keefe, A Woman On Paper
Masterpieces of English Painting—Hogarth, Constable, Turner
Gauguin
Monet
All The Paintings Of Masaccio
The Letters Of Vincent Van Gough
Gauguin
El Greco & His Patrons
A Life of Picasso
A Concise History of English Painting
Frieda Kahlo Brochure

AM August 7, Thursday

There is a very sexist statement, 'keep them pregnant and barefoot'—
regarding keeping a woman under a man's control, hampering, to
disable her so she can't stray away, become independent, etc. So too
it is used in class warfare, 'keep them poor and downtrodden. Poor
people talk all day about what they can't afford to buy or what they
can. Where are their great ideas? Their great art? Most important,
where is the realization of the true source of their oppression! So it is
a class design—to not empower the poor class who labors in their
factories and fields, to not give them enough money, by which they
might save up to buy armies of their own and overthrow the ruling
classes. Socialism 101 Dear Children. Anyway realized I spent half
of my hour long session with my shrink at the city health facility, not
in deep analysis of my broken childhood, and the cause of my
Freudian psychic damage; not in trying to work thru this, but in
talking about money I don't have—regarding foods for my diet, and
fear of loosing my small studio apartment due to the landlords raising
prices and the rich continual trying to overthrow Rent Control off
their backs!

> Dear Children enjoy your cheeseburger w/ onion fries. Cooks labor
> over a hot grill to prepare food all day & night 24 hours non- stop. I
> am food service. Food of a different kind…

163.

> A rich & abundant life
> —to laugh heartily.

This is all Transman asked for. A minor success in his arts —at the
very least, and this.

139

I am a common person with no titles official, nor positions past or present publicly acknowledged. So it is easy to speak my mind. When I say, rough and true, trans community stabbed me in the back, and gay community credited me precious little, ignored me, barely supported me, there it stands. So it has done the same for other low ones, like me. There are some of us in the public eye who will say, they are 'suffering from burn-out' which is a polite way to say the same thing. But because they are titled and still in the system, and have pensions and positions at stake they can't afford to take the risk of speaking the truth. They have dirty linen, which still could be gone back over; uncovered thru careful scrutiny of government files and departmental searches, so they dare not say what I say. I have skeletons in closets too, but so what! Nobody cares! Nobody is paying my salary to be a consultant or honorary member of any board.

I realize how important it is to have a support group---down deep reassurance of our masculinity by sitting shoulder-to-shoulder, knee-to-knee with other transsexual men. Those men too distantly far away by geography or by personality divisions get depressed. So, I must pick myself up and start again, drinking from various trans-wells here & there, little oasis's throughout the normal life, after the bad influence of my group. This last year and-a-half has been excellent; associating with mostly straights (who have been highly supportive & helpful for my work) but as they say, every transperson needs their 'transfix' on a regular basis. To check-in with our Motherload, so to speak.

> The public must understand what it means to be a minority—it means things like marriage which straights just take for granted, as a necessary chore, to us is a privilege, and we are overjoyed at the prospect of it... so this is what all this marriage hoopla is over— (AM Sunday July 6)

Up at Trans Space, the women are bitching over ancient gossip regurgitated, about one of their 'cousins' on the queer gender spectrum. This one number, in the words of the T girls insists he's a fag, but the truth is that he's a queen who don't have the balls enough to be a T.

Polk Strassa—she's a tranny girl who is at home in the gay bar—she's masculine enough to be accepted. She is a tranny boy/girl who is at home in the gay boy community---out of the dwindling queer digs of Polk Strassa she does still have a few taverns surviving & wanderers between them; weaving thru the pedestrians; a very tall figure amid a street of straight folks shopping.

Transman was a bit envious, eying her form in a sequined bluejeans suit, wishing he could have had the free choice—all these years since age 16: *there is 2 less watering holes for us—we have none-- & I certainly do feel cheated* & having been kicked out of his group he felt even more alone and without social resources. While, overarching the whole sordid mess, old age *—human timeclock is ticking down on me!*

> What appetites I had! Ran the streets. Get out to the gay bar night, in a hurry, the gay streets! Our gay music! The gay kids! Akahol! Drama, sex, romance, love, intrigue. We ate up life!
> --Red, RE his teenage gay days 1950's-60's.

The old man went around town that day with a smile on his face, because Sean was back & the bookstore was open—beside him his new fiancé, Ms. Lamb. Kensey Lamb. They have dated for 3 years; known each other ten. Desolation row is gone—the littered stretch in front of the closed store opens up into a bright clean vista. There, to the left of the cashier's desk, the sun-bright window-seat, my stack of reading material. My home away from home.

Thursday PM August 7
Nada.

Friday AM, Noon, August 8
Quit a bit of painting involves sitting, gazing at a picture, seeing what it needs.

Late PM
> God wants to know
> When people have all the secrets
> Of life
> Will they abandon God altogether?
> When they conquer death,

Disease,
Pain,
Will they turn full face away?
With never more a prayer said
Upwards to heaven?
When we know,
All there is to know?
 What will we do?
What tree will we plant
With this root of all-knowledge?

The quartet of vacationers/documentary cinematologists, brings back this horror story from Jamaica. One of the great founding fathers of reggae music had been surpassed by other musician's fame, and stardom—and international recognition. His contemporaries he once knew, who were better able to market themselves. Time and the attention of fans has passed him by. He sees those stars he use to jam tunes with, their names in lights, and on recording contracts; in fine houses, driving sleek cars, marrying Miss Jamaica's, & beautiful light-complexioned movie stars. Now this founding father has glaucoma. Can't afford medicated drops for his eyes, can't afford the corrective surgery. Why doesn't he get angry about this? Because he's a religious man.

> It's like a cage. Some people have the better part of the cage, higher up over all, others in a more low down position spend all their energy trying how to figure how to get up to the better part of the cage. Others will band together and say lets figures a way to break out of here---to break out of the cage altogether.
> --Sean, Bookstore Proprietor.

164.
Oh, just found out the answer to the great debate! If you gesso over a painting, any kind, oil, or acrylic, you can paint either oil or acrylic over it! So I'm ok, having gessoed with several layers, all those found paintings o which I kept the original canvass. Much hoopla back and forth arguments on line as to oil upon acrylic or visa versa—however that referred to painting directly onto to the original—without the buffer zone of gesso inbetween!

Felt sick on BART, must have a bite of yogurt-but afraid security might bare down on me, God I hate these people & their rules.

142

Feel quite sick today. Well, must mention—went by San Francis hospital. Oh yeah, checked myself into the hospital emergency. We are one of the few people who harbor great dark worry and have to check hospital bracelet upon admittance to see if the admitting nurse got our gender/sex right on the band. Worried about my heart.

8:14 PM, August 8, 2008.
Tonight, around 8pm, we entered 4 more pieces of my artwork onto imagekind.com poster-print on demand public art gallery, also to another site... Thai-born Shaun Roberts comes into Babylon Falling with this reminder: *this is the luckiest day of the century according to Chinese myth. Because the Chinese name for number 8 sounds like a lucky word.* —Previously, this fact was announced by the gambling casinos, to lure Pai Gow, dice, slot machine, trade. So, this has been, coincidently a most fortuitous time. Happens we entered the stuff in at the 8th hour of the 8th day of the 8th month of year '08! Will it be my key to fortune, and happiness?

Wee Small hours AM Saturday August 9
Born again Christians make more atheists then Madelyn Murray ever dreamed of doing. As a tomboy child, young Red was slowly twisted, transformed emotionally; green jealousy, yellow bile, blackened hate, growing in his young soul, while seeing the blind church staring at him in his pain—and dong nothing to alleviate it! He thus turned from the idea of God... It took 25 years before he found God again.

A jet plane zooms fork pronged in the sky straight up, viewed thru spokes of the bay bridge span; admittance to this modern day. When he was a child at play in his sunny Chicago backyard, a trans boy in jeans, plaid shirt, and brogan shoes, he'd stop listen to the approaching propeller sound of old-fashioned airplanes and gaze up at it for a full 3 or 4 minutes the plane took to cross the blue/white heaven dome which arched over his view. How time has changed things! As it slowly, inexorably marches on!

Sky blue, clouds blowing west, behind the backdrop of towering skyscrapers, glanced up momentarily, now the clouds were blowing west, in a wild confusion.

Sunday AM August 9

I want to have fun! And I want to do art. Have decided! For the remainder of my life —fun & art.

This is from the 19th century novel that most influenced Russian Society:

I have no great passion for money. You know that people have different passions, not all of them only for money. Some like to go to balls, others like to wear fine clothes or play cards. All these people are prepared to ruin themselves for their passions, and many do. No one is surprised that they hold these passions dearer then money.

--WHAT IS TO BE DONE? Nikolai Chernyshevsky, 1863.

PM Sunday August 10

It must be remembered that during her egregious sexual pursuits— courting woman after woman, and simultaneously having sex with 3 men nightly—The Countessa de Nies—of de Lago was not solely immersed in the desires of flesh, no, —in back of all that perfidery—the Countessa was hoping, hoping, even praying (for she was a religious lesbian) that one day out of this string of debauched nights, she might meet a life partner & Alice, she felt, Alice of Nies, was it!

The couple had recently married, under the holy auspices of a clandestine priest—the small city of de Lago would have been scandalized by a public display. This priest, known—in the biblical sense-- by her brother---the flagrant Count Nepthfu de Nies (De Nephew) ---was a secret closet case himself—who had given up sexual performances for The Lord, but was still known to fondle particular parishioners in the congregation from time to time in weak moments. This priest preformed the religious rites of holy matrimony, and the wedding was well attended by handpicked number of friends, who could be counted on for their discretion; but no other relatives were told.

All seemed well for the happy couple—until an unforeseen incident occurred, shedding light on Alice de Nies's secret past, unknown to The Countessa… (To be continued.)

165.

Down in the shadows of the city is still cold, but up atop Grace cathedral hill sun shines bright. Tourists walk up/down the blocks of

this tres excusive realestate; gay men sail past in sportcars with
mariachi music blasting as if life was a non-stop party.

Sat alone in the sun on a bench studying the tableau before me, tables
covered w/checked tablecloths; small platters of cheese & grapes; two
pots of coffee, two of tea; the crowd. I saw @ Grace, while milling
about in the pleasant church plaza—there is no one I particularly want
to speak with. —Why? They are far above me in class. —All. One
leatherman in full regalia, head to toe, he has no time for me, nor
anyone who was not male-born. Saw again at Grace gays, lesbians
must learn how to be more inclusive across the gender border—which
does not mean sex with non-females. Just as straights must correct
their damaging hatred towards us queers. Was soon gathered up by
friend Jay & Kathy, (she an acolyte, Jay a greeter) with whom I've
spent time. Had enjoyable conversation together in the pleasant sun.

> Tell My Truths, until their deadened hearts know My Word, until
> their parched lips speak My Name.

Once again, at the Holy Tabernacle, God woke me up to the spiritual
world.

People must realize there is a good & an evil; the evil which lays at
the root of all our ills, worries, pains, problems. Tell them, Jesus
said—so I do:

> Satan, you are not good, you are evil. Only God is good--& because
> of this God is Great!

Hate sin!
Hate the devil!
Hated his mother and would have tried to kill her if him & dad stayed
in that crazy place. Which was at age 13. By his late 20's his heart
melted. Recalling slowly day by day how she'd truly loved him as a
young child. Mental illness took her over and became her ruler. And
the real her, died. So began to realize, must hate the disease, hate the
evil possessing his true mother. She was a victim herself. —Of
losing her spirit to mental illness.

AM Saturday August 16

145

In the deep of the night where people do dark things & think darker thoughts; when the mask comes off & the animal reminder of a humanbeing is nearer; more base. It is here, at that level, to which I first learned how to access, how to descend into the underworld; when thinking up ways to kill my mother. To escape the regular world of school and run away into the highways of night; when to shed the roles demanded of civilized beings; of convention, normalcy, proper etiquette. It is from here and beyond, that killers and serial killers are born.

Tuesday AM
I think this world is divided up between people who are highly damaging, to mildly so, and those who are really striving for The Light—whither this be religiously, or in statesmanship, or in family/community life, scholastic life, scientific life, infinite ways. They are trying to be higher human beings, and better their own kind. One small, insignificant nation can spark a war, one individual can do horrible things creating mass mayhem; one individual can save lives, souls, even nations.

All the ills we stumble into; this is why it is so good to turn to The Light.

> Baruch atah Adonai Eloheinu melech haolam
> Asher kidshanu bemitzvotave vetzzivanu
> La asok bedivrei Torah.

> Blessed are You, Adonai our God, Creator of the universe, who sanctified us with Your mitzvot, and instructed us to occupy ourselves with the study of Torah.

Well, the 13-Galaxies Man has made his mark into the book of records--for 20 plus years this crazy Asian man in aging blue-blalck suit & tie has carried a picket sign around town, written with babble-words about the existence of 13 galaxies. A nightclub is now named after his dementia—The 13 Galaxies Club— today see a youth wearing 13 Galaxies teeshirt. Of course this man is too crazy to have patented his saying.

> Nothing ever gets done unless its done by a fanatic.
> --Martin Sheen.

AM Wednesday August 13

146

Enter Little Saigon @ Eddy & Larkin Street, rows of colorful stores & restaurants, Vietnamese names. Tamura Ching goes here for her noodles every day. My cheap Chinese market is at the end of this row—where a sack of chicken is one third larger for less money then any major supermarket.

Like I said, I've lived a very poor quality life—marginal, outcasted. These are some of the words, which come to mind. Inhabited all the scummy places. ---Never the rich, as my mother intended for me, in fact programmed me, the two of them struggling to send me to private school, ballet lessons, and reading to me at her side on the wicker sofa; showing me art paintings prints from the library—culture. Many of us have lived this scum life—of dives, barrooms, low-cost hotels. Of cheap hustlers, drunks, in-&-out of prison kind. Many of us, because we are queers. Dating back to the criminalized time, when our love was a crime written into the law books of every major metropolitan city. Transgender queers—which is the obvious sort. Much of my writing is about the Strange Men-Women of San Francisco.

There's your work & there's yourself. Transman thought he'd been doing a momentous job at the first & somewhat avoided the second.

Well, a diet of failure can destroy someone as well…

> Artist! Don't be disappointed! Continue! As many of the other Greats have done before you! Each brush stroke! Each written word! Each on-point ballet step! The Great Dance Of Life must continue! Must have you! When discouraged, listen to the others who have gone up this rough, stark mountainside before!
> -THE PASSION OF ART

Their voices call to me from out of the past; think of Rodin, starving, tottering down from his attic room of frigid icicle-festooned windowpanes outside into the snow drifts, dragging himself thru the wintry Paris streets to the Louve; begging them to give him at least a small room as good as the one in which his great sculptures were housed, in comfortable heated surroundings on display in the museum. He was turned away.

Early afternoon Wednesday, August 13

Committed to the idea of revolution—and that means change—
globally; & personally, with myself.

Transman dreamed of his soon-success. To be able to protect himself
economically. To move up into a comfortable citadel. Removed
from strife. No longer part of the common fray. Nerves wired up,
anticipating fighting over a plate of food at Trans Space because of
sneaky, greedy—and dirt poor—*trannys*.

T Space. Where else would you hear one patron ask another:

> Does--X-- want to be called he or she?

And the answer;

> Oh either, she doesn't care!

The thing about the corner tavern or ordinary hangout, to a queer---we
don't have a queer bar on every corner---being we are a mere 3% of
the population—so we must travel long distances. All except for
when gay districts go up. Then every bar might be gay in some few
square blocks of a major metropolitan city. He thought in a blast
from the past, how fortuitous it was to him that he lived just 4 blocks
from the only trans center on the planet earth.

Oh, overheard at Trans Clinic the other day, when a vile straight
person of an ignorant mind stumbled in for an exam; this is what he
yelled, at the nurse:
> Don't want no gay muthafuckas touchen' me! Don't want no gay
> doctor sticken' his finger up my rectum! -- You kain't say nothing to
> me I'm a patient!

Got to Trans Center, a counterpunch—yes my plate was still there,
waiting for me, a wonderful salad w/fruit & raisins; some cheese &
bread; —however, two pieces of chicken had been stolen off of it!
See what lying, stealing backbiting population ours is! However, not
to be daunted, Transman immediately began to scream, & holler:
WHERE'S MY PIECE OF CHICKEN! And soon two ladies of the
staff came by with food platters and a pair of tongs and he selected

148

himself some deliciously cooked chicken pieces & bread. Which he
ate later @ bookstore.

166.

> Red Jordan Arobateau is not technically proficient—his peas in
> Tiger Woman On The Water Dining don't look like peas! –They
> look like green sci-fi blobs.

> Au contraire! He was a po' old man! He couldn't afford to go out
> and buy peas just to study and paint into his picture! —He had to
> eat what came his way! If you're poor you can't just go out and buy
> peas—and throw them in the stewpot after you're done using them
> as a model! May not have had $2 to buy any peas!
> --Conversation about the Artist, after his fame, in the year 3000 ACE.

Well, the story behind Tiger Woman Dining On Peas On The Water is
that I wanted to paint the two tiger hands, big and small for
perspective, and noticed that the size canvas called for, which sat
blank, white, waiting in the kitchen, had wrinkles from being poorly
stretched, by myself. Oh well, am too tired to restretch. When I set it
on the easel, noticed it was lopsided as well! I'll manufacture that
right into the painting… I says, liking motion in a work. So naturally
if Tiger Woman is dining on peas, and a big green pea rolls away
from her, and the plate is sliding sideways and so is she---its because
'de boat she be a rocken' because Tiger Woman is On The Water!
Acrylic on Canvas; 29 ¾" x 30 ¼", irregular. Tiger. An 8-brush day.

AM Thursday August 14

> Tho the past of Alice de Nies was well hidden, for reasons we will
> see, it could be uncovered by meticulous examination—that she had
> a deep dark secret. Alice had once been a hooker—for women. Yes.
> And this is how sweet Alice, passive, compliant, and somewhat of
> an airhead, had learned the secrets of feminine pleasure—thru
> selling her body; her sexual services to various lesbian and bisexual
> women in every nation on the continent, and several major cities of
> the New World, America!

PM

God takes time, yet time always moves on, inexorably. I tried in the
ways I could. Now where my life is going I do not know.

149

AM Friday August 15
>
> The goal that I'm willing to accomplish is that I'm willing to go all
> the way.
>
> --Overheard on San Francisco streets, 2008.

Must Go All The Way. That's a title for a book!

Hashem, thanks for the plenty, we have more comfortablitly. Get this
from reading of the harsh life of the early part of the last century—the
1920's. There was no old age insurance, like Social Security. No
mass-produced clothes so people could dress decently at an affordable
price.

PM Friday afternoon August 15
>
> Don't be discouraged
> There is more to do.
> You must stay.
> You have work to do.
> Reparative work
> To the soul.
>
> Don't be sad
> When someone goes.
> They are going to a far better place.
>
> Everything in their proper place.
> Everything reported.
>
> **
>
> I have come so that
> One may be two.
> The Holy Spirit of God said
> And cyclically, love was back in my life.

Will again say I began engineering myself for fame when around age
14 toying about in my room with books, paper, pen and ideas I added
an A in front of my name which then began with an R, after years of
kindergarten and highschool torturously waiting thru the larger part of
the attendance roll call to be announced alphabetically as I trembled
in nervousness thru the lugubrious A's, B's, C's D, E, F, G's, on &

150

on. Today, an inadvertent blessing; how handy it is to find my name very near the beginning on literary anthologies.

> Rebel George who invented the gold brick swindle: The way to sell a brass brick is to bunko yourself first into the belief that your brick is solid gold—the rest is easy. The most successful bunko man is one who bunkos himself before he goes after a sucker.
> --YOU CAN'T WIN Jack Black, 1920.

So I have, over the last 4 decades as an author, and now, again, writer-painter slowly convincing myself of my supreme worth as an artist. I have bunkoed myself into believing it! Thus labeling myself, these last 10 years or so, as Master Author!

August 20, PM Wednesday.
Art—it is the world's, artist, —don't take too much credit for it!

PM early afternoon Saturday August 16
Summer Place tavern; very nice evening; establishment run by Korean lady, Sue, good time was had by me, two Shaun's the Lamb (Kensey), bartender Sue, a patron; w/Shaun snapping photos for an assignment from a local news rag. Place allows smoking however despite this; we like the joint & intend to come back but must discuss the wisdom of returning on a heavy smokers night like Friday.

AM Sunday August 17
New happening for the regular, commercial TV stations now broadcasting world Olympics in Beijing China,-- to hear them talk about *Chairman Mao*.

> I hate this city! Rich people! Snobs! Snobs everywhere! They infest this city like termites.
> --Alex Paez, a dapper young gentleman.

So it comes time once again, after all the pains & disappointments, a weary societies minds dimly turn to ideas of revolution—which the TV commercials advertisements of the day co-opt. But real revolution is when people with too-low paying jobs to live, throw off their yokes & bosses, somehow, don't ask me how, there have been many plans for this, some have succeeded others failed, all over this world, all thru time… revolutions….

151

AM Tuesday August 11
I have been very industrious in my life. I worked---yes I worked, for
37 years. Now have a small social security check. Plus stayed up late
nearly all my life writing poem after poem, novel after novel... Well
this leads me to the following comparison:

Socialism 101:
RE: Let The Good Times Roll.
Medieval times in Europe & even later, in Europe, the poor labored
all year in dire poverty, partaking in sparse dietary variety, often one
containing no meat for 8 or 9 months. Once a year the nobles of the
ruling class would open up the Great Hall of their castles and every
surf, or peasant, everybody under the nobles jurisdiction was invited
to eat all they want, drink all they want & not just for a few hours, but
all night long. Weddings too and other grand occasions, the Great
Hall was opened to everyone. These days you don't see the rich
owners opening up their mansions & inviting all their workers in; like
president to General Motors, Bectal, or owner Halliburton. As Sean
says; *"yeah, they've refined their techniques of oppression".*
Bums walk by w/ruined faces as evidence of their dissolute lives.

> The desire to possess land, whether inherent or acquired appears to
> me to be a sure safeguard against a wasted, dissolute, harmful life.
> --Jack Black YOU CAN'T WIN, 1920

Sunday AM August 17
A racist happening at church—old white man asks me if I can read...
* Well, thank God the old guard is moving out.
*This is what happened, old white man & his wife sat in the pew in front of
Transman; during the peace, where the congregation shakes hands with those
around him, he greeted T in a familiar way, as if he recognized him from
somewhere—which was impossible. At the services end, as we all milled around in
the people-clogged center aisle, this old man suddenly opened a billfold and showed
Transman a $10 bill, asking if he wanted it! Transman was stunned, hesitated,
looking bewildered at the money, then just as suddenly the old man snatched the
money away, then asked T "can you read?" Transman was speechless! He was
bewildered! Choosing the wisest of victories he hastily shuffled away from the
noxious scene; behind him he heard the ancient wife ask her husband 'well ----, how
did you like the service?' For several days after Sunday, this incident would pop up
in T's mind, and thru his bewilderment at this unjustified incursion upon him,
slowly realized it was racist motivated.

See my own non-stop sarcasm. As most queers. Because we have half lives. Only when you're out in the straight world do you see this clearly.

When Social Security was first introduced by President Franklin Delano Roosevelt, his Secretary of Labor was asked by a republican Senator; "Isn't this socialism?"

T girl we knew use to tell us, *"this is my restaurant. I go there every day. Breakfast, dinner; sit there with coffee for hours daily."* Now its closed. No longer *'her restaurant,'* Slated for some upscale removal-of-the-poor rich peoples condo's & cutsey bouquets!

> Christ fed the multitude with one loaf of bread,
> Poor people, there is something for you.
> --Damian Marley, Jamaican Reggae star

Must say a great dissatisfaction, which has possessed me most of my days, for as far back as I remember. First as a child, rebelling against unfair parental restraints, then my early teens, burning desire; yearning to escape security of my torture in the middle class, wanted to hit the highway of escape to freedom. I did escape a few years later. Freedom. Yet dissatisfaction haunts me still. Yearning pursuit of a woman, a companion for a happy home; but once in relationship for 16 years—itching for freedom again; was with God but still searching for something indefinable. Tried to feed myself, to feed this hunger; there was no answer.

Sunday AM. August 17
Higher thoughts. *Welcome.* --- The Word, the singing; his spirit soars. When he came in, walking up the center aisle looking for a spot in a pew near the back—as was his custom these days--- he noticed a black woman, very dark complected; in poor clothes, who kept changing her seat. She sat staring at some white people nearby for a while, giving them an up-and-down scrutiny, very openly rude then arose and changed her place, to repeat this performance with someone else. Her hair was in plaits with some fancy beads, thick nose and lips, very African-beautiful; also astoundingly different then all the 800-person congregation.

The sermon that day was about the Samarian woman. Watching the obviously mentally ill woman changing places to stare up and down at various parishioners, Transman had the following: *I think the Samarian woman is sitting right here in this congregation.*

Old Transman's eyes traveled up the height of the grey stone wall, to the vaulting stretches where the arches meet together for the apex. His eye stayed where all the separate arches conjoined at the very peak of the cathedral:

> Everyone will have a time.
> Everyone will be called.
> Like communion when the ushers move down the center aisle
> row after row;
> the usher beckons indicating the whole row, to go to the alter;
> some are first, some find themselves in the middle,
> others last — depending on how they were seated.
> Watch and hurry to your place
> when your turn is called!
> So don't be jealous or in a hurry
> as the others go before.
> Your turn will come — Be ready!
> Watch!
> Be mindful!

Realized he may have made the mistake in measuring The Howl. The frame he'd built for it is so solid—half inch thick strips of wood—that they never jiggled loose in 40 years of traveling, and bad treatment— like most of the other frames, who were now knocked off, partially, or all gone, or one, La Suena whose frame --thin one-quarter inch strips had two sides missing. So that The Howl's wood fame had morphed into the painting and taken on a symbiotic life with it, and I measured the whole thing inadvertently, being so use to it. So the size of the actual *canvas* is 13 & ½" wide, X 12" vertical.

Monday PM early August 18
People do not know what they're dealing with when they deal with a transsexual. The rules are different for us then for normal people—by necessity. Our rules are not your rules. Regarding marriage, relationships, etc., for instance. For years and legacy of meeting in the shadows, with no hope of validation for our couples, can't expect

that the trans person would entertain the same expectation of a legal marriage being a fulfillment in the natural course of a relationship— most of us have lived in sin always, and majority of our relationships short-lived, and non-monogamous. Straight people viewing this have no idea what to expect and if under their watchful eye their children are coupling off with a transperson, they might not be prepared for the course this might take—if they themselves don't step in and try to elevate this newcomers situation, suggesting and arranging a marriage themselves. This perhaps is now different in the upcoming generation, if the parents of trans children are enlightened, and their community in which they are a part of, supportive, then my words don't apply-- for they have already coached their trans child and the partner of their trans child on' the right way to live' but all too many areas of our country and globally, we still 'meet in the shadows' are criminalized, and any thought of legalized or celebrated marriage is not a possibility.

Walking the streets. No $. Heart problems. Age 65. Some people start preparing for their golden years at age 18; I begin at 64.

Poor old Transman had eaten only one can of tuna fish all day--- and had had to share it with the cat. That evening Transman returned home with 2 fish, some leafy collard greens, 4-cans of cat food. He put the fish in a pot and boiled them ten minutes. Upon returning he lifted the orange colored lid, and saw there was only mush left. But it tasted good.

What I'm trying to do is to be wise. I have slowly reduced my weight, and now, am again trying to give up the *purchase* of red meats, even chicken. And buy only fish, for homecooking. This means when I'm out being treated by a friend, or eating at a party, I will eat anything (no sugar nor substitute sugar of course) but what I eat at home is going to be strictly fish. So this means my beef/pork/ chicken consumption will drop to 20% or less, and the fish will zoom up to 80%. This is called Heart Smart. Today purchased a vegetarian burrito (yes cooked on a grill—not the best) and the two fish. Go in for heart stress test at hospital tomorrow. Wake Up Call.

Tuesday AM early August 19
Morning of my stress test @ hospital in a few hours.

Transman is ushered into a white walled room with large equipment; given a shot intravenously by which the camera can trace his heart.

Maybe there is a cure! The modern heart exam equipment is impressive. We are entering the super-future world, no doubt about it. A sci-fi world envisioned when I was a child. People are traveling thru outer space in a combination jetplane/rocketship. Technology & science forges ahead. Medical breakthroughs. Will I be relevant to this new world? Transman thought: *they will need someone like me*, and what he had to say.

167.
Thursday AM August 21
Religious Instruction, RE DOC:
I am a too large canvass upon a sturdy stretcher, well-built but too small for the canvas. This canvas is a masterpiece. Its beautiful pastel edges will be compromised—curled over the frame and tucked under in order to fit the too-small size. My love was great—the greatest gift. But the structure of my personality had been built up on hate, jealousy, rage, fear, envy, anger, competition, retribution—and smart retorts. The Angel Peace came to me, clothed in white clothing, with some gold & turquoise trimming, and began instruction this morning, upon awakening, groggy, from sleep:

> God is going to give you 20 more good years, maybe beyond that ten, fifteen, even more, —depending on what you do. You must begin this day, to live as God dictates. As a man of peace! I will work with you every day, every hour on the subject. Remember, your great love will be able to heal and change all these situations, involving your resentments & hates.
> --The Angel Peace to the Prophet Red.

The canvas is more valuable, ultimately, so the bones of its constitution must be altered to fit the canvas—which is Love. Each stretcher bar, must slowly be extracted from its current configuration—locked in to the rest in a mighty position of self-defense, and pulled out to fit the true love, in the size the canvas demands. Each hatred, each rage, each resentment, each jealousy, each gossip, each backbiting, must slowly melt under the onslaught of love—Love Divine, and be pulled out into a new shape. Ultimately, becoming a far more advanced humanbeing.

There are other tools, which work in the same fashion. A person in whom Love is not a dominant emotion—in fact one they may have little of--- might have a powerful desire to help others. And thru this fashion, slowly they will learn to rebuild themselves as well. Learning patience, toleration, acceptance, and begin to pull their stretcher bars out to meet the vast perimeters of their gift---as a helper of humanity.

Love is the greatest gift; it contains all of these others. There are many other gifts, and all can be used by the specific individual to pull themselves out into a bigger, person, a with more saint-like qualities developed!

List of Saint-Like-Qualities, each individual has at least one of these qualities, and thru the use of it, and contemplation on their gift, can use it to build a more saint-like self:

Honesty—in all situations
Compete trustworthiness
Forgiveness
Desire to teach others
Understanding of frailty in others
Generosity—expecting nothing in return
Encouraging to others.
Helpful to others
Loyalty to a just cause.

For the longest life possible, you must do this, above, in everything!

Hatred,
Rage,
Resentment,
Jealousy,
Gossip,
Backbiting,
Aversion to other humanbeings.

These are the tools you have forged for yourself---like an armadillo's quills, like a snail's shell---protection from the advances of a harsh world, a world of fist-fighting and self defense; this armament ultimately will destroy the soldier.

Evidence! The Evidence! The bleeding wounds. The broken heart.

*

I touted my own fame. I did it because nobody else would do it.
Thus, being defacto judge, & critic, I might have misplaced myself on
the scale of greatness.

> Fame is dangerous: it can ruin a journalist as easily as it can ruin an
> artist, and Thompson, who was essentially both, was definitely
> dammed by it. Though Thompson complained about fame, he
> embraced it. He played a version of himself on the world stage, and
> the minute he stated doing that, his best work was behind him.
> --Mick LaSalle, on Hunter S. Thompson, SF Chronicle July 4, 2008.

PM

> I'm in a period of time when I have money—I just don't have it
> right now...
> --Words of the Prophet, Red

The old man sat at his desk under lamplight. It was 10pm. Having
just finished his sojourn @ the bookstore. His eyes gazed upwards,
the bible, open in front of him at Luke; he pointed to the scripture—
take up thy bed and walk--- that's what I want Jesus! That's what I
want from you! To be healed! That's what I want from You—a
friend, and a healer to cure me!

AM Friday August 22
Nada.

AM Saturday August 23
The old guy felt sick that morning. Was it bad fish he'd cooked –to
save money—which festered in his backpack 4 hours while he sat
w/friends @ Summer Place? Was it the cigarette smoke, which fills
the club? * Felt bad. Worried about his heart. Sick in body. He got
up anyway and prepared his painting station. He thought; *I have to
keep working. It's my only hope of something better.*

*Sue, the sole bartender/worker-owner does not smoke, and dislikes it; (plus liquor
as well), but this is her livelihood, by which she's putting two children thru college.
Without smoking privileges the crowd would dwindle to one-fourth the size.

Great news! Sean has showed RETROSPECT to a book publisher...
Who took a copy back to show the other partners at his business!

Sold two more RETROSPECT'S also, and hope to sell one or more posters this Seniors Day at Grace. Thank God for Jasmin advancing me $100 in two increments about 3 weeks apart to keep me eating....

Well said a Rondo was 5 JOURNEY books, wrapped up into one big segment; but am going to close this current group at 3 only, a triumvirate, a triptych; (MY CONTINUING JOURNEY INTO SPIRITUAL, ARTISTIC & REVOLUTIONARY THOUGHTS) then on to another grouping— ILLUMINATIONS, or maybe ILLUSTRATION OF MY THOUGHTS might be the first title...

AM Sunday August 24

There is a little (under 5') older African-American lady political activist who is a presence here on our block, the length of which traverses thru district 3, who is working for a supervisor candidate, David Chiu. She goes up to people and business owners and makes herself known. She is advised of the law, regarding Rent Control especially; and we both agree, we must preserve this, one of the few preserves of the poor in this city.

> I first met Miss Daisy, this little older lady, she sees me and my friend sitten' out in the car, --our place is so small and cramped; it doesn't get any sun, so a lot of time we just go out and sit in the car, and one day this little lady comes up to us and sticks her head in the window and says; *Hello, I'm Miss Daisy, I see you all sitten' down here all the time... you ain't narks are you?* Narks she says! She thought we might be narks! And that's how I met her.
> --Meeting Miss Daisy as told by Veronica.

I promise you I will change my bad ways, Mother Teresa, if you just grant me this wish that my health be restored. Transman spoke aloud in the stillness of his studio. Then his wandering thoughts took him speedily to the place which he refers to in the introduction to this book. Must change my interior—otherwise I am a hypocrite—hatreds & self-aggrandizements puts me in the same category as the assholes of prejudice, selfish unholy greed. And then... After self-improvement is accomplished... what then? What good can I give to the world—beyond my Fine Arts!

Regarding possessing all worldly things, but still being sad inside, --
Sean comments how he has everything most cats would envy, a store,
a nice apartment, a beautiful girl, money coming in, but that:

> Now that I don't have anything to complain about, I find I'm just a
> miserable asshole.
> --Sean's Great Tragedy.

Transman stood in front of Babylon Falling as slowly the sun crept
across the street to the side where he was; and climbed up over the
curb, dark line of shadows inextricably moving, and was soon 3 feet
from his shoe tips.

Transman casually eyed a piece of fruit in the street hungrily—it sat
by the curb in the gutter—he had not enough motivation to pick it up.
People walk by all ages of life—ancient, old, graying middle-aged,
young racing along on skateboards... it's like time running out....
Young, then inbetween, then old... Old age—human timeclock.

The sun is about to disappear behind the tenement tops, street
darkening, subtly, in shades.

I am reminded of the scripture; work, while the sun still shines.

Being an artist is a different kind of discipline then being a nun or a
priest; but it is the same devotion to God's Calling, and should be
obeyed for the maximum performance of the humanbeing in point.
One would not pray to Vincent van Gogh, or Picasso—not even
Frieda Kahlo, although some do—as they would to St Francis or St.
Anthony, for intercession between them and God, to cure incurable
situations. The Saint is higher up on the ladder, but all of us have our
place and purpose!

Again, what the intro to this book says—

> You should know that one of these days the time will come to put into
> action the sympathies which you have held for so long, those close to the
> heart. Those issues you've spoken impassionedly about, discussed &
> ruminated over in your small study groups, concerning those situations of
> injustice on earth which rankles your ire to such a fiery degree!
> -- COMPASSION

160

Now what I said about Mother Teresa, (synonymous for a Saint-like Person) is that she went all the way with her love for God, proving it thru her Works and Deeds done for the betterment of God's Creation—Us, humans, and the world!

PM Sunday August 24

We were at the cabstand, and asked are there any hotels around here, and this big blond says, "Oh! The only hotels up there are for 1 hour!"
--Lev, recounting he & wife's incident while waiting for a cab, SF

*

This is the way Alice de Nies whored her way across the face of Europe, and visited America, in two cities, on the cheap---her clientele being exclusively female. Alice, nee Alice Dunngon, seldom could meet a lesbian or bisexual woman just casually strolling the avenues, or working in a cathouse for women—which are all but non-existent. Heterosexuals & gay men have their restaurants, bars, brothels all set up to facilitate their coupling. Lesbian society picks up along the edges. Thus Alice Dunngon was more for close up encounters—at parties, art gallery openings, university lectures---, and of course, the ubiquitous lesbian bar. Her technique was simple. To arrive with sufficient cash to pay her way thru the evening while meeting and greeting women and gathering a crop of phone numbers. Her follow up, on a date, was to go Dutch with ease in the initial part of the evening, but to suddenly fall short on cash, where by the mutual festivities could not continue—the wining, dining @ posh restaurants; shows, clubs, etc., without her partner footing the bill for them both, the remainder of the evening. It was this stratagem which led her like a diver (a muff diver) runs down the spring board (well) hung over a blue pool, then takes the leap—to maneuver herself easily into her revelation that she was in economic distress, and needed a Princess Charming to come to her aid---temporarily—was the line she used—until 'funds arrived' from whence or when, she was never clear… And by this fashion got hotel rooms paid for, meals treated, apparel purchased on credit, for which she offered promises, and good will.

Most all of her encounters were high scale affairs, involving wealthy heiresses, or very upper striving entrepreneurs whose salary was in 6 figures; but she was known to have turned a toilet trick when

161

necessity knocked hard. For instance that time in a lowclass gay dive, when, spying a drunken denim dike getting too loose with her weekly pay, spilling twenties and fifties out on the floor, then drunkenly scooping them back up helter skelter & stuffing them here/there into her jeans pockets, Alice sauntered up to the drunk dike, swinging her hips, hastily having undone her brassier so her tits bounced free, and lashing her long blond hair to and fro magnificently, like a wild, untamed pony, and propositioned her; the scenario went something like this:

Hi! My name's Alice! You're cute! Do yuh wanna make out with me in the little girls room?

Huh! *Yeah!*

Ok! Come on then honey!

(Five minutes later, a line has formed outside the toilet and the patrons are crudely referring to the closed toilet door:

What's taking her so long? Bladder issues?

(Putting ear to the door) Someone's in there giving birth, all that moaning and groaning. (Puts ear to door again) Humm, *two* people are in there giving birth…

Two people! Well! (Puts ear to door also) Shit! Their screwing in there and I gotta piss!

WELL CUM ON ALREADY!

When the denim dike staggered out, lipstick smeared all over her face—and her pussy---confidently and pleased headed to the bar, to refresh her glass, to pay for it she fumbled in her pants pockets over and over, suddenly realized, OHMAH GAWD! I BEEN CLIPPED!! Her weeks pay of $400 was stolen! ---And by then, Alice done gone!

168.
Have returned to painting on Self-Portrait—The First, Home Sweet Home. Oil on Canvas, 15" x 30".

A 10-brush day. Toxic oils & turpentine filled his studio, the painting was a mess of pastel lavender! Slowly he began to repair it with deeper color purple. Ahhh… An artists Life…

A 10-brush day. *Now I'm really painting.* Then he bustled about his studio, tidying up busily, and, being lonely, tried to invent a family in his mind. Describing each detail to himself.

Transman went out on his daily routes. He admired the city architecture. Buildings festooned with crenellations, bas relief's, cornices, everything short of gargoyles spouting rainwater. At the Trans Center he overheard this typical comment:

> I'm trying to get rid of my guy stuff and the only coat I have to wear is a guy coat.
> --New transgender woman.

These poor trannys are only so glad to put upon themselves castoff outer garments of females, courtesy the 2nd hand thrift shops, & worse. The old man trudged uphill towards the market. See seagull on peeked roof chasing pigeons. The crone who feeds them leans out of a different window—the one opposite, smoking. Gaunt, haggard, grey. Then, a jolting conversation overheard:

> --All the transgenders be up in here.
>
> --Yeh, ah'm tellen' yuh man—my momma came n' picked me up after work last night, she say, all these funny folks around, she can't stand to see it.
> --Overheard on SF Lower Polk Street.

To be nice & polite is easy for some people because their lives are easier. Don't have the additional trans baggage we have. T saw his own anger: *yet I am committed to a whole new life. I will take a humble walk… I will God, in this life---from now on.*

> If you're going thru hell---keep going.
> --Winston Churchill.

Get too close to people afraid they can hear me breathing. This is the sign of a hunted animal. This is a technique for self-protection.

Man stands staring; another, smoking, as I go past; realize I hate everybody—but, I love everybody too.

At the bookstore the young proprietor races around, handfuls of books, setting them here and there in some apparent pattern:

> Almost done with these fucken' things.

While a song floods out of computer amplifiers, coating the anarchist-socialist flavored shelves with a golden layer of appropriate music:
> The banks are made of marble,
> With a guard at every door,
> And the vaults are stuffed with silver
> That the old folks sweated for.
> --Old Wobbly's song—1900rds.

Every electoral official who is contender to high rank must be a millionaire these days—those of higher offices, have funds within the multi-million dollars. Yet regular folk who work 40-hour weeks and more are loosing their homes, the roof over their heads for want of a simple 3 or 4 thousand dollars. This is why America is no longer a true democracy. This is why America has lost the freedom promise she once had. When land could be had in exchange for hard work. Before the rich began greedily devouring land parcels into untold amounts of acreage, keeping all for themselves, whereas each smaller person wanted only one or two parcels for their families alone, and not for profit. Not to be exploiting others.

The human race has evolved down a long dusty trail and has moved from simplicity and cooperation of the tribe —by necessity—, to a great division among itself.

> We will soon realize the necessity of global cooperation!

AM Wednesday August 27
REVOLUTION NOW!
If we don't overthrow this tyrannical system today, we may never again have the chance—not in 1,000 years—until it atrophies of its own accord.

PM Wednesday, August 27

Transman thought about his stress—his heart, the inescapably cigarette smoke permeating his small studio from two chainsmoking fiend neighbors—the inexorable rising cost of living in this rich city, stress now making inroads to deluge his heart and how he could not escape this predicament trap Satan had set because studio prices had risen to $1,300—$300 more then he now paid. How he barely scraped together. Moving away was impossible, escape was impossible. So, he wrote this:

> Must remind you again this system must be destroyed, eradicated, fini!
>
> For you—reading this in the privacy of your home! For you already heavily involved in the struggle on the battleground itself.
>
> What kind of society?
> Hospitals--The sick person walks in & get as all the aid necessary.
> Education--Each parent sends their child to school for no charge and the pupil goes as far as their ability & desire takes them—into specialized degrees—with no worry of student loans, with no worry how they are going to pay room and board while they are engaged in the full-time job of study.
> Prison system--Which is corrective, not punitive—at least in the beginning of a criminal record, not totally restrictive and not persecuting. However if the offender shows themselves to be a career criminal they are totally restricted, and this not a punishment, but to protect the rest of society.
> The arts—Subsidized.
> The military—Mandatory 2 years of all able-body citizens, pacifists can choose a desk, cleric, or military hospital jobs.
> Work—Mandatory, each person guaranteed work after education and military is complete.

Later the old man went out. Honk horns, noise of the city, abrupt, surprise. Made his toes curl.

Glumly purchased 2 cans of cat food. He shared his sandwich with the parrots. Maybe that lady would purchase a poster @ church the next day and his wallet would be satisfied. Then, in 7 days, RENT due again!

Thursday AM August 28

A Cannon Lampen Thursday—Senior's. Bible study in an hour, it's 8:45.

> There are plenty of modern idols—as well as ancient ones.
> --Cannon Lampen, bible study

--To remind you that I have forgiven all, including the food fascists, here I am again @ Senior's Dinner, there they are—complete with ladles and tongs and platters---let the trial begin!! The trial of righteousness! Forgiveness! Tolerance!

> The Dalai Lama has never said anything bad about the Chinese who have taken over his home, Tibet. The Dali Lama got the message the Chinese had destroyed another Buddhist monastery & immediately he said *now we must immediately pray for the Chinese*.
> --Steve @ Senior's Films.

Sold The Arab to lady as promised. Can buy food!

Noon Friday August 29

Am 11-brush day. Good work Red Jordan!

PM Friday August 29

Walk back/forth from computer book, to easel, painting. Blue paint on the keyboard… Soc. Sec. check every month finances the bulk of it. So I can keep going. As for the rest, --sales. Acquisitions. Collectors. And, as a backup, Vincent van Gogh had his brother Theo, & I have Jasmin.

AM Saturday August 30

> We're all writing the same thing
> All us dead poets,
> living dead poets, dropped out, government check-
> receiving deadbeat, retirees, poor, won't/
> can't work poets;
> ranting about the system
> which has failed us as it
> failed our parents, but differently;
> well God forgives our anarchy I bet
> because we are so far dropped out of this
> Empire which lives by destroying other lifeforms,

sucks the marrow out of cultures, inserts its presence like a cancer
of strange of military-industrial powers..
We living-dead poets—
So far off the money track.
Much less guilty by reason of not being
 part of the problem.
Condemned only being self-condemning.
Having little hope—
 No money,
No-good lovers,
Not enough true friends,
No permanent home,
And too damn poor, stressed, under-appreciated, unknown, dead,
but living
 artists to be neither brick nor cornerstone of Empire,
Only mixed up in the rot at its base,
One in the sediment broiling
green-black at bottom, in dissolution.
Eating out the foundation of the Great Beast from its lowest depths,
 where the rich dare not go,
where the suits cannot see;
Us dead poets; some of us have become
lost ghetto survivors,
trailerpark white trash,
barrio blues mumblers
and the most severe;
wide-eyed insane zombies of skidrows
Across Amerika.
So read the 'zines,
As you would the daily newspaper
Clear channel, clean cut, clear cut
Commercialized, vampirized, whorized
America Once The Beautiful

Saturday Early PM August 30
A 13-brush day. Second Self Portrait almost complete.

Well my fine arts career is finally launched—after 50 years! Biz card
to arrive next week—with picture of Lost Dog on one side, and my
internet art galleries, and book websites on the front. Now this info is
also posted on the first, opening page, of my web-page; ---with links

to my art galleries, (where to find my paintings). 11 new paintings, a second RETROSPECT ready to gear up.

Band-Aid marks on forearm from the hospital heart stress test now just faint traces remain. There's been a difference I'm more tired now.

PM Sunday August 31
There's a distinction between filling out our day or living it. How did I get old all of a sudden? I was young! My life has been so lonely & so difficult, took so long to mature.

> Some take longer because they must be perfected.
> --God to the Prophet.

> Always hope for inner strength — thru the embracing of God.
> There is always hope.

> *

> Say you found Jesus at the end of the tunnel –or a clean pair of sox
> Thick, clean sox w/no holes where yer' toes poke out of em' —
> The clean sox won't last;
> Jesus comes back & back again forever.
> You will find this by & by...

Civilization marches onward, with all its great social services & humanities--which are only as good as the ability to enforce its laws. The moment chaos breaks out, the economy shrinks to starvation, these law cannot longer be paid for---its enforcers being for hire; thugs are waiting in the woodwork to come out, unopposed. So those do-gooders who would not consider the economic structure of a city or a nation, are sadly, just another part of the over-all problem. Those persons who, with a visible hand do good, pass laws to protect humanbeings, yet with a secretive other hand exploit others—thru what they do for a living, by their financial holdings, using their economic power over other people, ---contribute to the economic despoiling of a country, and to its downfall and thus reduce to rubble, all those sacred-held ideas about protections, civil rights, kindness, morality itself.

AM Monday September 1

Well there's a darkside, that is for sure. And you can find it—in motion pictures, books; in the streets, and in certain people, more pronounced then others. It is a choice for most all humanbeings, whether to venture up the wrong path, or to stick to the true path, no matter what happens, and do this thru prosperity and thru famine alike. Famine of all sorts—emotional, spiritual, as well as economic.

The sun makes a short cameo appearance; hovers brilliantly behind a building turret, which slowly devours the street in its long shadow. Transman went down the block to stand in the last spot of sunlight on the block. It was warm. A parade of young people each pushing a cart of different variety parades in an entourage down 3 blocks from their vacated substandard apartment to a newly leased overpriced apartment; this safari makes an appearance every 30 minutes.

Another older white woman, (middle class once?), stops by the bookstore to testify a little about SF history; how she survived fires, famine, floods, cable car rudeness, telegraphs stations switching headquarters, highrise buildings going up everywhere; but doesn't think she can survive condo development. She makes a poignant statement: *Artists are fighting to survive here.*

Noon, Saturday, September 1
Toxic oil wash—improves picture, body don't feel right; must finish Portrait-The Second, Home Sweet Home; then switch immediately back to acrylic. Cigarette smoke, shampoo, cooking smells; coagulate in the courtyard; next time must have a corner apartment, free view, not constrained nor hemmed in by 4 walls, which lock fresh air passage.

A 16-brush bang-up day.

Well life sure is different from what you think... but it is those wild thoughts of fame, of saving the world, of conquering the unknown, which drives us onward, so when you get like me—older—and reality begins to show itself, the raw truth, —that if anything you will be a very good artist, unknown to much of the world, and you are content with your secure perch amid the miasma of this whirling sphere of stuff—you can thank your early dreams for propelling you here, and

169

for those who taught you early, like at your parents knee, who read to you from books and showed you fine arts prints of the master artists.

People are given good gifts—in the personality department—but they fuck it up, by other parts of their personality, which are untrained, and untamed. They desire to help others—and do so, but accompany this with browbeating the other individual, and sarcastic criticisms so severe that eventually those who they help must run away. There are those who don't know the meaning of loyalty and as they befriend the person, they turn against them, stab them in the back—not realizing how very seriously the other person takes this—and again the flawed relationship must dissolve.

PM. Labor Day @ Borders Bookstore
Today Red went to art gallery—Wisenthal--- and 4th floor Borders, art section; perused art book color plates. Simultaneously informing himself via the highly intellectual text. Information is a good thing! T set his pack on a table, linked its strap to his green poster-carrying tube strap & hooked his cane thru them as a sort of lock so he could meander off to browse the shelves, briefly examining a Constable; returning soon, seated calmly now before a pile of:

> Monet
> Cézanne
> Carveleggio
> Dalai
> Gaugiun—in his own words; including pictures and his letters to various luminaries; art dealers & wife.

Suddenly Transman eyes grew wide at this statement:

> Monet was not one of the greatest painters.

Also, upon further Illuminations via text, Red had to confess— with pen, bowing deeply into the pages of his JOURNEY:
> Well, I guess Pablo Picasso did speak out against Fascism, which was sweeping Europe thru Italy, Spain, and Germany. —There's Guvernica…

Noon Tuesday September 2
Yes! It's a wrap! Home Sweet Home is done! Yeah! Now, 28"x 28"; dimensions of the new canvas—for my next acrylic.

2:45AM; Wednesday, September 3—(retyping the days notes)

As he pulled his picture-heavy cart up slant of sidewalk, sweaty, groaning into the golden sun Transman had a vision of billions of human beings who had struggled before him. —Coolie laborers in dynastic feudal China who survived on 1 bowl of rice per day. Woman, man, child, waded in cold water in rice plantations of feudal lords of untold wealth, planting and harvesting rice plants; until they dropped dead. Women give birth to an infant, cut the umbilical cord, wipe the blood off their thighs, then, 2 hours later must return to the rice paddies to labor for their 1 bowl of rice per day. They worked until they dropped in their tresses, the soul raised up to heaven, to their supreme reward.

> Yes I took them in.
> --God, The Creator.

Yes I took them in—to an unending golden bowl of rice. Transman saw all this, the shinning, blissful face of a Chinese coolie holding his golden bowl of unending rice, of peace, of prosperity, of cool breezes & fragrant scents of princesses & princes.

Thus enlightened he continued his walk up the slanted sidewalk into the sun, headed towards the Transsexual Center. On the way he witnessed an act of love. Dowist Love. As a woman passes by clutches to her chest her new baby—a majestic spider plant contained in a plain white pot.

Noon Wednesday September 3

Oil done. 3 acrylics minutely worked—touch-ups. A 10-brush day.

Noon Thursday September 4,

Finished checking last acrylic of the three, for the recent shipment to photog Richard, upcoming—now set aside while the lone oil among them dries, waiting to be driven there by Jasmin; then posters to be made at KKK (Koporate Kopy Center Kinkos); popped into their respective pages in 2nd RETROSPECT by Sean, along with studio photo shots by Shaun. So as you see this is a community effort. And all their kind labor is free to the starving, unpaid artist Transman; all but the grand processing done by two Koporations—El Diablo Grande, Kinkos, and El Diablo Minor, Blurb (for the art book) both of

171

whom require to be fed lottsa cash money for any action received, as they are expensive girls...

> Holy Communion/Self Portrait-The   Second
> Hunger For God
> Home Sweet Home/ Self-Portrait-The First
> Tiger Woman Dining On Peas While Traveling The Water

The 28"x 28", new canvas—acrylic---has become Our Thinking Caps On-- Perusing Books In the Bookstore, or something...

PM Thursday September 4

Love keeps us anchored on the good side, the positive--- a person who love has left is a skeletal shell; skin & bones w/no conscious, who can do anything with no remorse. Love is the anchor, which moors us to the positive side.

E at bookstore today—its ironic how E & myself, both the same age, both of color (Africa American) are in near desperate need of computer technical advice which the young men of Babylon Falling S & S supply graciously & for free. I in return, to the world give all this artistic labor—essentially for free, and for the last 40 years, unpaid!

Wonderful small dog came to Transman, nuzzling, today at his station in the window seat; a small dog; this dogs first year was spent afraid and cowering but in the next two he has bloomed marvelously under the loving care of a lady who passes by the bookstore with him on a leash. An animal rescue service connected to the place where Transman was recently a volunteer but dissed & dismissed—where previously he'd commented on how their love and concern for animals under their care was excellent, its just that their people skills were lacking—towards volunteers, people who inquire about pets there, etc.---Anyway this small dog was found shot thru the stomach, dying in a garbage bag with 4 other of his siblings—all shot and now dead. But this little soul was saved. Theory is that he was part of a genetic breeding failure. Some bastards with no conscious and no love, trying to make a million dollars breeding a perfect dog, breeds dogs over and over until they get the perfect pups. He was probably used to breed but his puppies didn't turn out the way they wanted—thus as a sire he was useless to them, and of course to love and be a

172

pet was not in their interests whatsoever. Often beasts like this are 'disposed of' in this most cruel fashion. A cruel plan, a cruel deed.

Noon Friday September 5
Let Us Put Our Thinking Caps On And Study In The Library is shaping up!

169.
Plans For Revolution. There must be revolution; and this can be as simple as change, when the people decide they've had enough of present system which is destroying them incrementally—the masses of them, while allowing a few 'dream children' to escape (movie stars, sports players, rock stars—who can command phenomenal salaries but whereas a holistic earth calls for a system which can help the optimum amount of people live decently. Not just a few 'lucky stars'). When all the people decide they will overthrow the chains which hold them down, by as simple strategies, for example, as en-masse refusing to go to work at their jobs--- all 250 million working adults—demanding a true democracy, housing, healthcare, education, civil rights, & liberties—then this will come to pass. All that has gone before in this country is attempts to educate—to raise the consciousness of the masses of citizens via demonstrations, a handful of murderous riots, protests, picketers with meaningful signs, small underground 'zines, art, and so forth. And tho more people might be educated, conditions are actually worse and more dangerously close to fascism within the borders of the U$ and far reaching, --- as her tentacles have pried into the economies and infrastructures of all other small nations of earth.

When this time comes—of the masses enlightened, when the people decide collectively; neighbors, co workers, relatives, friends, barroom cronies, beauty parlor habitués, etc., at the university, in the café, in the factory, on the road, decide they are ready to change—how will this occur?

We need then, simply a Plan For Revolution.

> SCUM will not picket, demonstrate, march, or strike to attempt to achieve its ends. Such tactics are for nice, genteel ladies who scrupulously take only such action as is guaranteed to be ineffective. In addition, only decent, clean-living, male women, highly trained in submerging themselves in the species, act on a

mob basis. SCUM consists of individuals; SCUM is not a mob, a blob. Only as many SCUM will do a job as are needed for the job. Also, SCUM, being cool and selfish, will not subject itself to getting rapped on the head with billy clubs; that's for the nice, "privileged, educated", middle-class ladies with a high regard for the touching faith in essential goodness of Daddy and policemen. If SCUM ever marches, it will be over the President's stupid, sickening face; if SCUM ever strikes, it will be in the dark with a six-inch blade.

SCUM will always operate on a criminal as opposed to a civil disobedience basis, that is, as opposed to openly violating the law and going to jail in order to draw attention to an injustice. Such tactics acknowledge the rightness of the overall system and are used only to modify it slightly, change specific laws. SCUM is against the entire system, the very idea of law and government. SCUM is out to destroy the system, not attain certain rights within it. Also, SCUM—always selfish, always cool ---will always aim to avoid detection and punishment. SCUM will always be furtive, sneaky, underhanded, (although SCUM murders will always be known to be such).

Both destruction and killing will be selective and discriminate. SCUM is against half-crazed, indiscriminate riots, with no clear objective in mind, and in which many of your own kind are picked off. SCUM will never instigate, encourage, or participate in riots of any kind or any other form of indiscriminate destruction. SCUM will coolly, furtively, stalk its prey and quietly move in for the kill. Destruction will never be such as to block off routes needed for the transportation of food and other essential supplies, contaminate or cut off the water supply, block streets and traffic to the extent that ambulances can't get through or impede the functioning of hospitals.

SCUM will keep on destroying, looting, fucking-up an killing until the money-work system no longer exists and automation is completely instituted or until enough women co-operate with SCUM to make violence unnecessary to achieve these goals, that is, until enough women either unwork or quit work, start looting, leave men and refuse to obey all laws inappropriate to a truly civilized society.
--Valerie Solanas, SCUM MANIFESTO

When you see Bill Moyers on channel 9 talk about a billion American White House Republican spent dollars on some oil fiasco—and how many American kids it could have helped house, feed, and keep in school and you feel pain; when you see other's care for a tiny tot and others, for global environment—your reaction to this—that is called having a *conscious*.

> The 1990 bulldozing of Mapoko left 300,000 homeless. Few Nigerians alive writes the poet Odia Ofeimun "can forget the sense of betrayal and the trauma of severance that was occasioned when it happened under military boots, it was memorialized across Nigerian literature in poetry, cinema, and prose.
> --Mike Davis PLANET OF SLUMS.

US Economists are saying this great economic slide is the beginning of decline of the American Empire. Economics, is its crumbling cornerstone.

It is still 2008, '09 just around the corner. Who knows what changes it will bring! Meanwhile Transman's thought he had:

> I been to date the beneficiary of a stabilized (tho horrible) economic & social fabric in this, the richest nation on earth & in history. Of course we know (again historically) that sudden change will occur, may occur during the passage of time; and sudden upsets in fortune can arrive on ones doorstep when least expected.

Noon Saturday September 6

You know if I decide to continue JOURNEY into still another dispensation---ending the journal part-- like I did PASSAGE, with another series (which essentially moved from AUTUMN CHANGES, the Unofficial Semi-Autobiography of Red Jordan Arobateau, into PASSAGE) an account; my views and observations of daily changes, passages towards reconfiguring myself again as a fine-artist, out of the 40-year drudge of novel writing, poetry, short stories, back into oil paintings. I will call it passion. PASSION. Oh, further notes. I have a confession to make; I have been masturbating my bird. No, this is not for perverted gratification. (At least not on my part!) Getting absolutely no erotic thrill out of birds, nor cats, dogs; nor small nor larger children. None. So there, I am not as degenerate as one might have suspected! Had the thought that this bird-masturbation might actually be aiding the mental and emotional health of said bird! This is the score—Over the years, on their nightly voyage out of their home (cage) to be free, my birds inevitably, and from distant times the distant birds of my teenage youth—cockatiels who inevitably after flapping around the room awhile, shitting on cornices, ledges, rugs, etc., came to rest on my shoulders, one on each side; as I sat, typing first on the ancient Remington stolen from my mentally ill mother, confiscated to our new house (a converted garage), and then the Smith Corona electric dad brought home for me, which drove me crazy learning to use it the first week. Well, over the years of the parrots, Bijou sitting on my left side---always she goes for the left shoulder--- and green Ariel on the right, --I'd periodically put my hand up to my left shoulder to scratch my head, or put my jaw in my hand, meditatively, while studying the text before me (for years on the Brother electric typewriter which failed miserably, and later, in exasperation having switched over to using a computer to compose for the first time—for sheer exasperation of the non-functioning electric typewriter, and later economy of it, having spent a Queens Ransome on disposable ribbons & correcto-tape) so that's where Bijou sat, white, solemn her grey specked feet clutching my shoulder, and she began to nuzzle my hand when ever I put it up there, so unconsciously I began to pet her, and one day found her hunching herself in a gross sexual fashion under the ministrations of my hand! And I dared not stop petting and pressing my hand on her back, yes her back, for she would not stop hunching and making strange noises. So, this has continued regularly several times per week for a decade now! Well one day at market saw a male cockatoo seated on the shoulder of its owner, a bird almost pecked nude so its pink flesh showed thru the white feathers, and was informed by the owner that the bird had done this to himself; because when cockatoos mature, the males at least, grow sexually frustrated when they can't mate nor raise their own brood, so they turn viciously on themselves, plucking off their feathers! So now I think maybe I'm helping Bijou with her 'problem' as she must be at least 15 years old by now which is the amount of time I've owned her.

> To edit your work 10, 20 years later after first written, removing embarrassing portions, juvenile revelations of ones ignorance, is to disregard true history. I prefer to let it stand however embarrassing. My battling against others; angry rages, & rants. So here is all this stuff for you Dear Children of the future to read— and you may judge!

No doubt there is no shortage of rich people; they're going to keep coming into the big cities & buy condos, so how can we tell the rapacious builders--- investors--their vacancies will never sell, they'll take a loss no one can afford them—stop building condos! Stop taking away the affordable housing stock for us poor and elderly! -- When in fact the rich keep coming in from all over this nation, and in a wider net, from all over the globe; first drawn by the microbiology stem cell research labs where they are trained to work at $100,000 thousand dollar per annum salaries; second the born rich, the entitled, the trust funded spawn of capitalists with privilege--they keep coming in; those with money. They have no conscious as to other less privileged people they are displacing—so we poor people will somehow have to put a hammer lock on this process and force the builder-investors to deed a portion of their condo units as affordable for the $10,000 per annum worker, or retiree & these condos are to buy and own! To intersperse these affordable-to-the-poor units throughout the affluent ones—so as not to create the repetition of a ghetto, not a segregated, set-apart-geographical island like those failed welfare projects that festered in crime and misery for the last half-century.

T had various musings as he sat, reading.

> He (Walter Benjamin's) greatest ambition was to produce a work consisting entirely of quotations.
> --Hannah Arndt from Illuminations.

And so he saw his own JOURNEY was fast becoming such. For instance:

Mike Davis:

> "middle class secessions from public spaces. The return to the medieval fortressed walled city. No more shared parks, schools, sidewalks, cinemas, restaurants, with the poor.

> The third world urban bourgeoisie "cease to be citizens of their own country and become nomads belonging to, as owing allegiance to, a super-terrestrial topography of money; they become patriots of wealth, nationalists of an elusive & golden nowhere. While local poor are stuck in their slums.
> --Jeremy Seabrook quotes by Mike Davis.

Which is exactly what I described in my Sci-Fi book, EMPIRE, akin to Orwell and Huxley as the nations poor travel the highways from city to city living out their lives in motorized caravans:

The 30-Day Ordinance, circa 2035.

Suddenly all over pre-Utopia in the nation still called Am-Erica upon which we now sit, there was put out into city streets the dark effluvium of grimy apartments, disgorged out of rat/roach infested, narrow walled rooms, people, squatting atop their belongings in a pile outside on the streets waiting for city sweepers to remove them to new domiciles. For those with insufficient monies, the abject poor, there was no place to go. So some 40 million were soon living in caravans moving every 30 days from city to city take advantage of local health care, charity food distributions, clothes; being in a strange limbo of economic exile, both protected of sorts, and denied, by the Federal 30 Day Ordinance--- which mandated that cities must keep indigent visitors inside the limits of their jurisdictions and not expel them, but must do so only for a limit of 30 days, after this, if picked up by police off their streets without a job AND lodgings they could be forced---by martial law, at gunpoint-- to leave, unless, the 3rd alternative, they were hospitalized. As long as the patient was in a hospital bed they could stay. Without a doctor's diagnosis of acute illness, and vital care, whenever they were healed, they must leave. Or, the last option was death. Those economic travelers who were better off, -- veterans of wars on soldier pension, those who received social security benefits, or pension from private industry from which they had retired after a lifetime of work, or those with small family inheritance stipends were somewhat financed, but if their money was insufficient to purchase a shared house, condominium, or even free standing individual house with no common walls shared with stranger's, they must stay forever on the move like vagabonds, like gypsy's
--EMPIRE, 2006

And, from Mike Davis:

--Poor people have found a Faustian bargain in a precarious ledge of land between a toxic factory and a poisoned lake. Precisely because the site is so hazardous and unattractive, it offers 'protection from rising land values in the city.
--Mike Davis from Seaboork's In The Cities Of The South

In one such situation from daily news, when 'one in 1,000 years flash flood killed estimated 32,000 people left, 14,000 homeless and another 200,000 jobless'.

That book was written 2005. Here is the newspaper for today,
September 8, 2008:

> Cairo—Hopes diminished Sunday for finding survivors among hundreds of people believed trapped beneath huge boulders that destroyed an impoverished neighborhood on Cairo's outskirts, killing at least 32 people, including whole extended families.
>
> Anger and resentment mounted as authorities failed for a second day to get heavy machinery into the devastated shantytown to try to clear the large slabs that split away from the Muqattam cliffs early Saturday.
>
> Survivors among the 100,000 residents of the Dewika slum were also left to spend the night without shelter, despite government promises to provide it.

According to Mike Davis:

> Arson has always been employed by wealthy landlords to get rid of slum buildings in order to rebuild a more profitable structure; create new higher rents charged; to circumvent the law and speed up the tedious court process of eviction and removal of the poor. Erlaro Benner adds that a favorite method for what Filipino landlords prefer to call 'hot demolition' is to chase a 'kerosene-drenched burning live rat or cat—dogs die too fast—into an annoying settlement... a fire started this way is hard to fight as the unlucky animal can get plenty of shanties aflame before it dies.
> -- Benner; Defending A Place; quoted in Planet Of Slums.

Again from Mike Davis, here is a relevant note (pertinent to that *superfluous* 'women's lib') regarding waste dumps of impoverished 3rd world countries:

> The content of the waste is sometimes grisly; in Accra, the daily graphic recently described 'sprawling refuse dumps full of black plastic bags containing aborted fetal bodies from the wombs of kayayee (female porters) and teenage girls in Accra. According to the metropolitan chief executive, '75 percent of the waste of black polythene bags in the metropolis contains human aborted fetuses."

170.

> Yakkedy Yak.

Take out the papers and the trash
Or you don't get no spending cash.
--Pop song 1950's.

I remember one job I worked in 1980's, along side a young man of
color who carried a guitar; tall, handsome, he would not work. After
a weeks employment in which he was adequate and was not fired as
some who couldn't make sales—he chose to quit & retire and stand
outside, down in the street below our window in the Flood Building at
Powell and Market, to play his guitar for sparechange from tourists
who gathered there at the cable car turnaround. Here he hustled up
coins for food and occasional room rent. His tourist performance-
begging was an even lower wage then at our low-paying job. I stayed
on. Not only did this carefree summer boy have no security and did
not squirrel away money, or live in a barely decently fashion as did
the rest of us, going from day to day; also, tho we didn't really pay
attention---he was putting nothing up for his futures survival years
later at an older age—in the form of Social Security.

Monday 3AM, September 8
Born into A World Of Trouble. We are born to this world, yet there
can be peace. Peace in the heart. It is the closest thing to heaven.
Otherwise, I belong –on the outskirts.

You wouldn't think that an artist would be against another artist to
such a virulent degree—but here it is. The Art College of San
Francisco is springing up everywhere. Dorms. Classrooms. Sprout
in an ill-growth on these downtown streets. Suspect that the
underlying goal is strictly for profit, so that now a full 3% of the city's
real estate, available housing stock, has been bought up by these Art
College people, one by one, to be converted into dorms and
classrooms. The College reaches out globally, attracting foreign
students from affluent families to bring here, to house in their newly
converted units at rent-gouging prices---and the students pour in from
overseas, eager at a chance to get a legal foothold in this country—
thru the comparative easy job of art study. More & more of them
access this route to gain entrance to the USA, thus providing capital
for the Art College Owner-Moguls to purchase, more & more
buildings. This subsequently drives up housing prices and forces
older artists (poorer ones) out of the city!

However there are a lot of other demographics pouring non-stop into this city. It is still considered to be a queer oasis. And most definitely a trans oasis. From Mexico, South America, every state in the union, Europe, everywhere San Francisco is heralded. (Meanwhile, black displacement now shows up as an embarrassing imbalance. After 880 small black businesses were bulldozed out of existence in the Fillmore district war zone years over 1960's thru 70's, and 30,000 black families were kicked out of the city limits. So that friend Marguerite says she feels she's the '*last black woman in San Francisco*' and when at Dolores Park with Latin friends comments she's the only black face out there except for a black poodle dog running around; '*the only black out there is just me and this little black poodle dog.*' M frequents the Mission district so she can be around some folks with dark skin & not be the only one.)

More about some very quaint inhabitants of this city who are also flooding in at an alarming rate, disrupting the demographics:

'X', was a trans girl who walked, stealth, thru the cities of the plane wearing an odd half smile on her face of one who has a deep secret that only those who knew her past understood and the very few knowledgeable, might grow to suspect, and this only after a time... 'Y', was 'a good job' but as before said there were tell tale clues--voice a bit too deep & strident in moments of excitement or intoxication; hands too large, sturdy (but not her feet which were fortunately of a small size); she was of an appropriate woman's height and build; but her head was a bit too big, hips too slim—clues that once a person had been given full disclosure of her trans status took it all in, in an instant and from this point everlasting their viewpoint which was now, immediately relegated to unconscious, was a reversal of their first, original impression as one totally female—a dike perhaps—now become one male born. There are some 'jobs' that are flawless; totally & height, voice (not strained nor faux) face, hands, body, demeanor, so completely perfect that even when you know their true story you still find it impossible to mentally replace the person of your first assumptions to be totally female—to do an about-face to them being male born—but instead since their 'job has been so good' they forevermore inhabit some twilight uncertainty of people wondering exactly what they are; their existence in persona, exactly where they are 'based' in physiognomy—further as is too, to some degree their personal lives. Many of these perfect 'jobs' were girls or boys who transitioned very early—beginning hormone treatment at 15 or 16 usually in my day thru criminal means; thus to circumvent the

181

masculinization, or feminizing process of the natural born body. Plus, as a side-effect, for better or worse, their social existence also changes in conjunction with their appearance; their experiences of ill, or good treatment in the world.

Monday AM September 8

Sometimes the streets of SF are like a child's wonderland, finding dropped, lost, or thrown-away items. Food. Cash. Bus Cards. An assortment of furniture. Clothes. Appliances. Silverware. Books. Music CD's. Video movies, et al. So that a quasi-destitute person as he was could go out daily upon their no-money routes, and entertain the very possible hope that she/he might find something of value to brighten up their day—often considerably... Found items within recent recall:

> $20 bill.
> $55 in assorted denominations.
> Art canvasses.
> Tubes of oil paint.
> Canvas stretchers.
> Several dimes.
> Nickels.
> A sack of canned goods.
> A $600 I-Pod.

Poor old Transman and his conscious! He sometimes had the thought, over his humble meal, that, because of global economic imbalance due to the bullying of his own, the most powerful nation, that he was now eating his meal and someone else's share across the globe somewhere, at the same time, off his plate of relative affluence—even if he had found this repast on top of an Amerikkkan garbage can.

> The time will come. All time will come, for everything & for the end of our lives. Only God knows the time. We can bargain for additional time. -----Did in the bible, and got 15 extended years.

Well you know we are little vessels filed with blood. Can easily be killed. All the blood runs out... and death's black blanket envelops us, dividing us from this earth & paradise, as we walk a silver bridge into eternity...

A letter from friend Eli, his cat Gardner must be put down. This is a good man, and he really loves his pets. Us, in this brotherhood & sisterhood of pet love/pet care. One right after another they go! All our loved ones die. Both human and animal. We all must die on this earth.

   --Just passing thru.

PM Tuesday September 9

Returned from clinic. Happy, drained. Found I don't have a heart problem. This event was probably due to 15 cups of coffee daily for months & months. Am off caffeine as of one month ago. Herb tea. Maybe will start some decaf—2 cup per day limit—in future. Thank you Jesus.

Made up with Sean at Bookstore after our Flagration Grande Mal, this Saturday. Believe we have returned to a state of peace --And some happiness, as I really like being on my ledge in the sun, and think he misses me and likes me being there. Amen. Well. Am drained by all this. Am getting next-to-final money this Saturday when cash in C-certificate, the last cash remaing from that windfall. Intend to save it—but not in the bank where the health department or/and SSI can seize it—if the account inadvertently goes over $2,000. Understand that if the Bancroft pays out a hefty sum (for 3 months of accumulation of stuff all at once) and this happens to coincide with my $900 per month grant—plus this C-certificate, it would put me over temporarily. —My rent comes out of that, reducing it immediately by $1,000; and the Bancroft monies theoretically are dolled out over several months. But to the eagle-eyed Zealots this means nothing! The government makes life so very difficult in this sense. It makes no allowance for one who might attempt to live frugally and put aside a few dollars every month—to grow into a nest egg. Instead the government system creates a galaxy of cheats, sneaks, and thieves, who learn to take their precious surplus dollars and hide them—in a variety of places—out of the prying government eyes. (In safety deposit boxes, under the bed, on trust in the bank accounts of friends.) Bad news! Bad for the individual! Bad for society! Bad for the nation!

I don't think poverty really drives people into evil. Poverty is a condition, which acts on people who are already weakened and cracks them up like a car wreck so that they begin to turn on their families and abuse them. But it is not the poverty itself. If a family has love, and faith in the Divine, they can weather many storms. My father witnessed extreme poverty from age 5 thru his childhood, living with his mother, who did not speak English, here in a foreign land, but she loved him and did not abuse him, and he turned out fine. You often hear stories of dirt-poor people and what they had to do to survive— scratching a living out of the soil—yet their families were big and supportive and none of them turned into bank robbers or serial killers.

All over the streets these days is talk of the up coming elections. Of politics. You hear people say that if McCain-Palin win they are going to leave the country. Others are going to go into their rooms and never come out again, just for supplies; vanish out of society for the duration –the duration of what we know not.

What is happening in our country has happened before. In other nations. In other times.

It is apparent from all the news which does leek some truth out to us periodically—that our country is on a downhill swing. This state, that all the revolutionists, anarchists, and left wing fighters could not achieve. Mainly thru the rise of other super powers—China, India, and other places in Asia, plus the united Europe. And, thru gross mismanagement of our own nations economics. —For the sake of profit. So all the prayers of all the nuns and priests and those sympathetic to the poor, to animals rights, to women's rights, to the sovereign rights of all peoples, can be vindicated. Soon, if this downhill slide of Empire continues, the US will be less culpable. Less guilty, less of a polluter, a warmonger, a robber of smaller nations resources. The prayers of saints answered!

On TV, the sound goes off every minute or so for 5 seconds—thus missing crucial parts of sentences, while the other TV—the sound per se doesn't go out—just the channel, so the screen suddenly goes blank, sound and vision alike. So impossible! For while one is fading in and out while the other remains constant is my method to fill in the missing gaps-until its reception also goes out entirely. So frustrating. While giving himself his T shot during this whole ordeal it made

184

Transman so nervous, he stuck himself with a needle accidentally. Luckily it was sterile.

They have nothing. It came to him. Looking around him he saw; *I have so much. 3 TVs! And at least some reception on each one!!*

There is no shortage of holy people, both dead; and alive, just coming into world prominence. I certainly would like to be one. Some kind of holy person—a minor league holy.

September 10, Noon Wednesday
9-Brush day. Let Us Put Our Thinking Caps On & Go Study In The Library. An African-American piece (the light & dark of it). Inspirational, educational. Books.

> Outside this fucken' store, There are the same jackasses every month; the same kids are lining up to get a limited edition hat. Its got so silly they all look the same, so fucken' corny. Every month this stores features, a new limited edition hat. How do they really think that shit is cool? It's like they're lining up to get their personalities.
> --Sean Stewart, Babylon Falling

PM Thursday September 11
I fought! I fought. Fights with friends. I run from enemies. Am still alive to tell my truths to you, Dear Children. My flaming firebrand to you; it's the relay marathon of life spilling onwards since before and after---before, back since the first atom 5 billion years ago given by the Hand of God(ess) the Creator! This is the end. This is the beginning.
> What the eyes have seen, the heart cannot forget.
> -Traditional Spanish saying.

Thanks God for your generosity in life length, in talents. Must say thanks; thanks Hashem, for allowing me the chance to tell my story.

It will not just be as the Valerie Solanas revolution? You must bide your time until the time is right. Wait. Even if it means to wait a generation. Two generations. Watch. Pray. Educate. Spread the underground buzz about the revolutionary way. When the time is right---including a confluence of things, natural disasters, famine,

185

attacks from within and without from great powers; then the people who know how to act shall strike!

Girls @ clinic talk about their ass-pussy, what lubricants, tightening up, about hard shit, like handballs. We are such outsiders! Such outcasts! Well how many people have the memory of being pulled over by the police---just for walking down the street.

An abandon blanket, stained, dirty in a doorway, which a homeless being vacated maybe by leaving off this earth. Just get up and walk away, leaving blanket, cardboard in the doorway which they've used as a crude motel room to spend a few fitful hours of the night.

Transman passes by the old woman who is always at her window; her pet seagull sits on the peeked roof next door, waiting for bread. Her apartment, frontal flat over the street at 3rd story; has informed him in increasing glimpses of her life, while passing by on his way to the clinic every few weeks and he has compiled a small memoir. A grey hag; pinched expression; a twisted face; too thin, smoking, nervous; over 60, maybe over 70. Saw her the first day tossing bits of bread to her seagull out of a north-facing dormer window; a ragged grey curtain pushed aside; then the following week at the opposite, south-facing window of this dormer; as she paced, smoked, and peeks from time to time from under a grey tattered curtain, as if waiting for someone important, as if in a Tennessee Williams play. But today, the three windows of the dormer are shut fast, their grey tattered curtains drawn; and the grey crone, flits, pacing & smoking inhabits yet another window down so she must have a very large space, the lucky hanger-on from a past, more cheap era, saved by real-estate rent control.

Another block informs Transman of something new. A building sprouted up to 8th story made of shining silver glass and cement, recently constructed—and it's city owned, for the poor. The old man peers in thru a window and reads the placard there, which has the statistics, to which he replied (to the thin air, as no one was around) this vitriolic response: *Hate these people! Hate them! $550, for a studio apt. $950 for 1 bedroom. Beautiful apartments, new baths and kitchens. Hate Them!* It is for seniors like him; but, has a price tag—

186

a $13,000-per year income requirement. More then he earns. How much money he could save! How much nutritious food he could buy!

Well, I'm off—like a prom dress; says Jason. As I approach my station, from across the street the bookstore looks forlorn, its awning dotted with white speckles of bird shit… And kapitalism is nearing its natural end.

Sunday noon, September 14
I lived a ghetto experience & remained on "that side" for all of my life to date—65 years. Realize this as we gain greater freedoms---that slowly as we get to ourselves, our final serf-realization; our public manifestation--we are becoming an anachronism, a dinosaur—when a the greater tolerance, understanding, acceptance of us extend services to our queer youth; including them into their traditional institutions, yet we survivors still as outlaws, barred from entry, we still exist on the outskirts of things----walking 'in the shadows' into perpetuity & myself, both in my life & my outpourings to the world. The crows nest observer on a sinking ship.

PM
Well, it still remains that the best brains of the whole universe thru millenniums of time have tried to figure out the human race—but to no avail. This is my effort added to the pot.

On my visit to the bookstore:
>Sean: --Modern technology say it saves time but it takes up as much time! This new technology…
>
>Red: ---Well at least it gets your message out to billions of people.
>
>Sean: --Billions?
>
>Red: --Well… hundreds & hundreds… or rather…in your case… dozens & dozens…
>
>Sean: --Fives! It gets it out to fives of people!

*

Getting close! So close I can taste it!
--Sean, while micromanaging store.

187

Noon, Friday September 12
11-Brush day.

PM
The children of today are entering into a world of toxic pollution, &
corruption—which is now visible, which is now talked about, as
never before in world history. Young people today, the educated
ones—which means they've come from usually a better-off family, or
they would not get educated in the first place, ---have a jaded air
about society—about politics, meaning they're seeing the dirty double
dealings of their nations. That this sexism is completely wrong; the
undoing of lives. And this is the hopelessness that many women
battle. You can see this in the women voter's hunger for a female
Vice President—since they could not get Hillary elected. For an
instent they even entertained the thought of retrograde Sara Palin. I
must say also when all is done, all the cards turned face up, with no
holding back; and the houselights are turned up bright, that men, by
positioning themselves so far ahead of women in almost everything—
a lot of back payment is overdue. Nature loves a balance. Demands a
balance. So what will happen!?

Noon, Friday September 12
Want to demonize the religious right—as if all the hatred towards us
emanates from them alone, like a single, blazing all-powerful sun. To
do this would be to miss the reality of many groups who are stiff-
necked, inflexible, full of hate and do not want to understand those
made differently from themselves. Who do not comprehend, nor
attempt to. Those without true compassion. Those with such closed
minds, that no bigger thoughts can permeate their skulls.

RE: These hateful Born Again Christians, I cry. I cry because there is
going to come a time we will wish we had of agreed on some
things… by then we will be so fragmented, there will be no coming
together, and we will perish as little tiny divided islands in a
holocaustic storm. A storm of such great evil I know not what.

I try not to harbor jealousy. Look at others success & our failing.
Well we are supposed to worry about our own journey. The
individual is who our Creator will judge.

188

I am going to be signing out for now; even as am setting up
JOURNEY Vol. 13, all this on the backdrop of the hideous 2008
election, the outcome of which may lead us more deeply into fascism,
and a police state. One with cleansing squads to *clear away, clear
away* with a good old-fashion military cleansing zeal, in previous
dispensations known as Nazis, Gestapo, Stalinist, Dictatorships.
Equipped with its elite soldiers; those granted licenses to cleanse with
deadly forces, to clear a wide as area as possible, leaving no one but
those identical to their masters.

This memorandum is to assure you that I am not a sex pervert,
irregardless as to what you may have heard whispered about my more
risqué writings; nor am I an armed revolutionary, determined to set
fire to this corrupt system by any means possible, and that what I truly
desire in my heart is to have a rich & abundant life—to laugh heartily.

Oh yes, Dear Children... being honest. Yes, that's one of the Ten
Commandments. It's always best. To be totally, utterly honest —in
the end. It comes in handy to have a clean slate. So this has been my
confessional...

To edit your work 10, 20 years later after first written, removing
embarrassing portions, juvenile revelations of ones ignorance, is to
disregard true history. I prefer to let it stand however embarrassing.
My battlings against others, angry rages, & rants. So here is all this
stuff for you Dear Children of the future to read—and you may judge!

> *Dear children enjoy your cheeseburger w/ onion fries. Cooks labor over a
> hot grill to prepare food all day & night 24 hours non-stop. I am food
> service. Food of a different kind...*

Transman looked up at the thin lengths of wood that held his small,
but growing stock of paintings... I am older. No longer see myself as
some great genius. —Maybe just a solid 2nd—or even 3rd rate
painter/writer of some fame. Think this after meeting all this parade
of artists, a host of 2-dozen art students, poets, activists, and
miscellaneous writers that I see myself more in perspective.

I thought I was a big shot---but time has cut me down to size.

I would say that this art is of God. I am just its workman; neither of heaven; or of hell. ... Stuck somewhere inbetween—in ordinary time—not saint, not completely a sinner. Dear God be my strength & my shield, and my deliverance.

--RJA @ Grace, 2008

Red Jordan Arobateau
September 16, 2008
3:30 AM Pacific Standard Time
San Francisco, CA
USA

MY CONTINUING JOURNEY ---
INTO ARTISTIC, & REVOLUTIONARY THOUGHTS

Volume 13.

A lot of art is predicated by what the artist/the viewer thinks art is or can be. For some its pastoral landscape, truly representational. For others, portraiture, which is photographically identical to the subject. For artists like me it's the inner imagination taken out of my head & soul and put down on canvas. The Illustration Of My Thoughts.
-- MY CONTINUING JOURNEY INTO SPIRITUAL & REVOLUTIONARY
THOUGHTS, 2008.

171.
Saturday, September 13, 2008
Got my $1,782.85 C-D Certificate of Deposit out of bank, (Wa-Moo) on the eve of it's financial collapse.

Jasmin & Red ran into a suburban branch of the nations 3rd largest bank & lined up. Red to cash in his C-D, and to give part of this money to Jasmin. The teller, an elegant 3rd-nation sister calmly with machine precision counted out his cash in $100rds, fast, while speaking of a new C-D he could purchase which paid *5% interest and matured in just 6 months*, but he wasn't going for the deal! All around him folks were lined up at tellers pulling their money out, canceling accounts, collecting on maturing C-D's—and not turning them over into futures. After the teller handed him his thick green cash wad, Red glanced back at Jasmin. The pretty woman stood way back in line—a strange smile on her face, and an air of purpose, --- when Red came over & attempted to give her $700, nervously she shushed him away. In a few minutes she did what she came for--- withdrew the majority of her funds. Then grabbed Red with a tan, smoothskinned hand, whisked him out of that ailing bank and determinedly walked across the broad clean sidewalks of the mall to another repository, of greater stability---Bank of America. There she took his proffered money; also added the sum she'd just withdrawn and put it in this account.

Red followed suit a week later, by opening a BofA account and re-routing all his online direct deposits to go into it. 5 days later the former bank, Wa Moo, collapsed.

Tuesday, September 16,
When finishing up a project his house temporarily dissolved into rack & ruin. Bathroom & kitchen floors not swept nor mopped—the one full of cat hair & muddy prints; the other, flecks of food, garlic hulls, dropped tidbits & likewise dirt-stained. Bottom shelf of the refrigerator not swept out... The studio was clear and organized, however only spot-swept/mopped, leaving corners full; effluvia from the birds; i.e. the male bird had taken to tearing up tiny pieces of newspaper from their cage lining which blew everywhere when they flapped their wings; and only spot-mopped to keep down the dust. And then his office... a paper-choked desk, plus an auxiliary desk swamped in crap—unread Street Sheets, Jewish Daily Forwards, miscellaneous news clippings, old envelopes, empty CD boxes--- whereas he preferred to work clean and organized, with everything in place. Nor had he lifted his weights in nearly 2 weeks! All of this disarray because of finishing up part 2 of the current JOURNEY (MY CONTINUING JOURNEY – INTO SPIRITUAL & REVOLUTIONARY THOUGHTS). And concentrating on the 2nd Art Book Retrospect.

Art students, photographers, writers, and saints come down to the TL-
--where fallen humans, now homeless, lay out on the sidewalk, drunk,
high, or suffering from mental illness. Each & every global art
student finds themselves inspired to do so, upon first seeing the place.
They do societal studies, pray; they lead guided tours for the more
affluent and less exposed in order to heighten their conscious; photogs
and writers, film documentarians, journalists write newspaper articles,
use their synopsis of the alkies, winos, crackheads, toothless, skinny-
shank, stinking clothes, long greasy-haired, beady-eyed, ratface,
dopefreaks; as treatise on the inhumanity of humankind. —They are
speaking about a shrinking geographical area; it is falling victim to
gentrification. All these streets form a noose, slowly closing tighter,
& tighter around the slum enclave, as all the students and nuns are,
ultimately, part of the problem! The sight of their clean-cut presence,
and shining angelic faces gives more courage to the realestate moguls
to move in following right behind them with potted palms, red
carpets, brass door hinges and extremely high rent boutiques and bed
& breakfast inns.

Here is some more about a person who has been in my earthly life
longer then anyone—30 years now, both of us artists, and lagging in
other skills like earning & saving money. Jasmin. We'd had to flee
by night. –Quite often. Once foreclosed upon after the repossession
bank took over our home, they changed the locks (on the iron grate
door Transman had installed) so we had to break back in to steal the
ashes of Jasmin's dead lover, which she had carried around for *10
years*. Now the soul of the deceased had probably departed seconds
after actual death—yet still we'd carried those ashes in a grey-silver
cardboard box (cheep standard cremation for those without funds,
from the Neptune Society) for a whole gawdawful human generation;
this silver box going from room to room, shelf to shelf, apartment to
house to hotel to loft. I told you we'd been thru a lot together. Well
anyway, there were these looks, which had passed between her &
me—looks words cannot describe—during the various incidents of
our roller coaster lives. Like the first eviction, the foreclosure—the
moving of boxes of belongings out in the dead of the night—the story
of 2 artists living together, and then, the fateful day when Jasmin and
I were helping carry boxes of stuff from out of the condo which her
affluent new middleclass lover had *defaulted on;* so once more, there

194

we were—Fleeing in the night with infernal boxes, and this lover not even an artist ... *yet here we were again!* So, we turned to look at each other a moment, as the brand new brilliant silver elevator descended towards the street, *la strada... the caravan... a gypsy life... this On The Road...* This perpetually traveling from place to place, *once again...* These looks. But also, other looks when, astonishingly once at Indian Gaming for his birthday, Red kept wining and wining over $1,200! All Jasmin could do was turn and look at him in astonishment! After all the books he'd had to pawn off (of his own titles with his own name as author) for $1.00 apiece at those little booksellers on Telegraph & Shattuck Avenues; to help raise their $20-a-night hotel rent) after all the standing in food lines with homophobic ex-cons & malicious mendicants to receive a box of canned pork & sacks of beans & rice, after all the stealing of x-tra food from benefits, testimonial dinners etc., in which *they were the entertainment*, scooping them surreptitiously into Styrofoam dishes and plastic bags...after all the turmoil of the poor, the worry, and despair of the underclass... now here were these hundred dollar bills fluttering down from Indian gaming Paradise. Equal to this surprised, incredulous look was the time when, after help from friend and sister transwoman Dominique, his play INHABITANTS OF A GHETTOIZED POPULATION WAS *produced almost to a successful performance...* and Jasmin walked into the large theater warehouse space of Carol Queen & Robert's Center For Sex & Culture (before they too were sadly dispossessed of that place by a prying narrow-minded landlord who inadvertently stumbled upon their Annual Masterbation-athon, a sex party/educational workshop attended by 100 people) where Jasmin witnessed the grand stage space 100 by 100 feet, the numerous chairs (80), the numerous cast— 25—and she could not believe her eyes, after all their failures. So likewise the time the windfalls of money came to Red (twice, once for $9,000, and once for $7,800) out of nowhere! They'd turn and glance at each other momentarily, liquid eyes, *window of the soul...* Those looks they exchanged, for better or worse, each and every time...

Wednesday 1 AM September 17
Transferred my small funds to a stronger bank—BofA.

Thursday Noon, September 17
6-Brush day. 45-minute session. Let's Put On Our Thinking Caps & Go Study In The Library.

195

PM

So what is genius? Talent. Dedication. Sacrifice. Sacrifice to the point of impacting health—sacrifice of not having a normal life as normal people, who work, mate, fuck, live in creature-comfort. The artist is alone. Is studying. Practicing. Working. A certain portion of her or his normalcy is cut out of them, and sacrificed to art. They will live like others only part of the time, the rest as aesthetics, as hermits, as prisoners in solitary confinement during the red hot fires of creation—their reach goes out ultimately to touch more people, and reach further generations then any one individual could ever do in an ordinary lifetime. Their work echoes thru the ages, its pendulum swing is greater. The sacrifice of privacy, —if the genius becomes known in their lifetime. Talent—that doesn't need an explanation, but a commentary, that it can be developed, maybe even created out of nothing—but pure dedication.

I love art, I loved inspiration; at age 15 or so—so, this urged me to plunge myself into true art—this had to include painting, tho I had already self-defined as being a writer—a true artist must have a beret, an easel, a painting at hand! At age 15 got use to, loved the smell of oil paints, linseed oil & turpentine, so this was total art—to do both!

3AM Thursday morning, September 17

Stock market is crashing! Babylon is falling. They say it can't get worse, but it can. To many of us America seems now in panic, and this Wall Street crash, is doing more then just skimming the cream off of prosperity; it's rapidly heading down, down to the reality of poverty—which is for a person to still be surviving, and not worse in the sense of absolute nadir of hell, just worse in that all the luxurious prosperity many have known, has evaporated. To someone who doesn't own their own house or simple condo of an efficiency size, how much can they sympathize with the crashing housing market? We have been thru this trauma *several times*.

Well the quandary is this. If I am able to move into the seniors governed sponsored building studio for $550 per month, I can save nearly $400 per month—yet, cannot actually keep more then $2,000 in a bank account or would get kicked off of SSI Disability & loose my medical benefits. Likewise, if my dreams start to come true and I rise into a more affluent income bracket, I could not longer stay in

196

this government-sponsored building. –Would be kicked out, into a high rental market, no longer covered by my original rent-control building! You must make at least 13,000 per year—but not more then 33,000. If I stay where I am I could make one billion dollars a minute and still stay in my unit—which remains under rent control. Confusing!

So, continuing my journal –JOURNEY. In which the reader can see all my ups and downs, my prides & prejudices, my strengths & failings, so you can know exactly what kind of person Master Author Red Jordan Arobateau truly is. In which I'll get a chance to apologize for being myself. Part of my apology being a redeeming quality-- that I am the author of over 80-books now, and a growing body of fine arts paintings—in dramatic color.

PM Thursday September 18
Look back and say those were the days—as a sex addict, for it was angst ridden, and pressed to the limit of raw sexuality, lust, longing thoughts, constant cravings; no to say that in my old age—65, whereas sex is lusty, but normal; and reduced to 3 or 4 times per week, as apposed to transition—three or four times per day, and menopause, which was wild uncontrollable frantic desire, must have it must perpetuate the species, *must live now*! Hot summer sun angst sex mating pressure; but those days of viewing B&D, SM, hot wax drippings, electric probes, piercings, cuttings, whips, chains, scenes, classes on assorted subjects of sadomasochism; now days its just normal sex—if you call being transsexual and bisexual normal, oh hum.

Noon, Friday September 19
If you don't provide for the social needs of people—they will get it thru criminal means, because it is a life-necessity. Weather this be housing, food, education. Gangsta style wrestling these necessities of life from the money-graspers hand. Men and women who sell themselves so their children can have a brighter future. Wither this be boxers who get their brains busted in the ring, waitresses who endure the everyday cruelties of callous patrons. Alas, to document the Great Wall Street Crash of September 2008.

Well, there goes my bank. —The checking and automatic deposits. All my little monies $ to a stronger bank—BofA, which has 10% of the nations holdings. Soc Sec, disability, Amazon, the fine art galleries, etc. Will keep old accounts with former bank as a side deal.

*

Dragging his silver cart, passed by David Chiu's office. If he gets elected, hope he does something for us—the grass roots poor. I've been touting his name wherever I go. Across the street stands a sleek tall, powerful glass & concrete & colored stone, perfect picture multimillion-dollar totalitarian corporate financial condo headquarters. Big money. There is no stopping place within its borders for the poor pulling a silver cart. Not la groceteria for one cheap tamale for your plate. Nor a grocery to get a single onion. No cafes. No coffee shops. Just money—behind glass, with barred vaults.

Midnight Friday-Saturday September 20
The raging frustration one feels—wanting to watch his humble TV program Transman looses transmission again & again

Monday PM September 22
Night. More hassles w/damned TV antennas.... Lonely, but busy. Powerful sound of fire engines in the night.

Noon, Tuesday September 23
Have neglected to tell you what's going on. Converter boxes must be installed to all TV sets or they won't receive reception after February 2009---due to analog receptor switching over to digital. A poor persons dilemma. Luckily Transman still had dwindling dollars from the windfall plus recent sale of RETROSPECT to Joe Pachinko who was introduced by Nicole Hen. Transman fiddled & fumbled around with numerous connecting cords, surrogate plugs, extension wires; moving his 3 television sets around, exchanging them here & there in different places for 3 days running, and so far did not seem too successful. Can no longer maneuver this heavy TV with my aged-weakened muscles. Must use platforms with diminishing height to wiggle TV set down to the lower level. Oh, and the stock market crashed a few days ago... This is bad. Not since the Great Depression. Government 700-billion dollar bailout —to be shouldered by the American taxpayers. Babylon She is indeed be a-fallin'. And one last thing Dear Diary, applied for that government housing--- an age 55-year requirement for at least one household

member. Wrote down me, & Jasmin. I don't qualify by myself (earning on paper less then the required $13,300 per annum. If I get chosen—by the random sort—will have no choice of unit, and must wiggle by with doctors orders on my pets. Blind luck will be my ticket if it is meant to be—there are only 110 units in this place; 50 already allotted to homeless.

Early AM Wednesday September 24
Old Transman thought, now stooping to pick up a dropped paintbrush; *Aw shit! Pain! Aw Mother of Jesus! I don't know what happened Lord, I was just living my life—all of a sudden I got old....*

The day is coming.
Tides of hopelessness wash
out into the city streets.
In irrefutable evidence.

We are the last free generation before
Thought-control.
Before eradication
 of the senses
by mass-media doublespeak & poverty.

The brilliant lives of poets cut short.

They will say—he died of despair & alcoholism—a free choice.
They will say---she died of a broken heart & poverty-- she could not change.
They will say s/he was a tranny hooker & died of complications due to HIV & Hep-C-- all her fault!

They will say:
> we believe in life
> religion &
> lots of money.

And they will say this
 over & over &
over again.

1950's

stay-at-home Saturday
w/radio
listening to Americas freedoms
dwindle like
dirty water drains from a Sunday night bathtub,
--but without a clue.

I've paid for my share of it
by hard work,
 in factories,
   offices,
      hospitals,
    restaurants,
how about you?

Then we will say
 the draft dodgers are now vindicated
by the evidence of the failure of 'Nam.

And we will say this
 over & over &
over again.

Jet fighter planes redfire sputum
strafes conscious
along the nightly news; --is
byline to moviestars & their
narcissistic affairs.
The heart is dumb struck,
paralyzed.
The last city bird left
trills its song
then is silent.

Me, not famous, not yet.
 Just simmering in a pot,
well done.

So don't blame me for it! Remember dear Children, -- regarding
The Powers That Be

I had about as much control over them in my generation, as you do,
in yours.

It will happen to you
 You will get old before you know it. Aches, pains,
Arms & legs loose strength,
Your face sags.
Its purgatory
Not quite hell, -- not yet,
 & still dreaming of paradise.
Still poor
 As you were in 1965 — and it's 2009.

(Watching Susie Ormen's budget on free TV;
having no money.)

So stay,
to the last day
possible
the last hour
because we are
the last.
Pieces of rock & roll lie
cracked & jittery in the sidewalk.

When our earth is an x-ray
Toadstool Hydrogen bomb
Negative
Life turned inside out
In reversal.
Nuclear holocaust

& over & over &
over again,
they will complain.
We will complain.

I will stay,
Till the last day.

Till all the earth

Is sick &
Dying.

The unborn fetus curled up
Like an abortion in a jar.
& dies
the worm
who crawled out to far on the sidewalk
 dies, dries to a crisp in the sun.

And all because you young muthafuckas
refused to vote for the right candidate in
 that 8 years past election!
And all because you hardassed oldsters
voted zealously for the wrong candidate
 in the 4 years past election!

Our freedoms were taken away
while we were all held prisoner
in the factory,
 as a waitress,
in the office
 bent over in the fields
sweat-laboring;
by the 3-piece suits; the bigger, meaner apes.

It will happen to you
 You will get old before you know it. Aches, pains,
Arms & legs loose strength,
Your face sags.
Its purgatory--
Not quite hell, -- not yet,
 & still hoping for heaven.

Noon Wednesday, September 24,
Photoshoot with Mr. Oto, —Shaun Roberts. Lights. Cameras. Is it
my cue Mr. De Mille? Always fun. Use these shots for RETRO 2.

AM Thursday, September 25
Transman Red recalled that he had received no vouchers from that
health and trans senior's focus group, promised him so long past.

Dead Promises. Take notice of the professional class. They prey on us like scavengers. Living off of us. Their agencies, doctors, professionals, social workers who earn a living 'handling us' in our health clinics, social agencies.

PM
We are living in a kleptocracy. The rich continually stealing from the poor. ---Root word is kleptomania—innervate stealing. Hopeless shoplifting of those CEO's, top corporate heads, governments, — powers in high places.

Noon Friday September 26,
Was explaining to Calf (Jasmin) that is it is difficult to show just one of a persons paintings; we now have her Lilly poster, but its best to show several others together, to give people an idea of style. So it is important for an artist to build a body of work—no matter how small. So she must keep painting! And take seriously his offer to have friend Richard P., photo her stuff along with his. At this point Transman has 23 paintings in his possession—plus those 25 scattered to the winds before. This to his name in entirety in the universe even if reduced to molecules.

9-Brush day. Jasmin's, poetry/dance event is tomorrow at Palace Legion Of Honor. These are my instructions:
> Let L. sit by herself.
> Don't beg for food.
> Don't follow L. around.
> Don't hiss or boo anybody on stage!

Am also reminded (by Jasmin) that at the last event he would not let her go anywhere by herself, and accompanied her everywhere she went. Feel disconcerted by this. And very alone. Could get depressed, or hyper-cynical. My purpose drives me forward.

Oh, Red enjoyed photoshoot with Shaun Roberts, and the next 2-days saw amazing shots of his painting storage loft, and his writing den— with himself included—with/without his black felt hat.

PM Sunday Night, September 28,
Everybody is a star, everybody wants to shine.

If you've had a life of drugs and alcohol, and procrastination, and do nothing, or do little—you can say, 'well it's my own fault, nobody else's'. But, if you have your best hat on and you put your best foot forward—each and every time, and you've done your job—but are still overlooked you have reason to get mad.

Another peril in the artists life is when success actually hits! People can be discouraging—even if they mean well. Maybe its better my success come late—after I've done a shitload of work. Once the complaints and critiques come in, the fan letters with well-meaning 'advice' it might be too heavy a burden to bare—have stopped others in their tracks. 'Uhh, his character development is poor.' Or, 'his plot's weak'-- (Etc.) '--so all I got was one book, not ten!' --- Well people do say anything! Like, 'your stuff is shit!' Or, 'your novels are misspelled—you use bad grammar!'

Noon Blue Monday September 29
Blue, but *active!* Hence, an 11-bursh day, finish up Put Our Thinking Caps On---, darkening all pastels in background, spooky deep green, & books, purple, blue, foreground.

T felt quite uncomfortable with his toes sticking out of his sox in various places, as he prepared to go out to Nicole's Cooking Class (free dinner) @ Trans.* (This Nicole is not The Hen, but an equally lovely, black, transsister.) Having packed his paint treys up off of the TV trey, and shoved the remaing unused brushes in their drawer back into the cabinet, unfolded the TV trey, stacked it against the easel, winding down on the days commitment to The Fine Arts, saving pigment-laden brushes which still rested in the open paint box & paint rags for one last foray upon the Work. Across the studio in his den, turned to stare a moment over at easel... —That's it! The blank white book hovering in space between the two studious readers—color it Yellow! Blazing light of intelligence! (Oh, a 13-Brush day.)

PM
A few times in my life I've had money and it's helped me over precarious times. When my dad died he left me a sum and I remember thinking in my hours and months of grief, also my resumed struggle with alcoholism (I 'd gone back off the wagon after 10 years) along with my ever-present insanity méjore, that at least I had this green money—it tided me thru—that if I'd had to worry about money

on top of everything else, I might not have made it. When I transitioned, suddenly there appeared that $8,000, just in time to get a surgery would not have been able to afford otherwise—a life answered prayer. When, after 40 years of procrastination, I resumed fine arts painting it came again --that Social Security reimbursement and afforded me, a whole new setup of acrylic paints, much needed brushes, 4 rolls of canvass, and other miscellany—paint drying boxes, art portfolios to display my work; it paid for the infernal KKK Kopy center to print my posters in an ongoing inventory that I sell at $20 a print. It paid for my Art Retrospective. That $6,000 re-launched my fine arts career.

Wee small hours AM Tuesday September 30
The soil of our soul is built on the firmament of God. Women of different faiths call upon the Creator. In low language; or high liturgy.

> I hear the heart.
> --God

Fed on a diet of meaningless commercials. Entertainment skirts the level of boredom, awful daily news the drama. Bad lives. Half-lives. Not satisfied, but for momentary wild inspiration, coffee-fueled. The artist has only their hope for recognition in some far off distant zone. To be feted. Published. Hung. Sold. Revenues received to better ones life.

Sometimes we dream of a great judge, because we want someone powerful on our side. Justice to be done.

172.
Well the city is ever-living, sleeping, awake, perpetually renewing its inhabitants; old timers curl up, die, but the city keeps on; alive, it is too big for all of it to die at once, too many new ones are arriving, being born, being imported from the smaller places surrounding.

So as I have said, more & more in this neighborhood can be seen the affluent class. The closer they live to the slums, the higher their gates, the stronger their locks, the thicker their chains, the more numerous police. Made the rounds up to Polk Strassa & saw quite a few shuffling oldsters in obviously worn, drab clothes, looking very uncared for. We are the last remnant of the old guard left over here. I saw & spoke with 5 people I knew, all because of the neighborhood-building of the Bookstore, and meeting so many neighbors. One is Nicole.

I like Nicole Hen because she is a poet, trans friendly & trans *knowledgeable*; knows all these poets & interesting artistic people. Today across the street, saw the older lady who was so instrumental for passing rent control back in the day, walks by downcast. She looks sad. Old & sad. Carrying a bouquet of purple violets on a green fern bed. Under appreciated? Non-appreciated!

> --Nice bookstore man. How long you been here?
> --It was a year in June... so, 16 months...

Noon, Monday, September 29
7-Brush day. Finishing. Called Richard & Jasmin, coordinate pick-up date for paintings—said I'd include "one or two" of Jasmin's---- the paper ones, Richard mentions, tho its same amount of work photographing them, they're easy to lift & carry, no problem. Want to promote a portfolio of hers.

Wednesday Noon, October 1
> There is a Holy One
> There is a Holy One.
> There is a Holy One.
> --Known by one Name in heaven,
> by many Names on earth.

Hashem gave Transman *words* to paint onto Let Us Put Our Thinking Caps On & Study In The Library, words which were titles on the books he had portrayed—Language, Biology, Math, Science. And he bowed his head, flushed with high emotion, a melting down of golden joy, thankfulness, & awe, nearly crying. When he was done, and set down his brushes, the books were appropriately labeled.

Noon, Thursday, October 2
I remember having money, at various times, once, when I had credit cards, but no actual cash, so I just kept using the fake credit card money; using the money & using the money—I was wrapped up in the creative process, and this facilitated my projects, feeling largest of

money I would go into the department store that had a food counter and use my credit card to purchase meals, thinking during this process at some point I'd stop spending, get a hold of myself get a job and go back to work and find ways to squeeze out the time to write etc.,—but until then I'd put on my best newly credit money charged clothes strut into the store go up to the food counter and get credit charged food for several days, go home, eat & create, go out to the club at night and party (on a few coffees) and *lived*; one day the credit limit was reached, had no money to pay. Hounded for debts a year or so, then POOF! the whole thing was gone! And my creative process had advanced! 'Mo Art!

PM

Must say, my ire at he constant trashing of Hillary Clinton and now Sarah Palin, has roused my feminist instinct—am for women, females. The more they trash these girls, the more I like them, and hate the male candidates. Bottom line, can't vote for Palin because of her anti environment dense no-nothing policy; her anti-women's free choice. And the probability that she is anti-gay, despite having very close lesbian friends. I think the whole thing has proven that women are now serious contenders for the presidency; and that women's vote must be appeased by offering female candidates in the future—for vice president and president. This has been well-proven.

All these protests, remember just 2 years ago, me and Kitty Kastro walked along the Trans march vigil together, with Dena; talking, laughing, dishing, shouting…

> They have poisoned America's lakes & rivers & oceans & seas.
> Don't worry—it will all wash clean—in a million years.

Noonish Saturday AM October 4,

The stock market has crashed. Wall Street has been whipped and is out flat for the count. Retirees have lost their life savings. Young investors wiped out. Beginning workers see their retirement pensions shrink from $1,000 to $5. The Government—Sitting President George Bush upon whose watch this gargantuan built itself up, greedily stuffing it's mouth with corrupt transactions, impossible mortgages, high risk venture capitals, totter and collapse—this same current government has forced usury upon the US taxpayers to pay 700 billion dollars to inject into this veins of this corpse to bring it back to life. Well the rich are just a filthy class of people. Me First,

207

is their motto. The Gimmie People. They climb like rats over the corpses of each other—fuck the poorer ones trampled to death under them. All the swindlers and White Collar thieves who caused the wreckage have absconded on golden parachute funds—personal bailouts to the tune of 10, 20 million dollars *apiece,* and there has been no talk of going after them to prosecute. It stinks. The stink washes in foul tides all the way up to the very door of heaven— where, thank God, it cannot come in. All the prayers of all the stock mongers in all the Wall Streets of Babylon—the World—have been said to no avail! The market continues to crash!

People are beginning to think in really big dominations these days. For a few days Transman had been griping about the $700 million dollar bailout, and others would correct him:

Uhm... that's 700 *billion,* dude...

The next notice he saw on an acquired bank was that its assets were in the trillion dollar range. What in the hell is a trillion? Is that a joke? Like a trill of a warbling bird?

So much for the talk of affluence & it s demise. A quick bus ride away is the Mission. Journey down Van Ness accompanied by decreasing affluence; makes a large right angle turn, then proceeds down Mission Street. Here, a jumble of colors, sights, & sounds. A lone bank blinks out; REVERSE MORTGAGES, a feeble advertisement for a service they can no longer do, in the dying economy. In curb-side stands ordinary poor people peddling los frutias & vegetables, cigarettes, & liquor speak in Latin language. Just like the bustling, hustling ghetto I remember of my youth. The dogs are bigger & mangier in the Mission. Not like the lease code enforced small breeds mandated by plutocrat landlords of Snob Hill. There are stains of crimson blood of fallen down drunks & gang violence, on the streets.

Here, in one of the many 2nd hand, used stuff stores, Transman purchased a metal suitcase to protect his fine arts prints from the rain, as he tugged them around the street on his cart, hoping to sell one or two per month. Then, a more lugubrious bus ride leaving from 16th &

Mission—Heroin capitol of the state—travels down Mission to Van Ness, turns, then climbs back up the hill towards home.

PM

I recognize my technical ability is not as proficient as many artists, yet I still want to be an artist. I will paint, regardless of my ability! Perhaps these techniques will improve with time. Rousseau is an example! His stick figures transformed into flesh animals & people with a high degree of perfection. Oh, am still a writer! Here, my artist's edict:

> Money stands between the artist and the Spirit. It compromises the creative process—even if only a little at a time. It leads the artist on a divergent path from their true creative genius with influences as to what will sell, & what won't, & they act accordingly; now to the call of money & not to their muse. It leads the artist into ruts & stagnation; over it they loose their art, & ultimately their soul. Tho you walk jangling money in your pockets you have become part of the evil; the wellspring of creative genius has dried up. Frustration, boredom, & deadened emotions will haunt you all the days of your sold-out life & you will live in self- imposed hell until the day you die.

The soil of our soul is built on the firmament of God. Not on the works of peoples insane plots!

Midnight, Monday, October 06,

Hello, my name is Red. I have a masculine wardrobe. I am a Transsexual. It all began in 1943, November; end of World War 2 would soon be over in Europe. *Tomorrow, tomorrow & tomorrow, creeps in this petty pace until the last instant of recorded time…*

> I was born in a howling hurricane. Jumping Jack Flash is a gas.
> --Rolling Stones

I was born in a red blood of my mothers womb in Provident Hospital a colored hospital on the South side of Chicago amid segregation, silent incest, unspoken, fear of communism, when it seems the true enemy is the enemy within—just as today--- I have attempted to speak out against those injustices well and as often as I could—and starved in the process. We are orphans of the world. I recall the twisted, deformed-of-limb French teacher so severely crippled by polio, rampant in the 1940's and early 50's. We met in college, and all hung around together; a band of radicals, Jews, Coloreds; half-insane; artists, musicians... He lived in a room-for-rent on the Near North Side, a busride from the college; his easel set up in the room beside the windows-where next to no work was done; his writing on the kitchen table. Mostly he was drunk. That was the beginning of his life.

The late part of his life, he had finally mastered the oeuvres. His art, no longer a drunk dream, pulled down from heaven and affixed on a page of paper; painted in colors blue, yellow, red, orange, green, purple, over canvas. One by one, Transman began to add accoutrements of his Fine Arts oeuvre to his daily repertoire—now a elevated recess on which to stack large canvases which would not fit into the 3'' space between the stretcher lofts and his higher Victorian ceiling--- a new waterproof suitcase to trot his pictures plus carrying tubes around in, next projected, a nametag: BUY MY FINE ARTS PRINTS! Likewise emblazoned, a poster—laminated to protect from the elements.

172.
The hand of cards is laid out—all can see 700 billion—corporate rotting stench, conceived by garbage minds who pull the levers and turn the wheels of machinery controlling our nation & the world.

It was so horrible—can smell the stench of blood & human sweat, tortured, unbathed human bodies 2,000 years ago as the Cross is raised up it boiling sun, 107 degrees; the blood, the flies, the agony, the smell of fear, the stench of dying corpses murdered in previous days, around which gather the faithful ones, traumatized, sweaty, tears having streaked their cheeks, the Beloved of their lives hung up beside the criminals both petty & political along the Apian Way.

The age-old story of humans searching for the Light. I enter once again the cool interior that is Grace--- grey stone, lofty arches, beauty. A temple built on faith. Faith alone.

Sorrow sadness, pain—then joy, release. *You believe in Me says Jesus, if I am for you who can be against you—for they are against Me.*

172.

210

The organ struck up chords & Transman was so on fire with the
passion of Christ that his eyes rolled around, his mouth opened wide,
and he fought to keep his tongue from lolling out of it—in sheer awe.
His spirit soared up to the stratospheres, up to the highest reaches to
meet God Who stepped down low to touch him from the lowest
fringes of the high holy place. Organ struck its last cords then the
organist departed. It had been an unexpected joy. Now a passel of
tourists walks thru marveling & talking in moderate, but not silent
tones. This is my cue to depart. 2 heterosexual lovers embrace—
caress---standing to one side of the alter. The SMACK of a kiss,
whispers, giggles, camera lights snap, snap, over at the foot of the
Cross. Yes, Grace Cathedral is a tourist site…

I have undergone several intense periods of religiosity in my life, no,
spirituality. Spirit led, the truth, the Path. And also coinciding,
became involved with the workings of the church or temple and
supported it in time, energy and projects, hence, the religiosity.

Eternally blue & trying to recapture in the night; recapture what? I do
not know. Lonesome hookers in the night. 1 hour preoccupations in
anonymous 3rd rate hotels/ motels, in which the bed remains made,
blankets and covers merely indented by human bodies. They then go
back to their separate lives.

> Back in the day when I was a girl police use to ride their horse into
> the church. I loved the sound of the horse hooves echoing thru the
> church. Back then they brought in all the big animals.
> --Overheard @ Grace.

Just a little bit higher. You hunger & thirst for God.

So good to see dogs lolling tongues happy waging tails, four foots
inside Grace Cathedral, seated in pews beside their owners, on leashes
on floor; one woman stood enraptured staring at the alter some 400
feet at distance, leash taunt behind her, her dog calmly squatted.
Transman stood, horrified, he was far away, the spectacle as the
dog… was it going to pee? No it took a shit! @ Transman promptly
turned around and left.

> On this day of the blessing of the animals saw a pigeon mounting
> another, the bottom pigeon held its tail up in the female pose split

211

seconds during which copulation occurred, then the top pigeon hopped off took a few steps away on the cornice of a 3rd story building; then the formerly bottom pigeon walked over and flapping its wings, hopped on top of the originally top pigeon and began mating with it—the now-bottom pigeon obligingly raised it's tail. So these pigeons were playing both the male and female role. Never before seen!

---Witnessed by Red Jordan Arobateau, on Sunday 3PM, October 5h, (St. Francis Day.)

173.

So its about the selling of the soul. America held us hostage. The workers of this nation, arms caught in a monkey wrench of its grinding machinery.

God how have humans gone so far wrong? Tiny infants, unnamed, abandon in trash cans. Cast up a prayer in love—love for their tiny spirits! Prey this child is dancing in paradise; dancing on the palm of Gods Mighty Hand. We are ruled by the average people, the majority---who vote in fear, repeating the same mistakes, electing the same master over and over into infinity. I ponder the decision to drop out, to not be part of the galloping clamoring hysterical throng; so much corruption, so much cyclical repetition of the same old tricks against the poor, those lesser then.

God stands above me—high above & says: Be true to your convictions.

So many people know the truth now.
> Strong-armed the people, twisting one arm behind us in a monkey wrench; if one signs the bail out bill—this administration will march off into the sunset with $700 billion of other people's money
> --Rep Daniel Issa, San Diego County, CA

There is outrage at it, but supposedly millions will suffer if they don't sign. Cuts to critical infrastructure, cuts to senior's financed by the state. Furthermore, every official running for president among both Democrats & Republicans is a sold-out crook, so what real choice is there? What real change can there be?

Time comes when the world would like to hear some truth; right now, today, we call upon the people of higher brow, the news rags of the week to tell some truth but all still spiel the same lies. Many of us would like to see what America is afraid to print, what America is afraid to hear.

All things I held so sacred, so dear, are dirt beneath these people's feet. Families, workers, are walking away from foreclosed homes— in such great haste-- so disappointed that they abandon computers, TV sets, stereos, photographs, furniture, furnishings—every other house in block in suburbs is deserted. The nations faux leaders have betrayed us while enriching themselves. Are great powers engineering this all in order to so horrify the population that they will agree to any terms? So the banks are falling like dominos, my new bank, Bo of A is the safest (?) Iceland, Ireland & England, --now *nations* are tottering on the precipice of financial ruin.

Well all my talking of picking up a gun & killing people (I.e. rich plutocrats) high rating & low degree corrupt politicos) spoke to the depth of my disillusionment and deep anger over this system & how it has both compromised & betrayed my parents, my predecessors & not me because never had any faith in it.

> One by one seen the lies exposed; this county perpetuates-- like our foreign aid programs are saving 3rd world nations when actually our government food aid to dissuade foreign governments from achieving self-sufficiency in food to feed their populations.

> What started out as a system of benevolent grants and loans to underdeveloped countries, at a real but moderate cost to the ample resources of America, has evolved into a strategy of international client patronage and dependency based on US political & military control over aid recipients.
> --Michael Hudson. Super Imperialism.

Noon, October 6, Monday
Transporting of the paintings to Richard; Photographer Day. Made milk carton crate stairs—one on ground, two, stacked beside it—to climb up reach loft and get cardboard dividers.

> God is the sum total of the infinite parts.

Sean's goal may be to have the best bookstore he can, and thru that save the world. My ambition always has been to be the greatest writer, painter, and thru this save the world. Doctor Sam has just become officially an Anesthesiologist, as well as a Pediatrician— maybe thru this is his secret idea to save the world. Well, if we all tried to save the world thru our gifts, this world would indeed be saved!

> Sean: Keep on asking myself, why do I have this perpetual guilty conscious.

> Red: I don't have no guilty conscious.

> Sean: I can *tell*.

> Red: But I have a perpetually poor pocketbook.

@ Babylon Falling I saw the pictures of Inferno by photographer James Nachtwey. This is a 'coffee table book' to be given to the rich, to The Gimmie People. Emaciated skeletons; chained, tortured children in insane asylums. Refugees blown-apart by war. Let it sit in its stark reality of human horror—caused in part by their grandiose lifestyle-- on each affluent table.

174.

The denegation of women is among the first, worst things you see in a barbaric tribe, at some point, more evolved tribes of people see that this means the extinction of their race, and learn to make a place and respect for women—albeit a controlled one, and not too high up in political or educational power. ---Otherwise the tribe remains ineffective, crippled, or extinct. In the advanced societies of today, we see how the constant disrespect of women-based functions, pregnancy being chief, followed by nurturing her family, has contributed to the upper-striving females choice not to have many children, if any, so as to advance her career and achieve equality with the high ranking boys. The misfortune is the loss to the tribe of what would have been very well taken care of, educated children to add to its numbers. In this worse case, women are abstaining having children at all. Every effort must be given to assure the equal advancement of women, including those women temporarily burdened by pregnancy, and to account for women with the constant

214

care of children—up to 20 years—so that they can indeed rise up to the rank of men, and help lead the world in which they live. I'll use this in Sedna!: *The world of 2050 was of more obvious gender parity then ever before on earth, tho not completely, sadly, not completely.* Use for SEDNA! Must begin my 4th Sci-Fi novel.

Monday Afternoon, October 7
Christmas Gaming Table, 24"x 24". Acrylic on canvas. Can't wait to get back to an oil. More control over it, because of not drying into permanency so quickly, which must then be painted over in white, and repainted to change. According to my style of painting by intuition or imagination. & mixing directly on the canvass while painting. A 12-Brush day.

All I had to live off was the crumbs you say. Well you better be ready at yo' table with yo' knife, yo' fok' n' yo' plate. Waste you life complaining, *all there is is these crumbs!* Be ready! Do what you can do, and get your works in place! I lived off the crumbs and this is what I've produced! Not, *I'm pissed about these goddamn crumbs, and ain't gonna do nothing, 'til somebody gives me the porterhouse steak!*

I been on holiday! Red spoke of his 8 month spending spree on his windfall, a respite from poverty. My shrink says I've made an investment—in those prints, paintings, art supply's… & money to eat out so I could save my energies from drudgery and pull together all my powers together to re-start Art. And how difficult that is.

Noon Wednesday, October 8
Christmas Gaming Table stands before me, centered in blazing lights. The work awaits. Thinking of selling a painting—Jasmin needs money. $50-overdrawn. She took $15 out of mutual account awhile ago. I can only scrape up $30 among my now 4 accounts at 2 banks.

PM
God please don't abandon me—don't abandon me to myself. Will use this for the end of this book:

> And as always I call upon Jesus to cleanse my mind so that I might be acceptable in Gods sight, and acceptable in my own insight that God has given me.

215

Blue Angles in town. To me it is a show of science. Not simply a
show of US power, of domination, but a show of technology.
People standing on roofs watch. 2 jetplanes---like sisters fly together
into the blue horizon with tail jet writing billowing clouds behind
them, mathematically locked in unison. Then, juxtaposed, a pigeon in
flight, winsome, investigating, changing its leisure course here &
there. The pigeons-- God's graceful creatures.

Transman saw a mailing tube first given him in the photographer's
shop; outdated now. Originally from when first he first began to print
up his life-long painting efforts utilizing this free gift of photography.
Time flies past so fast… steadily on its uncanny wings.

The dream on film. I've talked very little about photographers and
their craft, as part of my Art Journal series (OBEDIENCE TO THE CALL OF
ART, and, MY CONTINUING JOURNEY INTO SPIRITUAL, ARTISTIC & REVOLUTIONARY
THOUGHTS) but they have helped me in my adult professional art life as
a necessity to self-publishing, & as friends:

    Suzanne De Young
    Shaun G. Roberts
    Richard Politowski

Noon Friday October 10
Stock Market continues to crash. Global now. Iceland declares
bankruptcy—the whole country is folding; a year ago it was declared
a model nation. Iceland's debt is 12 times the size of its economy.
England, Ireland in trouble. China may have to bail us out, says
someone on TV, the Chinese are still working and have actual capital.
They still believe in saving mone, and are not a nation living on
credit.

Really painting on Christmas Gambling Table. A 10-Brush day.
Really going to town. Paint fast, lots of pigments, wiping off, brushes
flying in repetition, holding 5 brushes on left hand switching for the
right.

Saturday, October 11, Noon
We are a prosperous nation with immense resources. Says the faux
president. Those in power lying thru omission. Facts left out.
Sentences deleted, knowledge abridged, the truth gone unheard.
Meanwhile the worst week of the 120-history of the Dow Jones

216

economic indicator. In a ripple effect out from our nation, the world economy is on the brink of collapse. Gimmie people. Stockbrokers are gamblers in a gaming pit… TV financial wizards discuss what happened to your money. *What money?* Transman sat back laughing.

> Lock up your libraries if you like; but there is no gate, no lock, no bolt you can set upon the freedom of my mind.
> ---Room of Ones Own, Virginia Wolf

The phoenix who went up in flame. Jimi Hendrix, Basquette, Malcolm X, Janis Joplin, Marylyn Monroe. The world's unhappy children. Edith Piaf, Billie Holliday, Van Gogh. They produced such beauty!

Red was dedicated, yes, hours spent at the easel, the desk, but was not so dedicated that he did not go out. Had set aside 2 to 5 hours nightly to prowl the gay clubs, artist districts, and today, fast forward, 2008; his hangout was the Bookstore. That, and took time to exercise. The genius needed people and he knew it! They were his inspiration, and his hoped-for audience in some far off, glorious day.

We are supposed to be perfect humans. Perfect like humans can be— not perfect like God! Only God is perfect! We must try to be perfect humans, it is confusing, people think they are suppose to be perfect like God—which is impossible, and ultimately self-defeating.

Christmas Gaming Table (Indian). A whole lotta brushes.

I must confess something about the Darfur button. Andre @ Grace gave me a button:

> I VOTE FOR DARFUR
> AskTheCandidates.org

Red couldn't decline—as he agrees with this cause; --obediently pinned it on his shirt. Then few people passing by commented: *like yer' button*; etc. That evening went to take off his shirt, realized the button was on, rather then remove it, kept it on, because he wore that shirt again the next day as he sometime did if it didn't smell too bad. This button became a burden. Red's Cross, forced by conscious to pick it up daily. Having to take the time to pin it on, feeling that to fail to do so is writing off a million starving, subjected women,

217

children & men in the refuge camps of Chad. Wearily re-pinning it onto each fresh shirt—until the button got lost under a pile of stuff & he forgot about it.

PM
Sometimes the bar is set too high for the people to jump. Specifically the church/temple; where some display finery, so that a poorly clothed petitioner is made to feel out of place, shunned, ice-cold shouldered at hospitality hour, forced to sit in the back pews during service. Or by refinement of religiosity—agreeing with a particular doctrine, inflexible so that no other school of thought may be accommodated. Sometimes this temple is a 'house set upon the hill' as a light to all, but, so far up that goddamn hill, blocks and blocks of torturous ascent, nearly vertical, that only those who live up on the hill can get there... so the life struggle of those at the bottom, chiefly our Transman, dwelling in his halfway house (neither black nor white, neither uneducated nor degreed, neither destitute or well off, not a ghetto-dweller, but not high up on the hill by any means).

Wee Small Hours AM Monday October 13
Mailed EMPIRE! (His first Sci-Fi novel) away today @ Post Office to a NY house specializing in the sci-fi trade.

Noon, Monday October 13
Hashem I beg You for my life! No matter what life hits me with—more broken emotional ties, less success, that I keep going till the end, and see how far I can run this race—and be all that I can be, regardless; do not let disappointment strike me on the level of my cellular being so that my body withers under the world's onslaught! Keep me alive!

People think its handed to them, they don't know, we have to work for everything. There's plenty of rich people with all the opportunities who've fallen by the wayside—just that they are from such rich families you don't see them standing in the free food line, there are funds to back up all their failures, and financial ineptitudes and disasters.

PM
Static electricity. The shuffling footsteps of countless Utopians, generated enough electricity to power the hot water heaters, and

218

overhead lights of every floor. Hydrogen power, hydro—water power, solar and wind power all adjuncts fed into the gargantuan like power tubing system throughout the modern edifices of Utopia, with the steady fusion of nuclear energy to fall back on. The ever-dwindling supply of precious fossil fuel was used only now as starters to combustible engines--a drop at a time.

AM 4, Tuesday, October 14

For some it is a perpetual voyage thru the city of night—nowhere to lay their head, nor hide, but a pavement stone; at the end of day, to punctuate the hours of motion, feet shuffling, eternally being pushed on, on, on. He could not be like one of these, so he had worked all his life, for the lowest wage, but receiving a steady paycheck week after week, which paid rent on a small room, carfare & food. So there was always a place to keep his animals, his art; a place to dream his dreams. SEDNA! —is one!

The kitchen sink just coughed up a missing paintbrush…. Disgorged out of its drain… Thin red & white wooden handle, tiny hair brush; the smallest in his brush drawer.

Whatever you're doing, if it's for profit & not for love of the thing, it makes so much difference.

— Dear Jesus, keep me in your care, watch over me.

Now I tell you anyone who is great, who does truly great things; it is God working *thru* them, not they themselves. God chooses people; goes among them and chooses people by their thoughts, by their words, their actions, by their constant, feverent prayers. God goes among us.

God hears all prayers& can change all fortunes. God hears all prayers, & has from the beginning times. Because some races are 'chosen' having become more highly developed in their closeness to Her/Him by approaching God in doctrine, theology, discipline and in a conscious, rational act, and God can make very good use of them, does not by one fraction diminish the great closeness of the primitive, unschooled soul who wildly calls out GOD! GOD! –using no name at all! Unstoppable! Their hearts are in such fright, their lives so far destroyed by this earth. Those who need God so much!

Now, sadly to speak, him embracing Judaism—Transman attended a film in the basement of Grace Cathedral on the Palestinians. 2/3rds of the contributors to this documentary movie were Jews, sympathetic to the refuges of occupied Palestine territories:

> Those in power; lying thru omission. Facts left out. Sentences deleted, knowledge abridged, the truth gone unheard.

> 1/3 of all US dollars sent to foreign lands goes to Israel
> 6-8 million per day US aid to Israel

There was a tear in old Transman's eye as he saw Rachel's death as she bravely stood on the barricades, defending a Palestinian family's home; as, manned by an equally young Israeli soldier inside a bulldozer who aimed the vehicle dead at her; trampled onward, heedlessly of human life; crushed her to death under its massive ton treads. Rachel died at age 23… Like I said:

> Sometime the bar is set too far for people to jump.

Fire engine bass foghorn TOOT! A blast another honk, high trill, 5 red fire engines converge; fire hook & ladder; from separate parts converge on Nob Hill, 1,2,3,4,5 engines. They come wailing out of the distance.

I might have been undecided about a lot of stuff—but about my art I was not, whether to travel or not. Whether to make the pursuit of a companion my primary goal, after Jasmin he hesitated. All worked together, his focus on his work in anticipation —hoping it would pay off in the end in some wonderful way—this beside the sheer love of doing the work the' orgasm' upon completion of each piece.

> In heaven—one won't hurt another.

The newspapers of this day, everything I read—even tho I don't understand it its gon' be messed up, fucked up.

> When the mirror no longer will reflect me,
> And I pass silently on, as a ghost.

I am at a place have worked for an extremely long time. As the hardest battle is with ones self—that I have recaptured my fine arts painting, am closing in on a 2nd RETROSPECT containing 11-plus paintings, also writing (journaling); this to be perfected when I begin SEDNA! Have the 2nd RETRO out and in my hands, will then be working on an ART COLLECTION; then will be firing on all cylinders!

5AM
Cat standing guard over his food bowl, had now laid down on the floor, reclining, and fell asleep.

Noon
News, San Fernando Valley is on fire! Orange, red plumes of the element; earth, water, air, and Fire. He fell asleep to fire; that night he had a dream—a fire of a different sort:

> There is a table in a restaurant. The table has 4 seats. What will happen when God comes and sees the cripple, and the poor have been pushed out of their seats by the affluent rich young couples, each one of them now seated in the seats formerly were the humble people.

> There is an old red brick building 10 stories high, rusted fire escapes zigzag up; it is a very special building. It is the institution for the insane---don't look too close! Avert your eyes! Or you will see human wrecks flitting on the fire escapes, grey ghosts, skeletal; see the very old, the feeble minded; see them peering out of blackened windows dust coated at the real world.
> *So many turn their heads & avert their eyes...*

AM, 3, Wednesday, October 15
> Heaven is such a beautiful place
> & there we will know how much
> we are loved.

Regarding the aforementioned dream, we of a poor & landless class are being replaced. One by one. Substituted, each of us, by a rich, unfeeling, unaware, robot-minded psudeo-human; the soil of their soul is shallow. Subsequently they don't realize what they are doing. ---And they do it with disdain. Hate even. We are being pushed out of here. Person by person. Chair by chair. House by house. That's how the cultural genocide is being done. *The ghettos of my youth are all bulldozed down. Gone. Portraits from a Gone World.* So, this issue of the displaced inhabitants of Israel-Palestine, here is another bar too high to jump; as Jews fight for a space of their own on earth after countless diasporas, & evictions from host countries (Spain, Germany, Russia, et al). So some of us at synagogue sit shoulder to shoulder; one in sympathy with the former sole inhabitants of that land, the Arabic Palestinians; the one beside in favor of Zionism to a fascistic zeal intermixed with racial prejudice, and based on their knowledge that the Arabic population would 'wipe Jews off the face of the map' if they ever get the means. So the argument goes on. Kemperer, a Jew, refrained from escaping the Nazis by immigrating to newly formed nation state Israel because he compared the Palestinians to the Native Indians, displaced from their ancestral land of at least 8,000 years, America, by white settlers in wave after wave of tall mast boats, spilling off of the shores of Europe. Their covered wagons traversing the continent so there was nowhere left to escape.

My people work best in an atmosphere of peace.

ILLUMINATIONS—Journal Accompanying My Art Works. JOURNEY #14. That is the title of my next literary work.

2PM, Thursday, October 16
Dreaming Of Paris Streets Where I Have Never Been; 24″ x 18″, Oil on Canvas.

Late PM Thursday, October 16
Well we have reached the point in our lives—all those kids I played with as children back in Chicago, now we are in our mid 60's. Mortality has dawned upon us. Raised in the environment of grandparents, uncles, & aunts whose mortality range was 75 years; back then, that was considered old. We feel the twilight come upon us—yet, today with advanced medicine, 100 years old, not 80 is a possibility... where are those old playmates of my childhood? What are they doing? How are they prepared for their future in an America in decline?

Anyone raised in the African-American community, their life has been touched by racism—if not their life—then their parents lives; &

this impacted the way they came up; their resources or lack of, the mental, emotional climate of their household, of their neighborhood; the resources of their community—or dearth of it. So all of us had a less then ideal beginning. And also, among all these playmates were the few... the precious few like myself... queers. So there has been this rough background, then piled on top of that, the transgender life, carrying all these difficulties around for all 65 years...

> God created this beautiful little garden, with all we humans could want in it; we were with God every minute—then all this stuff happened, and here we are, in need, hungry, lost in gritty, grimy streets with nothing, looking for a dime or a quarter somebody might have dropped in the gutter.

To live to be old you have to tell the Lord—no matter what happens, what disasters, betrayals, sicknesses, *I'm in it for the distance.*

3AM Friday October 17
Foreclosures of American houses surges forward. Well I'll tell you we are all crabs trying to climb up out of the bucket onto dry land, to hold a place of our own in the sun. All people want a home of their own, but few can afford it. And many got in over their head with mortgage balloon payments. In the beginning they'd had an affordable $1,600 monthly payment for several years, but when the balloon payment kicked in, this immediately soared to $5,000 monthly which was out of their reach; so the house fell in around them. This combination of multi-millions of American homes foreclosing is what fueled the Stock Market meltdown; now America is in an economic crisis not seen since the Great Depression of 1929. Which is what I told people all thru these last JOURNALS---all human beings want, need, and deserve a home of their own! Completely rent free, lien free, tax-free. Theirs exclusively for life, even into their decrepitude and vulnerable old age-with live in attendants until the day they croak.

Again, Wall Street shafted Main Street. —The only way the suffering done by the poor will be remedied is thru collective action. Singularly we are too easily defeated. En Masse is our strength.

> Strategies to win a war the first point is to get allies. One man cannot win against another man, so, get 5 friends, ten friends, 20 friends, then go back and defeat the man.

--Transliteration from Sun Hu Dynastic Ruler of Ancient China; The Art Of War.

It's horrible, its not fair. $250 million dollar golden parachutes; enough to save 80-foreclosed homes. The first group, white collar crooks of high degree, the others, petty people, ordinary workers scuffling trying to make a life.

Scanned Naomi Klien's new book Revolution Now, disappointing. --- After her other brilliant analysis and exposes of stinking facets of this corrupt system that nips and bites at our very position on this planet, in a slow, painful destruction of the middle class, and squashing of the poor. By now this woman is the talk of the bookstore, her website often referred too. Maybe because she has fans clamoring for a solution to the madness she has concocted this book—or she needs the money to finance her speaking tours? Anyway, she is not alone; Plans For Revolution is impossible to write about... I keep telling myself—maybe its because we are ready for change; but now we must wait for the times to be right & then we will know what to do!

175.

> Everywhere I go in this city I get dick shoved in my face - & no pussy. No pussy that I want. Got one hot pussy runen' after me, but I don't want it.
> --Pre-T Transman; Overheard Trans Center.

> Trans woman be at work, she will overhear at least one person that day whispering in her direction, *"that's a man"*. When she walks down the street some guy is going to comment, *"there go a man in a dress"*. The next man she passes will yell, *"Say baby, how big is your dick?"* The next block she comes to, some man will ask *"Say baby, how much?"* The next block another man will say, *"I want to fuck you."* The man after that will say, *"I want you to fuck me"*.
> --Life of a Transwoman, testified by Andrea at Tom Waddell Tranny Health Clinic.

Regarding the Native American Way: a child in whose gender is in doubt is taken to the Medicine Woman or Man; the Medicine Person presents the child with 2 sets of toys, girl toys and boy toys; whatever set the child chooses and begins avidly playing with, is the gender the child must be raised as. The parents are obliged to teach their child accordingly. And to call them by their gender-specific name. There is always a place in community for everybody in Native style. No one is outcasted or excluded! Woe Babylon who devours her children! Alas, Amerikka. Hate is with you.

Friday noon, October 17
'France', 15-Brush day. Afternoon news headlines: recession; families loosing homes; meanwhile, customers @ Babylon Falling are spending like nobody's business. A true testimony to affluence of this neighborhood.

4AM Saturday October 18
Clear blue sky to the average citizen. To the artist-writer, clear blue tremelado sky, pink clouds. *The eagle who flies the highest.* To fly high---what else is there to do in this world? The secret is catching the very highest tree limb, before it begins to slip away; then hang on there by your teeth & finger nails, for dear life.

We are building bridges of understanding so written my Journal for the public to see so you can know more about me, & my kind. Poets are like prophets. As many of you know the whole bible is written in verse. Well, life is a puzzle to figure out—power, the government, as manipulated thru the most rich interests of this planet, must be put back into the hands of the people by all means necessary—Well some want to save the world thru Revolution. I want to save it thru Art!

Remind you dear friends that information is to be found in b*ooks*, i.e. England's Industrial Revolution, far from being a perfect advancement for all humankind sent into financial chaos & final hell whole guilds of accomplished workmen now replaced by *sheer in mee sheens* (sheering machines). —That from: The Making of The English Working Class, E.P. Thompson

Saturday noon, October 18
Painted. Mega-brush day. Put in Eiffel Tower, Arc de Triumpth. 'France'. Oil. Whole studio is toxic.

AM 3, Sunday, October 19
Nicole; her hair like a thick mane of a lioness. Sean & Red are having a terrific argument; Sean claiming Red had told him he didn't want fineartamerica on his website, when in truth it had been that Sean

225

didn't want to put it on there. (This had been 3 weeks ago.) So there they were having a reverse argument of what they'd had in the past, screaming and growling at an equal decibel, but about the exact different thing. —Both having forgot what their original opinions had been. Meanwhile Chris --C-3-- is painting a green hospital stripe around the walls of the bookstore for his Halloween Show opening. C-3 carries his drawings around in a 15" x 17" Leonardo da Vinci book to protect them, also to occasionally to refer to the Master for encouragement, technique; etc. Red then recalled he had a Diana Souheim biography of Radclyff Hall under his desk propping it up; someone offered up two short stacks of Lawrence Durell --The Alexandria Quartet--- used as bookends; soon all reveled various books they employed for more then just the purpose they were intended.

Sean's bookstore is on the dark side of the street—slowly the sun comes across asphalt, inch by inch. The Transman entertained self-analysis: *Why do I hate? Because I am an outcast.* He didn't think Sean realized at first, —the marginalization of queer peoples lives; that of persons of color—but he's starting too… In part, thru Red's eyes.

Later the old man returned inside, to the window seat and his pile of books. Here's the world from Mike Davis, Planet of Slums:

> Cities indeed have absorbed nearly two thirds of the global population explosion since 1950, and are currently growing by a million babies and migrants each week. The worlds urban labor force has more then doubled since 1980, and the present urban population 3.2 billion—is larger then the total population of the world when John F Kennedy was inaugurated. And; in many cases, rural people no longer have to migrate to the city; it migrates to them. After the fisherman's homes were cut off from the sea by a new highway their fishing grounds polluted by urban sewage, and neighborhood hillsides deforested to build apartment blocks, caused spiritual and psychic destruction.

This is also true in Malaysia, where Jeremy Seabrook describes the fate of Penang fishermen *'engulfed by urbanization without migrating, their lives overturned even while remaining on the spot where they were born'*.

PM Sunday October 19

TV commercials, fine cars, luxurious interiors of houses. Slim, young, well-dressed life actors. You are looking at the face of affluence. Out in the street, the reality: They crowd you out, they are younger, bigger, taller, healthier, stronger; they can purchase expensive foods—shrimp, delicacies-- prepared foods not in a box; they displace you, you poor, they don't know you, they don't care!

Powell Street, the thick metal cable of the cable cars, imbedded in cement under rails, is on fire! Scene: brownskin assertive stout blue – uniformed police woman, gun in holster swinging on her hip marches along the rail calling the emergency in on her 2-way radio.

I am glad am not an integral part of the bad side of Ameri(kkk)a—its greed, exploitation of others; hard headed & unknowing, rich ruling class. I'm instead a pariah, an old transsexual man with little funds, great ideas, a still functioning sex drive, pets in my care & a whole shitload of fine ART!

8pm Monday October 20

Diet kicking in again, slowly, inching down below 185; next interim goal, 179-180. At this point will be 8 pounds away from weight he was before transition, 10 years ago in 1998. He will be able to zip up his 2 new pairs of size-36 trousers donated by L.

The economy is in the news. Stocks on the market crashed, some will come back to life given enough time—but others are now dead. Dead Ends. Those investors loose their life savings. This is what the sitting president would have done to us on Social Security—his plan to base Social Security on the stock market! What a disaster that would have been! What a fool that man is!

The democratic contender for the presidency must be elected! I don't like him personally; but democrats are always better for the poor like me. The opposition has said he wants to cut Medicare! Then how will we live! The Republicans want to cut the handicapped, privatize Social Security, cut Medicare—all aid to the poor who don't have the resources the rich do! Murderers! They should be put on trial! Court held by a judge, jury of the poor! String them up by their heels to dry out in the sun!—The light of disclosure!

227

'France' is working well; got photos on internet for a beret (tam), the French flag (red, white, blue) some landmarks-- Eiffel tower, Arc de Triumph, and left over ruins of the aqueduct constructed by Roman conquers 400 ACE circa.

PS, sold 2 postcards to transwoman writer.

176.
X says he was a member of an Indian Sweat lodge; to go to a sweat is a holy, mystical transformance. Naked or with small towels you sit around with other men; only men are allowed in the men's lodge; chanting, singing, meditating & sadly, there in, he started his period, forming a red pool of blood under his towel; —there are distinct Indian rules for women on their period; they must go sit in the women's hut during menstruation.

Women are exiled, women are put in apartheid women are excluded—due to their physical bodes and female functions. — Must say at a meeting all this notion of the high spiritual elevation of the Dalai Lama---an older Jewish individual pointed out last night, the Lama has been surrounded by his monks much of his life; all these man & boys none of them women—what does this say for women's liberation?

True; have not seen any female monks portrayals in the movies & documentaries made of the subject.

Early AM Tuesday October 21

Why do I hate? Because I am an outcast.

Well what is an earthly paradise? Each nation has an independence and it is bound together with other nations via webs of economy, trade, tourism, sharing of art, science & technological information, education; with each citizen having a home which they own from young adulthood to the end of their life—no matter how sick or frail or incapacited. This shall be a solar and green heated, powered home, each home will have a small plot of land for the human to farm; as well as their participation in larger collective gardens nearby, including some farm animals.

228

France. I try to make the picture move around a little bit… adding space to left hand upper corner, edging out a sliver of the Arc de Triumph; when you go to write a book you might write the most fabulous passages of prose—but between these is text, paragraphs which get you from one passage to another---all is necessary; it adds to the body of work. If a picture (France)* is not so fine as a Blue Dog, a Ho's Bath, it is still necessary to add to the body. Viewers will want to see this, they will look at it, as they view the collection, pausing only momentarily perhaps before they proceed on to the next oasis which happens to be true greatness—there to linger awhile to savor each line, huge color strength, motion, meaning, symbolism—statement. So to discard lesser works out of a collection would be stupid.

*(Unless they are French themselves.)

--By the way, submitted e-mail to SF MOMO, with my art galleries on line info, and offering to show them my art.

6 AM Wednesday October 22
Investors are coming in buying up 2, 3 foreclosed houses—for realestate investments. Sharks. Capitalizing on a broken families misfortune. Could you put a bullet in them from hate? Well God asks us to do something, different then this. To not become part of their reality!

Painted AM. Still on his job, that afternoon now found Transman in Oaktown to P.U. contents @ mailbox. Junk mail mostly; but a nice packet from Christopher Robin; —Zen Baby 'Zine, & other literary paraphernalia.

Bus rides to where the bay bridge splits in half, spread like a ho's legs proceeding into Treasure Island.

All well comported on bus; friendly brown-tan oldsters this afternoon, scorching hot Oakland weather, street corner slo' walken' lip smacken' stereotypes of yesteryear where remember Ruby, a San Pablo Hotel hooker in 1973, days of my youth. Seems just like yesterday.

Transwomen can be cruel; silk stockings swish, legs shaved, tall, bewigged, boisterous, lipstick large mouths; walks with her sorority sisters for protection, they come upon some innocent antiquated oldster glare at her; hiss-voice gossip; the oldster crone shuffling along, too much bright red lipstick, powder caked on her wrinkled face; the tall young trans beauties laugh; one with falsely sweet voice artificial under which comes a snake-hiss:

Oh has Halloween come early this year?

Overheard at Trans Space:
Why would a 76-year old man fuck a 7-year old boy? It really fucked me up! Why would a 7-year old boy get fucked in his ass! You see how big that thing is? It really fucked me up!
--A transwoman's trauma.

Remember My Arms are everlasting & far reaching.

*

Grace. T arrived @ end of service. Got a free coffee, which he immediately diluted w/milk & hot water in his thermos, according to his greatly reduced caffeine regime, after having had to go to hospital to undergo Stress Test—which was not pleasant. Sat out in courtyard awhile. Contemplated his interior landscape. Felt himself—the aggravation of being human; aches, pains, irritations, fears, allergies.

My Chinese friend J. who sings traditional opera, trained on the Mainland as a child, comes by; she tells me to promote my art:
Your work is better then what I see at the modern art museum. Be aggressive! Go there! Show them this work! The ones who are aggressive, they promote themselves but your stuff is better then theirs!

Midnight Wednesday October 22
Scanning thru Christopher Robin's Zen baby 'zine. See accounts of others who have sacrificed their time/lives to outpourings of their souls—felt very connected. Transman felt proud and satisfied that night. He was one in a legion of an army of counterculture artists who were nowhere.

Oh the artist! Their beauty lives on after them. They gave it their all.

> Sometimes I buy their bad art for 50 cents or a dollar because I feel
> sorry for them. They gave up their art dreams way too early, but
> they are over it, they don't care!
>
> --Christopher Robin; If Hipsters Were Garbage Men.

Noon Thursday, Seniors Day; October 23

Birds chortling on his shoulder; green, & white. Opening mail from
mailbox; BNI, Richard Freeman's 'porn 'zine from Ohio is shutting
down shop—Richard is suddenly unemployed & out of funds. -—
This before the Great Stock Market Crash of September-- letter dated
July 30. Transman infrequently got to his mailbox. Another prisoner
letter —this one from Mule Creek State Prison, Ione, CA. A former
pugilist (boxer), mob enforcer, and FBI informant who was betrayed
by police authorities is languishing behind jail bars. His story has
been on CNN evidently and he seeks to find promotion for his book.
Transman got mail from prisoners, would-be-authors, and others who,
while squatting in their jail bunkers probably were sending out
blanket ad campaigns, and confused his tiny self-publishing-only
press with a larger company who could do some good for them. Sit at
my desk with Christopher's list of Prisoner 'zines; contemplate again
how if they (men primarily) had gone straight to the *pen* or the brush,
they never would have fallen afoul of the criminal law. This of
course does not include fellow political prisoner caught up in protests,
demonstrations against this corrupt system, etc. Once locked up
where they cannot longer roam nor get in trouble—at least not in the
greater free society---they begin to look inward, like the Buddhists
suggest all human kind do, and begin to produce materials from their
minds, skills & talents! Raising up pen and brush to illustrate the
wrongs of an unjust society. This gives me cause to think how a
female-born persons life, an educated persons life, a queer persons
life may be more circumscribed in that they would never join a street
gang, nor be allowed to join one—and thus being de facto in 'jail' of
sorts already, do ascend to the higher levels of intellectual
productivity in due course, missing the penitentiary, the jail, the gang,
the criminal underworld. This reminds me also of Dorothy Allison,
the well known writer from white trash southern redneck beginnings,
her testimony how she, as a lesbian, was the first of her clan ever to
go on to college, and graduate with a degree. Why? No pregnancies.
Why? Different from the common herd. All this to add that we
queers, we female born, we intellectuals must assert our cause

everywhere! As we pick up & help to advance our brothers/sisters in the lower levels of this world, they too must embrace our struggle as well! No one way shit! Again reference Dr. Sam's sojourn in Africa as a medic in the Humanitarian Medicine team, which flies around the world to strange, wild, uncivilized, destitute spots to give aid to those who have never even seen a doctor. As his skills bring the patient relief—he must wonder—*would they kill me if they knew I was a queer?* --Due to the archaic tribal beliefs of many of them. This world will be whole one day—and it is a two way street! No reverse-racism! No one left behind! Not us queers, not the poor, not even the rich who have allied themselves with the call for justice, balance & harmony on earth in all things tangible, economic, life-sustaining.

The way we raise animals for food, it should be different. The way we treat prisoner in institutions, it should be different.

PM
There is no way our nation could have engineered 9-11. We could not have paid, bribed, coerced all 20-odd Arab nationals to drive passenger planes to their death. But we could have found out about this plot early in its formation, and instead of stopping it, warning people, making arrests, allowed their plot to carry out to its unbelievably horrible conclusion—to use as excuse for entering mega war in the Middle East. —All in the sake of money. Oil money.

Deepak Chopra says you and I are the eyes of the universe looking at itself. Well this is my look at it.

2AM Friday October 24
I don't recommend seeing the movie Cry Of The Snow Lion, because you are crying & anguishing along with the Tibetan people at their brutalization and subsequent raw cultural genocide at the hands of the uneducated Chinese.

At church a saint upholds a translucent chickens egg. Ancient riddle; what came first the chicken or the egg? Jesus answers; *I am the beginning and the end.*

After worship service, lunch, then Steve showed us a film. Everybody assumes Tibet is a tiny little bitty place, but it's a huge mass of land stretching along the China-India border.

The Dalai Lama is a Buddhist Bod-a-nistra; this is one who is reborn again to help guide those who he has taught in a previous life. Faithful Tibetans view him as a living God—a God right with them in flesh & Spirit; where as our Christian God dwells right here with us--- invisibly, in Spirit only.

Now at last Transman saw female nuns-- Buddhist nuns; captured and tortured by the Chinese soldiers; beaten, electric cattle proud in their vaginas. Always this fate for women. The young nuns testify, of the rape; one tearful; will not give her name. Her devotion to her Faith has grown stronger.

A monk, Pauline, beaten, tortured, electric cattle prod inserted into his mouth, and anus; shocked repeatedly. Left for months in solitary confinement; spent 33 years in Chinese prison.

> Its impossible to have economic democracy without social
> democracy coming along shortly behind
> --Diane Feinstein, D. Senator

Solution for Tibet is for individuality of each Chinese person; for each to form a conscious; assert their individual thought and self-identity divergent from the party line.

> I dwell in the heart. —Jesus Christ.

> Metanoia---Greek. Metanoia to turn around; change of conscious.

> When exploring outer space could be exploring inner space; what is
> more important to land on the moon or the understanding of the
> human mind?
> ---Dalai Lama

Noon, Friday, October 24
So many obstacles were in my way. Ah shit. Feel like I'm an old dog who somebody has left outdoors in the cold & grown mean in the process.

I just want to feel good, I just want to feel happy, and to find a *placement,* somewhere in the greater art world, outside myself, so that I might know where I stand, and of course to be recognized as such by other people.

*

France. This person is definitely on their way somewhere—to France, to France in their dreams… to the actual country of France… France of memory; France of escape from segregation, France of hope. A new continent! A brilliant sun! A blazing sun! Furthest upper right hand corner! Green bird squawking his little head off in office—driving me crazy! How to capture that sun! To turn it from a shaky little dot into a SUN! Eiffel tower fairly *dancing* off the canvass upper left! A 16-Brush day.

177.

Must report that these days we are laughing at the stock market. -- Every time we hail one another. Such is our great hate for those richer then us:

> First person: The market lost 300 points today.
>
> Second person: Ha ha ha ha!
>
> Both together: HA HA HA HA HA HA!
>
> First person: Well, see yuh, I got errands to do. I gotta go to the bank.
>
> Second person: Better *hurry!*
>
> Both together: HA AH HA HA HA HA!

This is because none of us has any money in our pockets much less the stock market, and all of us hate the rich investors who have robbed small people blind. Often this exchange will be interrupted by a blast of guilty contemplation:

> Second Person: The market dropped another 300 points today!
>
> First Person: Ha ha ha ha!
>
> Third person, joining: Ha ha ha ha!
>
> All: HA HA HA HA HA!

First person: HA HA HA… Whoops… I guess I really *shouldn't* be laughing huh? It's not really funny… (Pauses a moment, then tips up head once more) HA HA HA HA HA!

All uproariously: HA HA HA HA HA!

It's a maniacal laugh. Maniacal, desperate laugh.
--Jay S. @ Grace

10AM Saturday, October 25
Peter, upon this rock I build my church, and the gates of hell shall not prevail against it. All what is going on today in the financial economic political market is a web that cannot be untangled—it is the web of hell, and we are caught inside.

After completion of this entire book—consisting of 3 parts, must switch to SEDNA!

Above! All good things come from above—not horizontally. It is God Who frees up the gifts that pass from one human to another... *Many good gifts I will give you.* Says God.

Noon
Jesus With The Blue Hair. Oil on Canvas 25"x 25". Thirteenth painting in 2nd RETROSPECT. The Christ is giving communion to pews of parishioners—and to you. Of course the red background as told to me by the Spirit a week or so before—blood. The Blood of Christ.

A 14-brush day; very crowded pallet! Must change it. Meant to change after France, but Jesus just came along down the pipeline, so will use this pallet to the end of it?

Whoops! The Blue Jesus just became female—2 breasts.

8PM Saturday October 25
Behold! The black iron neck-shackles of black iron; a slave is the cleric collar around Blue Christ's neck. The left robe-sleeve of the cleric robe is a chain of thick black links—God chained to the holy & compassionate service of humanity!

Debating wither to spend $2 on a coffee @ coffeeshop T discovered himself coughing from noxious fumes at the curb, reading a newspaper (The Onion) on a bus bench @ side of the road. Finally made up his mind to go in— purchased a $1.50 cuppa' decaf, and set a stack of used newspapers on a table; seated himself; and this is what he read:

> ### BAN ON TOMBOYS
> Malaysia's main body of Islamic clerics has issued an edict banning tomboys in the muslin--majority country, ruling that girls who act like boys violate the tenets of Islam, an official said.
> --SF Chronicle, Oct 25,

All the 'race news' clustered together on the same page—death of Dreamgirls Academy Award winner's mother & brother; a black man death by dragging in the fine state of Texas.

We are living life on a one-way street---not in hindsight. Criminals repent after their violent action, *after* they are put away behind bars— some for a lifetime.

9AM Sunday October 26

Times in his life he'd performed the most outpourings of oil/acrylic painting was those of the most poverty. Likewise many great poets & painters of history. Christ was born in an animal's stable. In 1968-70 in the condemned building now, 2008 living hand-to-mouth; social security disability income $120 less than his rent, so as having to hustle and scuffle up the remainder thru his fine arts outpourings, & poetic prose; 1958—when he'd first begun while living a home with his dad in a small rental house which was a converted garage. Nothing fine. And how he hoped for one day to have a small self-sufficient place he would own, in which to work and to be happy with mate, companions, dreaming of the stars.

Must tell you the current political scene—which is moving at a frantic pace. Very difficult—painful, to see the hate Proposition-8 has generated. This is a bill put on the upcoming November 4th election, which would defeat lesbian couples & gay male couples in their right to marry. Hadn't we all fought for these rights back 5 years ago, and then again back in the 1970's Briggs Initiative; the Anita Bryant Orange Juice Queen scandal? Defending ourselves from Those gangs of homophobes who lurked outside gay bars and assaulted us in the 1950's?

At last I'd relaxed into my art, no longer worried about controversy. A painting is not as direct as words, which directly inflame the reader. They are usually not as challenging, not as highly diverse from public approval. Now this Prop-8 business, which has flooded the streets with religious gay-haters carrying their infernal signs—SAVE OUR CHILDREN FROM LEARNING ABOUT GAY'S IN SCHOOL! YES ON PROP-8! Which would overturn gay peoples right to marriage (and subsequent rights of hospital visitation, mutual home ownership, last wills & testaments, inheritance rights, adoption, immigration, being 'domestically partnered' in one state of the union, but not right across the state line in the next; all these rights that other married spouses have); all this hate is agitating my soul, suddenly looking at my art work carefully thru this new, foreign lense, thru the scrutiny of those haters I see what controversy my Blue Christ—with breasts and a Star of David—might cause, even *without words*! Or my hermaphrodite Pool Shooter… Or Hunger for God, (the red-dressed old sex-prostitute reaching out to the symbols of God, multifaith religions, including Wicca, Islam, Buddhist, Hebrew & Christian) to name a few.

From this moment on decide I will occasionally use 'sex-prostitute' to describe a whore; as opposed to wall-street prostitutes, or real-estate-prostitute, political-prostitute. All these highly placed whores who have sold our country down the drain.

One big ray of hope—and I do mean big, been notified my Social Security is being raised to $823 per month from $706!
> Red J. Arobateau;

> Beginning November 2008 we are not reducing your benefit because of worker's compensation and public disability payments. We do not reduce benefits for months when the disabled worker is age 65 or over.

> You will receive $706 for October 2008.

> After that you will receive $823 on or about the third of each month.

Thank God(ess)!

Now it was just to wait and see if the infernal mechanization of government *would deduct a portion* of this wonderful raise from his disability check—a much smaller percent of his income, yet a vital one necessary for survival—and if so, by how much? They had deducted from his raises before, but only by a few dollars… Then, there was the *rent.* By law (rent control) the evil, cold-blooded, reptilian landlord could not raise the rent more then 1.7% per year— which fell greatly beneath the fabulous new raise; *however,* also by that same law the landlord could pass on the cost of any improvements to their property directly to the tenants. And the building had that year installed a new electrical system, bringing it up to code (since then there had been no power outages as in the past— frequently incapacitating them for one, two, even 3 days; once for an entire week). Would there be a deduction, & would it eat up his entire raise?

Two more things as well! There had been an approved Federal Social Security budget raise for 2009 of 6.8%, an increment not seen for a quarter century! Did his new $823 per month reflect this raise— which wasn't supposed to begin until January—or was that yet to come? Which would be even more astounding! AND, finally, there was the matter of the original lease of $1,150 he'd signed some 8 years back—which they had never held him too, after the dot.com collapse, when tens of thousands of rich yuppies ran out of the area, scurrying back to the regions of the world they were from, as one after another their lost their jobs in speculative company failures; the dot.com dream collapsed like a pack of cards, subsequently renters began to flee, abandoning their overpriced units. And landlords reduced rents by $200 in desperation to keep any tenants they could. Once before they'd threatened to raise his then $997-a-month rent back to the original $1,150, plus charged him $3,000 for back rent plus interest—until it was discovered there had been a computer error-- and he was reinstated back at the $997 level. So you can see old Transman lived a quite perilous life; up/down riding an out-of-control roller coaster-- of stuff he could not prevent. This threat of a rent-jump was ever lurking on the playing field, and the landlords loved that; using it as a monkey wrench to tie up their opponents while they were sucking the blood out of them drop by drop, month by month until they were dead, just as a venomous insect uses webs to bind up its prey, then devours them.

Well, as usual, praying to the Good Shepherd that the victory will be mine; and for peace & salvation in my life here on this dusty earth!

178.
> The Cross, the tomb, the Resurrection; the longing for Christ's return.

As Transman trudged uphill that Sunday morning, towards service, he had these thoughts:
> Well, have lived 5 more years on earth then my father (dad died at age 59.) In that time restarted my fine arts career, undertook the great journals of my life, plus my theatre masterwork Stage Door, and 4 wonderful 3-act plays. Plus wrote my first sci-fi novels, 3 of them.

The very second his old ears heard the religious singing pour like golden honey out of the 10-foot metal doors of Grace his thoughts changed dramatically:
> Dear God I can't take it any more! Not my own pain but more of the great vast Beauty of You, the service of Your church Your songs, Your Might, Your Holy Communion, Your Holy Presence!

The small band of humans in Holy robes struggled up the aisles baring the chalices, icons; Cross uplifted, the little procession proceeds. *The pilgrim, Oh pioneer!*

Transman feels a great lifting; a great empting, a great release.

> Well---see now, is not enough for me to have 1 dog and 1 house 1 woman---I want all the world who wants this, craves this, to also have 1 home, 1 dog and one companion-for-life. Then this true expanse of my soul in which God has given me to do will be satisfied.

On his day off he just wanted the time to pass swiftly in his life which was not much of a life socially, nor love-wise; tho highly creative, brilliant! With a truly great production. Yet & it was not a good life.
> The countess Denise de Lago had heard of the nefarious sex-capades of Mouissure de Pitieu (see PASSAGE) the profligate transsexual—chaser, a minor magistrate of Ptieu, Italy, who officiated there in a splendid uniform

with epaulets and a ceremonial sword; & tho they lived in a separate time & place she felt a kinship towards him, and was *ignited* sexually by her fantasizes of him—after reading of his perdicellos which were greatly her own. In an unholy kinship across generations & continents. No longer satisfied by her boring, tame lesbian wife, the Countessa had also sadly outgrown the thrill of being fucked by three biological men---heterosexual fucking-- these the handsome studs in sequence, nightly—only a fantasy of the magistrates hard cock would work! Those nights @ De Lago were a hoot & a howl.

PM
Yalla. Arabic for let's go. Maybe I'll close this book with Yalla!

Computer database petaflops, --- can perform a quadrillion operations per second; and xaflops, do a quintillion ops per second. This is the new technology now used to spy on Amerikkka people.

179.

Via Appia. The dramatic figure, arms outspread—in a sort of crucifixion-- stands on a surrealistic cross. This is a suicide, in progress; maybe he, or she won't jump. The Apian Way was the place of execution in ancient Rome—Christ was crucified there, by Roman soldiers who nailed or hung up thousands of crucifixions of petty criminals, and political agitators against the Roman state. It was a main thoroughfare, and self-murder too is a common route some take. The figure is androgynous. He/she has stepped down onto the via—or road—which is also the crossbeam of the Cross, and voluntarily is stepping over it, out, off into oblivion—his legs hesitating to step off into space over the deep blue sea. A cluster of small figures assemble on the other side, women, men, children, and one figure morphed symbolically into an ear. —'Let those who have ears, hear.' The fascist police/army stands ever watchful blue-uniformed in the lower right hand corner. This person is being hemmed-in by the evil dark powers of a fascist state; she/he could be one of the uncounted self-murders of the world. The sun is breaking however, red, violent right behind the head of this person. A fierce sun rises up over the horizon, maddening, energy packed, gold/red whirling out of the clutches of night's blue depression. If he can hang on long enough, it will be a new day! Inside the bowed head of this prisoner of defeat, this captive of the dark force of the 'blues' is a combination of three faces, two of his own including the low, barbaric face of self, and selfishness, and another one who wails; it is the face of his-her mother, who will mourn after, if her child departs from this earth.

Along The Watchtower. The castle is on fire. Figures in the lower ground heads bent, carry sacks of money. A black slave has been decapitated; green money and blood gush out of her neck. A large hand encompasses this scene, spilling out jewels. Fire licks up from the bottom edge of the painting. The horrified face of an old woman, above all, it is her hand, she holds all the riches, she controls the workers carrying sacks of money—yet she is bewildered at how it has all gone wrong!

Evening Descends On The Poolhall. Repainted on found-canvas along worst part of San Francisco's Market Street, @ 6th leaning up against garbage can at 10pm. Interesting part about my history is that I led the queer life, exclusively; not the artist life, not the university circle; but the taverns, and 'certain' streets of homosexuals; AC-DC's, lesbians, trans folk. All those cold nights in drafty bars. This painting is the setting for so much of my life.

Wedding Day. Of course the 'day' is not day, but night, deep blue over a fierce skyscraper silver glittery city; a wicked city—the light or day being an emanation from the holy temple (of many faiths) centermost at top, in which sits a bird outlined in white, over a blue background—it is the Bluebird of happiness. The wedding couple, an African woman and a brownskin man, of some native heritage, young and somewhat gender ambiguous, touch, arms extended. He holds two wedding rings. The temple theme is repeated within the torso of both partners, symbolizing that the holiness will hold them together (despite the evils of the city). Beams of yellow light stream down and around, embracing both of them.

Raiment Of Love. Raiment Of Love, upon analysis, in which is portrayed the duel conflict of human nature—love (symbolized by the valentine shaped heart thru which the black evil head of the snake((serpent-wisdom!)) appears) bringing its pain, truth and ultimate vindication. On the left side of the person's chest, plain, unadorned is the shape of a heart, which has been removed. The heart is taken out of the chest and seen red, openly. Interwoven in the African curly hair, on top of the person's head are the words, written in script-- ANGER, VENGEANCE. The meaning (or statement) of Raiment came to me in 2008—not 1998, when the work originated, with that Colored face, oddly tilted. Didn't know what the statement was going to be at that time.

Holy Communion/Self Portrait-The Second. God has given me a vision---a red stain in the cup of this Self Portrait—it is Blood! The Blood of the Lamb! Making it a Communion Chalice! A fleck of blood added in the corner of Red's mouth, the cat's mouth, & a tiny speck in each of the birds' beaks! A crowd of male figures in derby hats is seen, stepping, or dancing symmetrically in the background. Holy Communion, the second self-portrait, I have done.

Hunger For God. In 'Hunger', it is God who hungers for Her-His people! See the red tongue extended out of the heavens, from surreal parted golden

/crimson lips! It is God Who calls forth—baring a platter which holds icons of some religions of the world: Islamic Crescent Moon & Star, Women's Crescent/Moon, a Chalice, Crucifix, Star of David, Menorah (symbolizing a miracle worked for the Hebrew people), Buddhist Om, for the people to take their pick, and thus enter upon the Royal Road, The Path, The Journey to greet the Most High—this being in all dignity of the individual—no matter how poor, nor smelly their clothes; no matter how blackened their heart with evil done, nor how crimson their soul with stains of sin and shame; in all reverence on the part of the person, awestruck at The Eternal's Great Majesty. This is what the people shall see in 'Hunger,' the old prostitute, arrayed in a fine, but gaudy low-cut red/purple striped dress & matching headgear, unabashedly showing expanse flesh of her bare chest; large breasted. Her old face, toothless, upturned. Her hand, ---portrayed center foremost in red & light blue once clenched in as fist, now opens, fingers extended. The Light shines down, licking around her, and also inclines towards another small brown figure possibly a young boy, canvas left (by A., -- signature), who is preoccupied by the sight of nude figures frolicking on the green. The light travels up becoming the tongue of Gods hungry mouth.

Tiger Woman Dining On Peas While Traveling The Water. Note sailboats pictured in top, distance. Well, the story behind Tiger Woman Dining On Peas On The Water is that I wanted to paint the two tiger hands, big and small for perspective, and noticed that the size canvas called for, which sat blank, white, waiting in the kitchen, had wrinkles from being poorly stretched, by myself. Oh well, am too old & tired to re-stretch. When I set it on the easel, noticed it was lopsided as well! I'll manufacture that right into the painting... I says, liking motion in a work. So naturally if Tiger Woman is dining on peas, and a big green pea rolls away from her, and the plate is sliding sideways and so is she---its due to 'de boat she be a rocken' because Tiger Woman is On The Water! Note sailboats pictured in top, distance.

Home Sweet Home/Self-Portrait-The First. Red peers out of the canvas in a purple wash hue, with flesh tones overlaid, 2 green birds sitting on his head, and two dogs at the bottom of the canvas. A keyboard—for composing books, and a pallet with which to paint are shown. The city rooftops of many domiciles constitute the background, upon which a plaque reading HOME SWEET HOME is written. My very first self-portrait in all these years!

Let Us Put Our Thinking Caps On And Go Study In The Library. Two young African-American children in the Library reading from a pile of books, appropriately labeled Writing, Math, Biology; they wear red 'thinking caps', also pictured the favorite of young people, cans of soda pop.

Christmas Gaming Table Indian. This older Native gambler sits, jaded; weary; satisfied, eyes half-closed, holding a wad of green money; in front of him, piles of silver dollars; he wears a Christmas hat, red & blue.

Dreaming Of Paris Streets Where I Have Never Been. This symbolic portrait of a brown skin person, masculine in identity, who yearns to go to France—a place of freedom, or escape from his present reality. He holds the French flag or a travel-ticket; is right hand fiddles with a ransack. A brilliant sun-- furthest upper right hand corner. Two dogs are at his feet. The Eiffel Tower behind, surrealistic, *dancing* off the canvass upper left. This person is definitely on their way somewhere—to France? To France in their dreams... To the actual country of France... France of memory; France of escape from segregation; France of hope. A new continent!

Blue Jesus. This Christ is female, or transsexual—2 breasts. S/he holds the church in one hand. Blue Jesus is giving communion to pews of parishioners—and to you. The red background—blood. The Blood of Christ. Blue Jesus' cleric collar is a black iron neck-iron of a slave. The left robe-sleeve of the robe is a chain of thick black links—God chained to the holy & compassionate service of humanity! The Golden Chalice foreground drips Blood. The loaf of bread reads *Me*; it bares the Star of David.

Noon Monday October 27
Can't believe someone would still be searching for their place at age 65.

Blue Jesus. 15-brush, 2 –pallet knife day.

AM Tuesday, Dentist Day; October 28
Dentist apt—finally—at Dental College—2 months later--- while tooth is rotting & jaw hurting. No wonder I'm a socialist! Fuck this lousy system! The thieves on top with their golden parachutes of 30 million dollars! Have heard the wise say publicly on media how those on top have underestimated how harshly the average person took the sight of those filthy ultra rich scum million dollar financers robbing our nation blind—causing a global tidal wave of depression —and getting away with it, being bailed out for 700 billion dollars by that sitting president—how seriously we have taken this robbery by the rich; and now the powerful rich expect people to go on spending, investing in their rotten system and behaving like before with no

repercussions? They wait in vain for the market to go back to the 'good old days' of their robberies and frauds!

I don't know why women are the beggars of the world. The gypsy entertainers of high fashion trying to please their way to success; using sex & charm to access the avenues of power towards the top. Is it male's brute strength alone? The ability to teem up with other men enhances men greatly. Why don't women do this? Is it that when they do they are shot down by men? Fragmented? Or is it that they are betrayed by other women within their ranks? They find other women withdrawing from the team struggle, and their group grows smaller, smaller, thus less powerful. Another reason I will be watching future politics, intending to see some high placed females!

Do think socialists, communists, union organizers, radicals—left wing people-- will throw women's rights, our cause of feminism aside during their fever for change—at any cost and no matter whose backs they must step on, or whose heads might roll. Saw this in the presidential election when Hilary Clinton, first woman candidate for US Prez was sacrificed on the alter of change, in favor of a black man. The first black man! People howled! And the fact that Hillary would have been the *first woman*; went unsaid. There are those of us with who this registered. Another contest of woman vs. man—with color thrown in to whet the appetite of liberals--- was years back in SF Mayoral election. Atchenberg, a white dike with a left-of-center viewpoint, was running and all gays were happy about it; she was, of course, their candidate-- but at the last minute (a lot like this presidential upset) a new player, the most personable Willy Brown, African American Speaker Of The House in the California State Legislature, decided to run for the office and immediate all the white gays and liberals switched over to him—a black man must be a champion for peoples rights—they reasoned, since he, as a black has 'suffered so much discrimination in his personal life'. Brown easily beat the much-less popular white dike who retreated back to her post in Washington DC. What kind of mayor did his Honor prove to be? One who sold out the black people, and the poor people of The City. A dapper, personality-plus mayor who wore $1,000 hats; attended any assemblages of The People in grandiose public appearances, shaking everybody's hand, even common folks; while he devoured the homes

244

of generations of working-class black families in Bayview Hunters Point thru Eminent Domain.

My point is, that lip serving radicals who've taken up the flag, the march and the drum since I was about 13 or so, who believe in all the right measure's--- save the environment, save the animals, women's rights, minority rights--- still cannot be trusted not to secretly prefer and switch their votes to a male candidate especially if he is minority. This aside, I am waiting to see how well Hillary Clinton, and the wild crazy likeable—but certainly not vote-able Sarah Palin (for Republican Vice President) will pave the future road for female candidates on this highest level.

     ***

Women chained herself to her foreclosed house; says she won't be moved. Last week a man completely destroyed—vandalized the inside of the home he had been forced to abandon. Sickening fallout of the wave of foreclosures. —Up 25% in California. The bust of the housing market causing the national recession—and global recession which follows. It is because all of us desire to have a home of our own, but this goal was unreachable. So the greedy lenders dreamed up schemes to get people in the door of a house, at affordable mortgages –say $2,000 per month; which a year later ballooned out into $6,000 a month payments which they had no hope of affording. —Rule number one in old Transman's litany of Social Change; a House Of One's Own (See EMPIRE, PASSAGE, JOURNEY et al.)

2 hardworking, retired elderly black people, inhabited their house for 30 years. Police kicked down their door, handcuffed them and dragged them out of their foreclosed house; setting them out on the sidewalk. It was their 3rd visit. Now this property is owned by the bank. It sits vacant, boarded up.

Countless properties—about 25% of housing stock returned to ownership by banks which can't possibly market them, not even pay for their temporary upkeep—i.e. lawns mowed, windows/doors boarded, premises periodically purged of housebreakers, squatters. — And the banks have failed because of the trillions of dollars lost— gone up in smoke---as such a tidal wave of owners sadly cannot pay their new adjustable mortgage payments. This black family had paid

$400 per month for the life of their 30-year mortgage. Trouble came when they got a re-finance—which ballooned from $500 per month, to $5,000. *I just don't understand what's happening* says the dazed black ex-homeowner, a retiree, furrowed brow, her hands cuffed behind her back, seated outside on the curb in front of their former home.

Incidental—more sharks are buying up these defaulted, foreclosed, boarded-up proprieties, then raise the rent by $75,000, and resell them to those desperate for a house. The price is way down from what it sold for in the golden days of realestate boom, just one year ago. But now higher, due to the *shark*. These *sharks* are acquiring properties, and reselling—flipping the property--- is the term used. They still have not learned their lessons! Those whale-sized *sharks* greedily flipping property after property--which steadily fueled the increase of home prices several years back, contributing to the great spiral of sky-rocketing housing prices, was the cause of this mess! Of course these sharks also help destroy the little person's hope of her or his own personal home ownership---they wait for property to be affordable to their small working persons budget, but along comes the *shark,* who swoops up the property up with a lot of cash, in hopes of resale for profit—not to live in, nor have a life in--- thus driving the house cost out of reach of the small person! I hope they get stuck with all those properties and not be able to unload them and have to pay multiple property taxes and loose their shirt, the greedy MF's!

Here's how it works:

> House cost in the golden day of realestate speculation--
> $500,000.

> House cost greatly reduced in the black stock market crash of foreclosures--
> $175,000.

> Shark buys house, re-prices it for sale on the new rock bottom market of pain--
> $320,000.

So you see the house is still greatly reduced, but not as low as it was, and could have been on an open market of first come, first serve, small buyers, each to inhabit one property. May the rent speculators die! —In flames!

24-7! TV blares. *Retailers say they will be at work 24-7!* See hos' slang, race patois, queer vernacular first envisioned by the street-poor has worked its way up the ranks of popular use, until it is installed in official usage.

PM Tuesday October 28
Dorothy Day earned her money by giving talks, by writing, by begging.

I want food, I want sex, I want coffee, I want a condo, I want my mommy! Art—is comparable to the life of a priest; no food, watered-down coffee, scarfing up fistfuls of stale crackers he'd saved for the birds in the lining of his coat pocket... Transman had made his choice and @ Grace sat in a comfortable downstairs conference room for prime showing of documentary on Dorothy Day. He could have been down the hill at a testosterone & needles discussion; a topic which transsexual dearly love; with snacks of cheese, avocado dip, crackers & fruit... But tonight the Spirit won out over the flesh and found him in the basement crypt of the cathedral @ Will's movie group.

Grace, I'm here to learn things of Spirit. There is no food! No coffee. Stomach rumbling. Topic; ----documentary film release, w/filmmaker, on Dorothy Day. Mostly well-heeled crowd. Like myself they all are religiously inspired but unlike me, all have eaten their dinner. Where is mine? Don't Call Me A Saint. Photo of Saint Dorothy, cigarette dangling in her lips; communist, religious believer, activist for the poor!

Noon Wednesday October 29
Blue Jesus.

Only God knows, we can only suppose.

RE: Social Security. The government will end this fine program started by the worldly saint Roosevelt in the 1930's. For all of us over age 30 they will keep the program, those under will be refunded all monies they paid into the program plus some extra at a regular rate of interest earned. Somehow they will shore up extant Social Security benefits with monies raised here and there, such as bonds floated over a 100 year time period—then it will end as the last oldsters die off. For the youngsters now growing into old age with no Social Security net, there will by then have been installed national health care in which all citizens have mandatory participation including the ancient Social Security recipients, themselves. This will eliminate the need of indigent future oldsters (youngsters maturing without the Social Security net) needs for health care money. Housing will have been nationalized to a sufficient extent that the working or retired indigent will have housing they can purchase at the *rate of their ability* to pay for a normal working person—even if they've worked minimum wage all their lives. They will thus own a house. So a poverty-stricken oldster of the future will no longer be cast out upon the side of the road to die as are the old in foreign lands, nor put away into a poverty level almshouse to die, stacked up like dusty merchandise as in Americans past, nor having to depend on abusive or uncaring family members to take them in. The poor oldsters who are of a non-criminal past, and have worked all their lives—tho earning very little—will thus be housed decently in a domicile they can afford, have completely free medical coverage as all Americans. This will only leave food, transportation, and clothes. Something communities can furnish via their religious institutions, charities etc. The oldsters will be cared for and the government can get rid of the Social Security of the future since they hate it so much! Of course nationalizing housing and national health care smack more of socialism then Social Security did--- too fucken' bad!

PM
Am I seeing the well dry up at trans space? Influx of youth—under age-- who are primarily male born; MTF's, all of us crowded over 3 computers, a weary clothes closet, and very little food. A regular-size coffee pot, which makes 6 cups of coffee at a time; and not a commercial 30-cup coffee pot. Addendum—this same sorry coffee pot was later hurled against a wall, breaking into smithereens by an insane, abused, mentally-challenged tranny street girl, furious at Luke, the director. She was summarily dismissed from Trans Space, sadly, but deservedly.

6AM Thursday October 30
1 day before SSI payday. Never before in my 65 years on earth do I recall news media uttering the words; socialism, communism, nationalization of US banks… Is that what this rightwing Republican administration has done for us?

T-train to Richards. This is the old Bayview-Hunters Point district, referred to in my books of 30 years past as 'Hungers Point' a notorious blax ghetto to be feared. Finally it has a convenient rapid transit—just as it is being destroyed, rebuilt, gentrified, and affluent whites starting to purchase expensive modern condos there. They sit elbow to elbow with vestiges of the former blax population, still muttering & complaining, in poor, cheap clothes, who they are displacing.

Iron I-beams planted in the ground, stand reddish-brown with rust; litter scattered in the dirt around them; efluesuvia, wind-blown, a sagging cyclone fence demarks property lines. Projects now discontinued because of the steep financial recession. The T train passes the wind-swept tumbleweed, abandon, decayed factory district.

Transman walked around killing time since he could not afford an expensive yuppie cup of coffee --$1.65 for the smallest. Down in the inner city decrepit brick buildings of Polk Street one can still find a small cup for $1.50. Even $1.35. (Finally a modern Chinese tacky palace--$1.00!!!) He sat on several fire hydrants sequentially, beside rusted, sheet metal-covered factory's & long-ago dead warehouses, consulting his cell phone watch, sipping self-concocted 'decaffeinated coffee' from his fine found metal thermos. Here is his recipe:

> I boil a cup of water, pour it in the thermos; add 2 small milk's stolen from the supermarket coffee kiosk; then at one of the facilities on my route, add a quarter cup of their coffee—thus diluting it. Try to drink no more then this one container full per day.

PM
Intuitive Art. A new style/term used today in Jamaica. The newly-returned Sean tells me this is what my art reminds him of.

Sean said he liked the 'Via Apia' bunch of paintings better then these but he liked Self Portrait The Second—Home Sweet Home. (Oil.) To bolster his ego on this matter Transman thought:

> Must remind myself of my adage, keep all your art---don't wipe off the lesser pieces to use their canvas again—while you tussle & struggle to execute that one very good one to keep. Even the ones' which are not so good---they still build your oeuvre, your collection.

249

And I immensely enjoy these. Sean liked the expression on the old rich prostitute face in Hunger.

1 day before Halloween. 1 day before SSI payment and can purchase meat! --Get my strength, energy back. If cannot find some up at Trans Space, or elsewhere (replating on the street). ((That is eating from bags kindly left atop garbage cans, building ledges & fire hydrants.))

180.
> The Spirit gives instructions.

—Transman wrote down fragments he saw; glimpses from dreams, on a sheaf of paper beside his bed. Then he stuck these pages in his drawing book. After each painting's completion there would be 1 to 5 or 6 loose pieces of paper, these fragments of instructions for future paintings stuck in between the pages of the drawing book—which was otherwise very seldom actually drawn upon. Many of these instructions were words, mostly they were line designs, outlined figures, placement of people, shapes, lines of perspective, gestures, & positions of hands, --where this all should be on the new painting. This is how some instructions looked:
> Rich red brilliant crimson, small canvas. Purple lines with green face similar to Watermelon Eater, jutting jaw purple/blue body in brown pastel outlines browns purples. Paint in breasts, iron shackles.

Then he'd turn the page on a finished painting—proceeding to instructions for the fresh canvas. —Using what God told him.

PM
Put up so much merchandise, memorabilia, in Bancroft boxes, when this library re-opens will receive mucho moola—a fine time to begin SEDNA! For which much time will be needed to actually craft a novel, comparative to rapid-fire journal style—by which he cranked out book after book—at $100 per tome---plus an additional $25 for the print-on-demand edition which was slightly revised & spellchecked, -- plus an additional $50 for the finished bound major work which housed maybe 3-5 smaller 'books'. He could float himself a loan this way for the time needed to write a novel –time, which could have resulted in twice or 3 times as many Journals. All

this in lieu of a *publisher*, & an *advance* of *cash* & honestly paid *royalties!* Well from distress good things are born. There definitely would be a much slimmer JOURNEY if he was funded.

*

> That each person can draw like a master. And each person can play a piece perfectly after only hearing it one time. All of us have savant abilities.
> --From news piece on savants.

This program discusses the great intense concentration savants can summon up to apply to the execution of arts, mathematics. A heightened focus of the brain, compensating for the loss of some other brain process due to injury in the left cerebral frontal cortex. Such as the blind person's mind is freed up by its lack of sight, to open greater depths in the region of hearing.

Paint like a savant!

Noon October 31, Halloween, Friday
There are at least 11 symbols in Blue Jesus--can you find them? The green/yellow Crown of Thorns suggested around Christ head; the crimson Cross in background, the golden chalice foreground, the spilled Blood foreground, the Star of David on the Elements (the Challa/Bread) & a few more.

I am a symbolic artist. A 17-Brush day.

4AM Saturday November 1
Talked to Kerwin S., last night at C-3's 'Within This Institution' Halloween show. Somewhere beside a green stripe, which runs around the room between baring C-000 and C-8; grotesque illustrations of peoples worst fears-- portraits of patients & nurses in forlorn, decrepit hospital ward, Linda & Kerwin and I talked art-iz. He, recommending an on-line journal, where Transman could submit both an image of his work and a text. Kerwin illustrated fantastic covers for magazines and Hollywood stuff back in the day, earning 25 centavos per poster, while the fat cats exploited his art, purchased luxury houses, & drove around in limos. Now their day is done. They are gone. He lingers on in poverty, still working but holding the originals of his art. Transman suggested he put his images on line and

exhibit them at some of the galleries his own stuff now was installed. They all looked at Red's RETROSPECT with minor humm's, huh's.

PM Saturday November 1
Exhausted from APE Bookfair. Walked home 30 blocks. Oh presented my biz card to Jennifer Joseph—publisher of Manic D Press, while in the company of Nicole Hen who was talking up a furious storm to Jennifer about children, being a teacher, etc. Will any good come of it? Overheard someone speak of the bearded bear proprietor of Last Gasp distributors, how, at events like this he is accosted at every turn by writers seeking a publisher; they approach him using a variety of subterfuges, small talk, attempting to work their way into his good graces—and a book contract.

Noon Sunday November 2
Intend to go back to APE, have a 2-day pass courtesy Sean; Nicole to call in early afternoon for a lift; on my way to Grace—Coffee Hour— right now one green bird sits preening on right shoulder, Bijou the stellar white sits majestically on her perch, left—until she marches cross across my back to terrorize Arial who carefully claws his way over my chest to the left. And on and on, ad-infinitum, as ten thousand other days. The two birds now are housed in separate cages, which is a great trial to Transman. ---Having two cages on stands with wheels occupying twice the space in his tiny studio, but as the fighting between the two—beaking—as he calls it, had grown more furious as of late, and the sympathetic T., afraid to open the covers over the birdcages one morning and discover poor little Arial's green body laying on the bottom of the cage, injured, dying because of a battle-gone-out-of control—had separated the two. They only got together when they were out flying free, perched on their respective shoulders, whereupon many a furious battle transpired.

Transman's humble home had 3 basic windows; around them clustered a jungle of plants, green, straining from their pots in geometric configurations, inclined towards a faint sun which would appear over a building top, pass by in full for an hour, then be partially blocked by other buildings, resulting in a dim white light until it set--& this seasonally. And here also the birds sat, chortling, preening, dining, drinking, fussing about in their respective cages.

252

There were 2 more windows; one in kitchen, where a forest of green plants sat in smaller pots relishing greedily the light; and one in the bathroom, which faced an airshaft thru which voices & noise plus noxious odors from the studio apartments on the floors above could be heard & smelled.

181.
Light that filtered into the 2 main windows into the studio that dim morning, 2nd day of the Small Press convention. First, ascend the Holy Hill.

Soul raising, soul lifting, music; poor parishioner shuffles with cane wearing raincloak, ankle length like a monks robe, lofty music, the majesty which is Grace, symbolic of the Divine, Heavenly throne. At the convention last night Satan was the tone. At APE no God seen anywhere down the rows & rows of well-executed illustrations. Took Communion. He needed it.

Body of Christ; T closed his hand ferociously around the Element.

Will you share?

Yes.

It's important.

So he had to share his bread.

T's eyes wee moist as he left the communion rail.

God bless you Red, for you have sought Me diligently.

His soul expunged from the first of the 2-day Godless-convention after communion at the rail, Spirit told Transman:

I will pull the veil off of it* so you can see.

Just a bit. A brief glimpse.

So, now, today am waiting for this brief glimpse of hell to show its true face—but just a glimpse & not too much to bare. This is what he found:

- The people here are innocent, not knowing, tired, afraid.
- Using Satan's name frivolously not knowing what harm it does to humans
- Unknowing of God, little knowing of self
- Ego supreme, believing self is God.

Ego –me supreme. Remember you're a *part*---a very vital part of God's entirety, working together.

That AM @ Grace he got intoxicated on the Spirit. God ignites human souls… *Generation unto generation; age unto age!*

> I Will give you a high place. An instrumental place.

And Transman thought; when I get famous I will tell them about the ho's on the corner. How the vagina is a sacred gift; that is defiled. It is like defiling the purity of the Virgin Mary… He had these thoughts about his past and what he had seen… then said, concerning his art:

> I can lay it on as thick as I can.

And God agreed, concerning God's Workings on earth:

> I'm laying it on thick.

> **

APE Convention. Transman was a notorious gossip and he wondered if it was a bad trait causing people to avoid him. Sat there on his fold-a-stool he had brought behind the Babylon Falling table piled with books as people circulated among the crowd. A few he knew seemed to shun him, while others came around and talked.

> You guys just opened up recently right?

> Ah… it's been a year last June.

Conference. Time when the bathroom floor has gotten wet & toilet paper trials out the men's room door.

254

These plutocrats with cars give me a pain.
--Sunshine Mary, 1930's: from Boxcar Bertha-- referring to richer hobos
who had their own jalopies.

Deju vu to see a Near North side joint The Front Page mentioned in Sisters of the Road, the 'faux biography' of fictional Boxcar Bertha. –remember that nightclub as a dive where he saw, in early afternoon thru open barroom door, emitting foul stale hops beer smells, a white transvestite pelvis pump up/down, in/out; skanky white ass bump & grind shimmying her skinny white buns; sexually inviting.

Rain. First in a while. Cart decked out in a raincoat-plastic garbage bag. The wandering poor can't search for tossed cigarette butts to re-smoke; but dollars & coins weather the storm just fine!

Transman carried a spoon around with him—not unlike the 'bindle stiffs' of the 1930's boxcar hobos, riding the rails going to and fro, from one end of the continent to the other; who carried their own tin pans, cups and cooking pots & forks & spoons.

Noon November 3, Blue Monday
Began new painting using orange & yellow lines in the form of one larger figure, seated, holding a second, smaller or baby. Don't know what the title is yet. Oil on canvas; 15" x 30".

PM
When powers of Empire open the lid on our hideous ghettos, peer inside, and decide—for the sake of ultimate controlling of us---to study us, categorize us, and find out what's going on with us, they hand down monies for officials, and conduct searches for the best suited of these ghetto inhabitants then give them well-paying jobs, with benefits and chances at moving up along lower rungs of Empires structure. This is beneficial to the ghetto in one way, as now there are a handful among the thousands and thousands who have good jobs; our community has role models who are 'making it' and more legitimate money comes into our community, instead of only criminal or welfare money. The bad side is that now we have divisions. Those in the official positions are bosses. They have control over their former friends with who they once the inhabited an equal playing field.

Trans Space. The sound of weeping from the community room. A tall, willowy transwoman. Berserk crying:

> Distraught Transwoman: I DON'T KNOW WHAT'S WRONG WITH ME!
>
> 2nd Girl: No one knows what is her problem.
>
> 3rd Girl: Does she need meds? Is the problem her meds? Drugs?
>
> Red: She's having a bad life. That's reason enough.

Another conversation, about miserable conditions in their cheap hotels:

> A Transman: How do you shit on the walls?
>
> A Transwoman: Serious shit!
>
> A Transman: Every morning you go in there there's shit smeared all over the walls...
>
> A Transwoman: Every day?
>
> A Transman: Intermittent shit.

So this is illustration of how we live, we, the poor, and as have documented, the reason (apartheid) that many of us remain poor, and without jobs.

An elderly pigeon, black, oily feathers stuck together, unpreened, sits against a building. These are her-his last days. Her-his last winter. T stopped to open his sack; crush some tortillas into crumbs and tossed them to the pigeon, happy to see her dine.

AM Tuesday, Election Day; November 4
Feel drained by this constant barrage of TV watching, prez-campaign, stock market crash; Obama is not the best candidate—of the originals—McCain would be a disaster for our country; remember his words '*to look into* Medicare/medical'. He wants to take it away and give people back $15,000 and their choice to travel across stateliness to get better healthcare; what a joke! Some destitute poor can't even get out of town—buses no longer run there! No car! Remember the

sitting president—who ruined the country during his 8-year term—plea for us to put Social Security on the stockmarket! And 5 years later—this hideous September Surprise—the Stock Market Crashes! The worst day in history! Hillary Clinton was my favorite and am still pissed about the abuse she took—as a woman, I believe. Obama will not soon recover in my sight because of this. If Sarah Palin had had a righteous policy regarding environmental, alternative energy, women's rights, and gay rights (she's the first candidate to openly say she has gay friends and gay people in her own family) I might have considered switching to vote for HER, as vice president; but stupid McCain gets a running mate whose politics seem more ultra conservative & ruinous then his own.

Sick & tiered of the constant stream of political ads for and against propositions. Everybody's lying, everyone's telling just half-truths the disgrace is the amount of money—73 million dollars—spent by Religious Christian Right-wing challenging gay peoples right to marry, and the corresponding defense we gay people had to mount to fight that. The Hate. *Hate.*

Drained by this shit, and will take my T shot a day early I believe—as it has run out of my system like a car runs out of gas after traveling too far. Too much stress. Very irritable and frustrated. Sexual angst in my loins. Must re-center within self. Be happy with my art/writing production, although am recognized almost nowhere.

People put material goods before spiritual gifts because these are harder to get. Industriously Transman transferred used pyramids of paint pigment onto a fresh pallet paper, greens, blues, purples, browns, yellows, reds, oranges, lamp blac; it had begun with a glob of titanium white which he no longer had space for on the oft-used sheet; fastidiously his fingers plucked the page up, crumpled it, bagged it and threw into trash.

One must be bold if one is creating. Once I have something I like, I leave it—and it adds to my collection, but the next fresh canvas will again attempted to push the envelope, develop technique, push the borders of perspective, of facial expression, and hand gestures. Wipe off a face, a hand, with drenching of turpentine repeatedly; *develop* the canvass, so I have something greater then before. Seems oil works better for this as said; time and practice with acrylics will decide.

--You must erase the satisfactory face, and paint, straining your technical ability, your view; your inner view, to capture the elusive spirit-sent further face. The feet. Whoops! The toe is on the outside of foot—should be the inside! Do not change it! ----You are doing abstracts, don't forget! Why mess up a perfectly inspired dancing-line wrong toe, to wash clean duefuly, slavish to reality, just to paint in a satisfactory toe. If the toe is spirit-sent, and fabulously placed in a once-of-a-lifetime gesture, captured, do not change it! This light inspiration, this grace, this motion, is what you are striving for! Your face looks old and weathered in the mirror, yet inside you too are dancing, because you are pushing the boundaries. You are doing great art. The face is developing! Keep working keep working! Pieta At Sunset; Oil on canvas; 15" x 30". Imagine, Artist! Imagine!

Blue paint on keyboard; it's hard to paint with latex gloves on. Birds chortling in respective cages. Cat slumbering under blanket, his plate of tunafish devoured.

The tork of the body, twisting, demonstrative. Albrecht-like perspectives pushed.

Need a left foot? Whip off your sock! Wiggle toes! Look! Paint!

PM
Waiting line only a brief moment at his polling place. He began filling out the ballot in line, not caring who saw his choices. The first, drew the line beside Obama, Biden. Then worked his way onward.

Even if Obama gets into office and does nothing, it will be infinitely better then getting the Republican in office to continue cutting up Disability aid, Social Security, and other government programs upon which the poor exist in partials, within this monied society where they no longer have a place. Transman clutched his ballots to his chest! It was his sacred right! Serfs of Mother Russia, and European peasants fought years for these rights we have today. One by one his slim, yellow hand fed his ballots into the counter. His were numbers 6,103; -04, -05, -06. T had made his choices as humanely as possible.

258

Very sick today. Queasy stomach all morning, which he dismissed, but which got worse as the day wore on. He bought vinegar and sipped it; drank water. He had not eaten all day. Friend came by and they went to coffee, but no food purchased but a yogurt. At the FTM trans group again, no food! Transman scourged thru the kitchen area, found a piece of wheat bread.

When he left the group got to Babylon Falling, his stomach roiling and boiling; there, it all began to explode up his throat in a volcano of puke. He, managed to step outside and vomit geysers out of his mouth; he threw up violently 4 times. Then he felt better. All liquid. The entire contents of his guts. Sean's tall form appeared in the hazy backdrop of the old mans eyes, as he promptly whirled out of the doorway with a mop, bucket, & disinfectant. Patted Transman on the back, inquired *r' yuh OK Dawg?* He was kind.

Every time I work in oils I get sick!

As the old guy tottered home, dragging his cart, feeling relieved, there was cheering in the street, around 8pm, OBAMA! YAHOO! YAHOO! This country must get better now! No infernal power grabbers on top eating up the people's civil liberties.

When he got home, the rival, republican was just giving his concession speech. Scent of oils heavy in the air. Talked this over with Dr. Sam and he suggested I put the oils aside—no matter what great progress have made. Jasmin agreed later when called her after my vomiting session in front of the bookstore. So, the oils will drift out of the air, and no more for them for several weeks at least—then, just enough to finish pieta at sunset; then back to acrylics *for a long while!* I think it might not be my Hep-C acting up, it's just that the toxicity makes my system more vulnerable for any bug that comes along. This is my theory.

Cheering in the streets on TV continues for the new president elect. I hope we will now have a more humane dispensation. Also, am waiting to hear the news about the Hate-8 campaign, also Help The Animals-2.

Obama is making a speech, I don't need to hear it. I voted democratic, and helped put him in office for the good of people like me, that is enough. Also must mention have been a bit nervous upon nothing bad happening to him. (Assassination fears.) He has made it thru to the election, and now hope he makes it thru to the inauguration and at least 1 year in office! Anyway, most important to return to inward self, and feed and nurture self. Many I talk to have been avidly watching TV, the campaign and the stock market. The stock market is terrifying so many middle class yuppies they are flocking to the shrinks in record numbers. These are trying times!

The fabulous facts are---the Democrats have swept the house and gained in the senate! This is a win win win situation! Give us more Social Security! More disability! More Medicare! Shake loose the coffers like you did for the rich—700 billion given to thieves! Give something to the hardworking poor!

Many of us poor will hope now the democrat Obama will bring about raises in health care; Medicare, social service and disability and keep in place city's social programs for seniors, the poor, the disabled veterans, the homeless, which the republicans have slowly been hacking away. However our group, queers, a dark cloud still hangs over our heads. To think that one half this city voters hate us enough to vote against our right for marriage together. Oh, the hate on Proposition 8 to stop gay marriage was funded by lot of interests out-of-state. —Mormons from Utah, and Religious bigots from the state of Missouri.

Transman fairly danced when he heard the farm animal's bill had passed 2 to one! 70% to 30! He had not yet heard the gay marriage outcome.

5 pickups for seats in congress and senate!

Later that morning he got the news. Feel bad about proposition 8 not going in our favor--of queers. Hurt. So much has gone into this—us pushing at state level at Sacramento year after year; finally the current governor passed the bill, only to go down in defeat less then a year later. They hate us. Blacks have got their black president. The animals got their compassionate rights—on passage of the humane treatment for farm animals. But queers are still hated and shunned. This takes a toll on me emotionally. Hate is a killing thing. Its race vs. race, race vs. gays; hate! In every configuration that is humanly possible. When will the voices of reason take over? Tens thousands of doctors, psychiatrists and clinics who have treated queer patients over the last 100rd years can testify that being gay, lesbian, or transsexual is not a choice, it is something you are born with. But for preachers and churches to declare their 'opinion' that it is a choice— based on nothing but their opinion and what they extract from their very confusing bibles—is cruel, plus it is a lie. It is proven by blood, sweat, years; years of pain and clinical study that we are born with the hard drive of queers, of trans! They won't listen to reason ---yet if the same doctors order them a diabetes test, or a cancer cure, the same bigots will go flocking, trusting to these doctors for personal relief! This is so stupid! We queers will have to begin our uphill fight once again! We have numbers on our side, tho; our own growing population as queers, and those in intimate association with us who have come to recognize our side—siblings, parents, cousins, childhood friends, co workers—that just leaves the bible thumpers to finally see The Light of Christ who has informed us of tolerance, of love, of acceptance! ---Too bad bigots can't read! Or *think* for themselves!

Thousands of people massing in the streets, toy horns blasting, it's like New Years celebration on Obama's election! A crowd in front of White House hollering OBAMA! OBAMA! Into the face of the evil, grotesque, ultra right rich, administration which robbed Americans for 8 years. Crowds in Berkeley, San Francisco. A record day.

People are thankful at last a black individual has broken the race barrier; people are relived, deeply, that the long 8-year reign of a murderous republican president who has nearly destroyed our nations economy, made enemies for generations against us in the Middle East, cut back funding for schools, social programs, health care—glad that he shortly will be GONE! Toot the horn!

Wednesday, November 5, Noon.
Feel drained and no energy from not eating—because of sick stomach. Jasmin has informed me to throw my oil paints away. Will not finish Pieta just now, poured glass of turpentine to clean brushes,

261

down the drain. Everything else was put away last night. Will return to it in no less then 2 weeks, maybe longer. Back to safe acrylics. Jasmin advanced me $160 for rent, from money I had her keep for me. It's crazy; money back & forth. Scuffling for survival.

The fat cats sit up there, on top of the pile, they see their money disappear, so they panic, and they begin to chop at the foot of the tree---take away from those lowest, in order to prop up themselves---when it by reason stands that they, possessing so much surplus so much more should cut away at themselves! The Boo Hoo Tears of financer Funt from Leyman Brothers corruption, who complains of having lost 2 million on the stock market and leaving him with only 4 million!

Noon, Thursday, November 6
Day after election. Nations continued economic slide. In the streets. All the earmarks of poverty. A well dressed African American woman begs *'Can you spare just 10 cents?'* Groups of men in scrubby clothes, black, Mexican, white—these, crackheads. Standing on 2 different corners, the crackheads midway down the block—in front of a drug paraphernalia store.

The moon had distanced herself from human affairs, still a half but so far, far, away up in the heavens; blurred, a halo of gauze surrounding.

Later in the dentist chair, he happens to glance over at his file, which lay clipped to a folder on the counter besides a trey of silver instruments. There, on a sheet of paper was his drivers license, and below it, the State Medical card. – The cards had been enlarged. On it a big F—instead of M for male. So the sheet of paper had both male and female on it.

Noon, Saturday, November 8
Sick. Since Tuesday. Stomach feels constantly mildly upset. Sleeping a lot. Not much work done, but subsistence—writing. No painting at all.

Will go out to bookstore—Sean has said will put captions on next 5 paintings and send them to on-line galleries.

Another war with Sean about asking to use his computer while a customer was in the store. Bad for business. Wonder what will I be like when I get rich—no longer have to ask for charity.

> I get no respect in this MF! —I'm trying to run a business in here!
> --Sean, Proprietor.

Luckily have money from Jasmin, which she saved for me: will buy deli-food. Thought of cooking (other then microwave) is the furthest thing from my mind. Urgh. Am stuck.

> You made a fence around me with Torah.
> You comfort me with Your Word.

This earth will pass away. Only My Word will remain. Our hydrogen sun burning itself out, gone in 500 thousand years.

Oh, twenty more pages of this book... Am setting up for ILLUMINATIONS, (JOURNEY Volume 14.) The idea of this next Journal is to document my paintings, as I continue on, concentrating with fiction—my mainstay 40 years. In a Sci-Fi book.

PM
Transman cleaned out the insides of his microwave oven with bleach. It was crusted, stained; full of blackened debris. For it occurred to him he had perhaps been poisoning himself with bacteria every time he heated his food inside.

The opposite bookend of my life is coming nearer into sight; my last dog Husky a big dog, and my very first dog, a collie very large, I loved him. They put him away—called the animal shelter while tiny Transchild was asleep. Animals kept disappearing from that house—my dog, the cat, and her kittens... I learned not to trust them, and hate them still for this! After 60 years! *Animals are dirty; they leave dirt in the house* was their petty excuse.

He had a bad childhood, but some elements in it helped him succeed, and come out of it----this was a passkey to a normal life—but he wasn't a normal person. He was a damaged person. Not evil, not cruel. Just fucked up.

I stand before you, the despised of the human world, hands open with all I have done, and left undone. I 'm glad my crimes were petty.

> Mother, he's very poor—even with his job he can barely support himself!
> ---Natalie Wood; 3 Coins In The Fountain.

PM Sunday November 9

@ communion rail that Sunday Transman Red paused, waiting to receive his Bread, then bow defiantly before the Chalice he could not take, and, The Spirit answered:

> —Jesus you're right here!

I'm right here with you!

Give me my healing.

Healing in My wings …And *hope*. A fiery burning powerful *hope*.

As he'd planned to, earlier that morning, Red checked into emergency at hospital. Was there from 2 till 6. Blood and urine tests came back normal—thank God. Panaceas and liver OK. Lady doctor said not to eat spicy foods 3 weeks. Wrote him a prescription for reflux/ulcer medicine.

One of the triggers for this sickness is stress—this election has been a terrible stress, and it on the background of the financial collapse, stock market crash and growing insecurity.

About prop-8 it brings back all the wounds I've experienced in the past as a queer. Yells, derision, violence, accusations; heads turned to stare at the *dike*, violent cars speeding past screaming, hurling bottles; snickers, have spewed out of violent mouths.

Mixed race is another category. It brings high discomfort to me during this election. Obama is identified as bring black and mixed race; he is mixed race (one white parent, and being raised as a child in a white environment by his white grandparents) in his case Red is mixed race—tho neither of his parents was white, nor any 4 of his grandparents white; he had been raised in the black ghetto behind segregation lines from birth. He had walked the walk and talked the talk from day 1. Where as the president elect had not—yet, he, being more black in appearance did not have carry the burden that does a black who can pass for white. Transman's angst was that as a light skinned black person he was never acknowledged; & was passed up, hated and misunderstood by both sides.

Noon Monday, November 10
Being gay, lesbian, trans impacts person's life greatly—due to the disapproval of greater 90% society, even up to loneliness in old age; less income, little support, or care.

182.
PM
He left his pain in the darkness & awoke. Now offer me a love story.
He returned to his secret citadel of power. –The pen, the easel.
Pieta At Sunset Two; 38" 42" Acrylic on Canvas.

> His (Van Gogh's) aim was to bring out with simplicity in each painting the human feeling which he believed the subject could express most strongly. As he put it, his desire was to bring consolation to those who are unhappy.
> --Van Gogh Paintings And Drawings, a special loan exhibition

If you come out of art school you will have ability to draw realistic human figures, faces, hands, feet, the ability to use shading, and perspective. The untrained artist, poor, with no funds or time to go to school, who has a desire to paint and an *expression* to make should not be deterred simply because they don't grasp the geometric elements.

Noon Tuesday, November 11
Transman remembered his first semester of Art College (he had had 3, total.) He had been working on his first collection of poetry. As he'd walked up and down the halls of the Art Institute Of Chicago on the way to various classes, he thought of this collection, sitting on his desk at home on the South Side, and gloated. He was proud of his accomplishment. The best part of Art School was lunch. There he'd found his place at the brown-black table. How was he always identified by others and invited to the 'Negro table' his, out of the sea of white faces, seen for black? Before, in public high school, that colored table, that strange, artistic table, then public college, and others.

If you are an educated person—and this shows—if your lot is cast among underclass persons, after awhile they will see that you aren't the same as them, and some may find they hate you for it. You are different, thus it is good to be in the company of your peers. Thus the artistic, individualistic thinker who is in poverty must somehow find their own.

> If the last king could be strangled with the entrails of the last priest—then freedom would reign.
> --Thomas Jefferson

John Adams one of the founding fathers of America, designed our Constitution; in mind was his greatest fear that the new America would fall into the hands of the aristocracy who would take control over the nation. Is this coming to pass here in America today? And if so, is it, the greatest concentration of power the world has ever known, in fact, the Great Beast of biblical prophecy?

> Rebellion to tyrants is obedience to God.
> --Benjamin Franklin; 1780.

Oh, last night my mailbox contained the returned EMPIRE! W/form letter from editor that it's not for them.

Transman stopped to rest from his blustering & clutterings around. Having had to switch immediately out of oil into acrylic, leaving Pieta One only begun—well begun. He now chose a very large canvas formerly intended to house The Arab, but which was just an inch too small. Having had to wash clothes in sink, prepare green's shake for dinner later, fuss around with the details of placing the giant canvas on easel, anchoring it down, setting up lights etc., felt himself tired and sat down to document his work:

> This pieta might be two homeless people on Sunset Boulevard in Hollywood, LA or somewhere; not that I've ever been there. To be more certain of my locations—it could be right down the hill here in SF's Tenderloin. Cobblestone streets of a generation past, now become red brick and asphalt. Blankets, the larger figure clutches the smaller.

Oh called Bonnie @ Bancroft, good! Will be able to take stuff in next week! This means a paycheck 2 months earlier then I thought! May be the only money I get extra unless Renters Rebate finally appears.

Drip, drip, drip, of his worn black trousers, shirts, and white teeshirts & sox & padded crotch boxer shorts hanging over the sink. Occasional chortle from parrots in their respective cages. Took down electric saw; tomorrow must put down cross beam of easel so I can lower it 6 inches. The painting as it is now is too high to properly place brushstrokes along its top.

4AM, Wednesday, November 12
> I found it was the home of a group of lesbian dopefeind hustlers,
> who, in all the experience I have ever had were the most abject,
> pathetic, forsaken humans I have ever encountered.
> --Sisters Of The Road

Red sat in the window seat of Babylon Falling watching the street traffic. Watching/being in the street, as he had so many times before. Occasionally he'd put down his current book—Boxcar Bertha---go outside and stand, leaning against brick wall of a building front. November---death of the old year, harvest done, stubble fields, smoke wafting up from chimneys, logs cut piled up to warm the hearth thru long winter months. All of a sudden feel I've returned full circle. Since the'60's Civil Rights. Proposition–8 demonstrations are growing daily, no, hourly in California. And across the nation. A list of all businesses who made contributions to it have been made public & now receive attention from us, attention of what kind I have no idea

Some people lowest on the social ladder can be the most prejudice. Case-in-point; are many many conservative thieves, thugs, sex workers, drug dealers—(especially those who don't use themselves). Ho house scorn for lesbians. He would never forget that gay white pure-of-heart preacher in our little church in the ghetto; proclaiming compassionately from the pulpit that we should have sympathy for our sister out there on the street, we should go out and minister to her, as she stood shivering in a wig, full length coat & high heel pumps hour after hour. Red sat in the congregation feeling uncomfortable. Because that evening befo' he had stood out there on the same ho stroll talking with those girls, long after the church was darkened and locked up, and heard the disdain spew from their mouths, hatred for gays.

> I'd let a rat pimp me 'fo I'd be wit' a lezban fo' my man.

And, frequently:

> Date honey? Looken' fo' a date! Shiet! Gowan' den faggot! I hates me a faggot punk piece of shit anyway!

Standing on the darkened street in front of Babylon Falling he again saw the terrible loneliness—an old lady shuffling along non-stop talking to herself.

Back inside the store several customers were having a discussion regarding their current reading about the anti-Christ:

> The anti-Christ its not just one person, it's a group of people. And the anti-Christ is already here.

> Could it be that the anti Christ will arise in our own country? This mysterious group of people who are working together to take over the world?

God has given us free will & this is against God's plan to take away peoples free will.

Noon, Wednesday, November 12
Friend Marguerite appears in bookstore pretty chocolate woman; she removes off her coat and cheerleader-like begins to chant:

> **O-bam-a! O-bam-a!**

PM
Well here is the latest on the race track. Today is the group Black Stylen', which is held at Trans Space; Transman was embarrassed that he had to explain his rightful place in this group; he was by far the lightest one in it.

As before said there are many slightly crazy transsexuals, especially on the MTF side, in which there seems to be more damage. Perhaps, because while growing up, the role of a 'sissy' is intolerable, where a tomboy isn't a magnet for as much hate. This particular white MTF has a cheerful outlook and had been supportive of Red in his art—

promising to buy a book or an art poster for 6 months, but as yet had not done so. She suddenly walks into the Black group, and sits down! Anger spewing from her mouth, that she is excluded from our assemblage:

White Girl: You let Red in here!

Red: Don't bring my name in to this! I really am black, I'm part black and I was raised black and I don't appreciate you comparing yourself to me, you never said you were black before!

Black Girl: She don't know what she is.

White Girl: I might be an alien!

Another Black Girl: From a different planet?

White Girl: Yes!

The insult was so stupid he couldn't even think about it without his head twisting around & smoke billowing out of his nostrils.

Evidently Red having joined this group had created waves of envy among the other clients, (non-black) all of whom liked to eat & were poor. They had not realized Red was part black before, although he was obviously not white. Being part black was his passport to being in Black Stylen'.

9AM Thursday, Seniors Day @ Grace, November 13
Am setting up file for 3rd RETROSPECT, to differ from my first two, shorter art collections. This book will take longer to execute; have put in slots for 30-paintings, all new work. Plus text; planning on having less text but that might change. Copyright page pre-dated for 2010. Must paint non-stop, while working on SEDNA! And keeping up the Journal (ILLUMINATIONS, JOURNEY 14)—but that, infrequent.

PM Thursday, November 13
Almost 65 years old! Birthday! Oops, building almost burnt down tonight! Fire alarm ringing distantly. Masturbation paraphernalia assembled on the bed. For a moment before his indulgence, Transman sat at keyboard, thinking he heard a faint sound, but believed it to be his computer going haywire, greeted this with sour

fatalism, as just another thing broken, another expense of monies he did not have. When he got up, moving out of the closet he heard this noise louder, it was actually distant timpani of the fire bell clanging up and down halls; and immediately he called emergency 911. An African-American sister dispatcher responded within seconds:

Dispatcher: Police, fire, or medical?

Red: Fire, oh hum; its probably a false alarm, the alarm goes off every 2 months.

Dispatcher: What address?

Red: xxxxxx------.

Dispatcher: That fire has already been called in. Do you smell smoke?

Red: No! Haven't had time to check!

Dispatcher: My advice is to leave the building. There's a fire on the 5th floor.

Being nearly naked, Transman hastily donned trousers, a hat, a shirt, some leisure shoes to go outside; *so it really is a fire!* Waded down hallway thru waves of the high decibel alarm bell; firetrucks wailed in distance; as he neared the entrance they pulled into port. 6 trucks, including two hook & ladders. Firemen and a few firewomen wearing heavy fire retardant gear came storming up the entrance; he held the door open and let them in.

It had been a fire after all. On the 5th floor, a food fire on a stove, and the wall next to it had caught flame. Red felt thankful. He returned to his unit. And to his fun.

183.
Noon, Friday, November 14
That morning when in basement dumping his garbage, Red returned via the front door, on it was a notice from the Fire Department:

Fire alarm for this building disabled as of November 14. Do not remove this sticker under penalty Of the Fire Marshall.

Noon, Saturday November 15, 2008; my 65th Birthday

Am to meet Dalora for my Birthday dinner; Jasmin called to say they were on their way to Civic Center for a NO ON PROP-8 rally. L. has become radicalized by the events of the last year. Eight years ago they didn't even vote; having lazzie-faire attitude of voting not interesting them whatsoever—now are voting by mail and attending rallies. Transman was highly inspired to see via television & internet all the queer people taking up the challenge—rallies being held all over the state—and the nation.

Jasmin & L. are walking around the victory garden @ Civic Center, and said; *the rally is nice, with music; they aren't going to march anywhere, just stay out here*. I must meet them there half past noon.

Oh, went to Temple last (Shabbat) night. Inspired by the presence of God. Service followed by a congregational potluck—food delicious! Two plates. Satisfied the soul and the whole being. Transman, coat & cane flying, over hill & valley; walked home fast; got to the bookstore just in time to argue with the young proprietor. Which, afterwards, as usual, we made up. As @ Grace so low profile gays, their presence does not stand out enough to convince a newcomer that there is a queer presence in the church—so younger or wilder gays don't stay here. Argued with Sean last night about gays in Jamaica. Much he does not know—about gays, about trans. There will be a growing presence of queers on the Island—chiefly because more and more queers are being born, and see others around the world gaining independence and want the same for themselves, even if only a small portion—and they are too poor to immigrate—leave Jamaica; America won't take them; so poor Jamaican queers will pull together their resources and go to parts of Jamaica itself in which there is a queer underground established, and this will be the launching pad for the movement there—just as it has been all over America & the world. Sean said; *gays can't grow as a group because they don't reproduce,* which is ludicrous, as my parents were straight, and the majority of queer people's parents were straight—it is God(ess) Herself who is reproducing us! Generation unto generation! Insuring there is a stockpile of queers in every age, time & place! A goodly storehouse of us!

The kingdom is full of dark secrets.

4th fire in as many days. Arson? What kind of mind would do this?
What kind of mind dreams this up? Turns out it was *Mother Nature.*
Embers carried to diverse places by an unusually high wind. State of
emergency in LA county. 1,000 homes burned.

Oh, found $5 on escalator of BART subway station, green, crisp. Met
Dalora in the midst of a sea of gay activists and other participants at
the rally, in library. Picket signs everywhere.

Sunday, long day at coffee shop (alone) —glad have God/Jesus who
uplifts my soul upon request.

    & S/He will wipe every tear from their eyes.

This national disaster is a 'correction'. God is tired of Amerikkkan
greed, has cut us down to size. Many have raised up their prayers for
the end to this crazy gluttonous real-estate, gas guzzling huge cars, the
whole materialism, artificial Hollywood falsity; and The Almighty
has answered. A correction—like a sick bloated body needs to be
purged, with vile medicines.

Lovely little snack this AM @ Grace; nuts, grapes green/red, cheese,
& croissants. I'm just human. Enjoy eating. 2-half cups coffee; the
other half milk.

Motherfucker is practically a word of endearment, we use it so much
around here at the bookstore; regarding those MF throwing bags of
money $ out the White House window into a procession of limousine
stock brokers, realestate moguls, CEO's of Korporate Kapitalism.

    As an artist you are minting your own money.
    --Al Farrow, sculptor.

PS, her administrative superiors at art college informed Marguerite:
*you have a good little teaching style that would be better off done
somewhere else.* Her contract for the next semester has not been
renewed. Alas, the powers of Babylonia.

Tuesday, November 18

No entries for awhile. —Bancroft Monday, earned $770 for the Arobateau coffers—to dole out to self over the year, supplementing Soc Sec income. Dentist today; am in a hurry. At the Dentist: a page rests open on cove-- a page pulled back so it shows an enormous E. He was too exhausted by life to be embarrassed. Simply sat back in the chair, resigned.

Transman's schedule had become fierce. Crowding out the first thing to go—his fine arts painting.

Thinking about attending Shabbat Saturday plus torah, at Sheriff Israel, so this will cut into my art production Saturday mornings.

65 years old. I have inhabited this space and this birthday nearing three fourths of a century; I have walked in these footprints...

West Oakland on BART; whenever he was *there*, he couldn't help but think of the last woman he was with—had dwelled there--& was sad. We were so insecure, not knowing our future (which is now) moving very precariously; had recently been on the run financially, skipping from bankruptcy to foreclosure, to eviction... managed to shelter ourselves here at this affordable price & was back working my minimum wage job once again—low pay, but steady, continuous employment vs. our declining housekeeping jobs--- was composing AUTUMN CHANGES on a tiny desk 2 feet by 3 feet wide, with only space for the typewriter & one stack of paper on it; all publications had stopped from New York and elsewhere—only my own; this, what he thought of upon glimpses of grey cornice of that landmark hotel.

Bancroft was officially still closed after its retrofitting earthquake, and remodeling, front door locked; so had to approach it via the Doe library. He was tortured in endless corridors, confined in a coffin-size elevator; and asked directions of students who also did not know their way; plodding dauntlessly on thru the Kafkaesque castle despite growing claustrophobia, dragging his silver cart laden with literary & artistic fine shit. All around him he saw students. All young students. T was old enough to be one of the professors, thus he belonged on campus. He thought, regarding the young students: *I know all kinds of stuff. Stuff you'd never believe. If you're lucky you'll never find out.*

He remembered the college graduates, working towards higher degrees who came around Tom Waddell tranny health clinic, clipboards/tape recorders in hand doing their thesis in surveys, dissertations by interviews—in which we, the common populous remain anonymous, no-royalties or payments from the fruits of their projects. They'd come in, donning white clinic coats, ask questions over several weeks—then disappear, forever; we never saw their forthcoming books nor dissertations. Some of us got jaded in the process. Some of us felt used.

> I wanted to help the social workers & the social scientists. But the more I investigate, the more convinced I am that they are but cheap, unenlightened tools in the hands of a powerful system.
> --Boxcar Bertha, from Sisters of the Road. 1919.

I saw the grave-slab slots of parked cars; the city blueprint freeway overpass where we parked Jasmin's van full of the dogs to protect it from prying eyes of the meter maid. Grey dust kicked up by truck tires. Roar of heavy rigs axils over giant tiers overhead; below we sat, protected by a simple white demarcation lines framing the slots.

Wednesday, November 19
> He ate his breakfast with a platinum spoon.
> He walked barefoot around the frieze of life.

Minor miracle! Found neatly folded up $20 bill last night (Tuesday) on way home from Bookstore. Nice talk with David Ball, artist. Had 4 slices of pizza—at FTM meeting at Trans Space, and bookstore. Hope to put more paintings on my website soon.

Called Richard to invite him to bookstore party this Friday—blax brother's book signing; he had been held in Angola State Prison, Louisiana, 29 years! 25-of them in solitary confinement. Friend Richard is very nervous about the economy, his company and hence his job. Selfishly Transman thought I must get these next 5 paintings to Richard *soon!* Sooner then planned! Yet is this selfishness? Or the CALL of ART asserting itself into primacy! A God-Given Call!

Friday, November 21

You hear the cries of desperation jump out of the trans community, here and there:

> If I have to live one more day like this I'll kill myself

> I'm really going to end it.

> The next cop I see I'm gonna shoot him then kill myself.

Any time you see pictures of trannys around town advertising this benefit show, that trans party, their photographs like a FBI Most Wanted display posted on the wall of the Post Office, you see the risk each girl or guy takes as they reveal themselves, standing up soldiers in our queer army.

Dellicious food at Trans Space; dignitaries & trans-soldier troops arriving. Tenth Annual Transgender Day Of Remembrance. After, we filed downstairs. There in the cold night air were 4 squad cars, w/ double occupancy of cops, 2 bicycle cops, one, black, totally effeminate gay man. Back in the 50's and 60's, if you walked out of a gay club or hangout and saw police squad car outside it struck raw terror into your heart! You might run back inside if the place had a rear exit, or else you tried to walk as fast as possible away down the street—before they had time to come to the door, a squad of blue uniforms, silver badges shining, and trap you inside----for arrest. Now they are here to protect us! ---From street thugs—one element that remains constant all these years—but that their number is greatly reduced, and the penalty for violence against us at these bully's hands is greatly increased and today, crimes against us are prosecuted.

Former officer herself, tall, stately, Teresa Sparks stands outside beside thick pool of police vehicles; her redhead bent into windows of squad car.

OH YEAH! Childish squeals of fun. Polk Street is roped off, we proceed downward; traffic barred—We trannys take over the street!

STOP THE VIOLENCE, END THE SILENCE!

Chants rise out of the chests of 150 transfolk; a hemisphere away from the vice cop harassed gay bars of 1950's.

HEY HEY, HO HO, TRANS-PHOBIA HAS GOT TO GO!

Cattle find solace pressed against the flanks of one another. When a cow or bull is cut off from the herd, it panics. A bull is led into the bullfight ring between two nurtured bulls—steers—the presence of their flanks against his acts as a tranquilizer... 125 transsexuals were beside him; buxom beautiful trans women, high femmes to modest, and drab housewife's; small men, some muscles buffed out from testosterone steroids & weightlifting's of youth, others old hair gray, w/canes; beside us, our police escort because now we are a political body; two police cars stand positioned across Sutter street, as we cross; light turns red, then green, without no interference to our parade.

STOP THE VIOLENCE, STOP THE HATE!

Transman kissed one last transwoman, was clutched momentarily to her buxom bosom, then he veered down into the dark streets; *be safe!* she calls into the night, with a lilting voice. Before him the grey, littered streets, empty—almost-- with his cane the little old man, more or less straight appearing went on.

After the procession passed, before Transman on either side of Post Street, two thugs, walking; one white, one black; the black one shouted in mockery of the gay tranny call for justice *HEY HEY GO HOME,* to which his contemporary across the street laughed in a course, rough, mocking, tone.

Transgender Day of Remembrance, ten years past. It began during the first year of Red's transition; a lot of stuff was sprouting up then; chiefly the dawning of the Trans Male, a here-to-fore, very small minority of stealth travelers:

> When they kill us they not simply killings us but the brutality of the killing; stabbed repeatedly with knifes, slashing our throats.

Red remembered that first day, some organizers from one of Kitty Castro's support group and Tom Waddell clinic, going to a

276

demonstration, so he was there. Was still with Jasmin at that point; her waiting for him, cozy, soft & warm back at their hotel.

Miz Sparks reminds us of her Film on U-tube: The first Transgender Day Of Remembrance, 1998. Setting, out in the rain @ Castro Theater under umbrellas. As the film ran by on computer at Sean's bookstore he saw faces now gone; now sick & old, now dead.

This is the problem with it the men 95% who come in this bookstore are affluent, young, strong, bio-guys, well-educated; and have access to tools, computer skills, opportunities, which they take for granted. Here was Red's predicament. This is the problem. As he stood/sat in the window seat of Babylonia Falling, Sean laboriously doing computer entries to the old mans website; in came 3 young white men who bantered aimlessly about intelligent stuff—*distracting Sean from his industrious work on my website! These guys have all privilege & me waiting to have stuff done!*

Now this is wrong! And he knew it. It was selfish thinking—but he was desperate!

Noon
He will never be the type of painter who does fine meticulous work. He has cat hairs in the oil paint tubes, Transman sadly discovers over the crimson red.

Working fast now, because Richard may loose job and hence no more photographs! Pieta #1 (oil). 14-brush, 1-pallet knife day. Cat shitting in his sleep. House stinks. More work for me. Green Parrot screeching his head off. Must finish paintings before the great stock market crash engulfs Richard's business!

Saturday, November 22
15-brush day. Hurry! Jerk off, then, out to bookstore.

Sunday, November 23, PM
Notes to type up. Darkest night, when the roaches come out to play.

Monday, Noon, November 24
So I was an observer; a fly on the wall; seeing but not noticed myself---the best cover for an artist in the throes of creativity, the white

yellow hot molten sun; unheralded; & *stealth* historian. Reminds me
I belong to the world and belong to nobody else.

Tonight, Friday, is the Bookstore event:
> I was born in the USA. Born black, born poor. Is it any wonder that
> I have spent most of my life in prison?
> --From The Bottom Of The Heap, Robert Hillary King, --2009.

He spent 31 years in jail. 29-in solitary confinement.
> I born fair skin in Chicago, bourgeoisie, from a severely broken &
> fallen home. Is it any wonder I'm not insane or dead?
> --Red Jordan Arobateau

Am getting ready to meet this gentleman myself.

Kind of feminine manner & vibe; of an old man, a man whose life
hard edges has been worn down so that they can be withdrawn,
hidden; occasionally booming voice raise out of him and this edge of
violence, wildness reappear. He has been locked down, bound,
restrained, shut up. Soft, warm, large, hands. His job as he sees it to
continue to stomp down on the rats tail of the system which sought to
destroy him, which took 31 years of his life.

He has a shy, sweet smile. & Just an inkling of devilment.

Oh, gave K. Lamb the Epilogue of AUTUMN CHANGES (My Semi-
Unofficial Diary); that begins on page 1,530 or so. She's taking it home to
read—mistakes and all.

Clean house, pet care, fix food—1 hour 15 minutes left to paint, then
out to Trans free meal and computer time. Got more pages of this last
Journal to Xerox.

PM
Red came out to SF for Queer Reasons. IE; to find *love*, as the
hippies proclaimed; Free Love in the streets. That is all the eager
young 23-year old Transman needed to see! A beam of salvation into
his trapped, grey-blue depressed life without end. And it was not
summer which drove him there—but fall. Red's birthday looming
ahead; the glorious summer of young people with tan bodies, lovers,
decked out in beads and costumes; as he, back in the Midwest, passed

time dismally and solitary, haunting the near north side taverns, alone. He, and 100,000 thousand young people heard the siren call:

> All the leaves are brown
> And the sky is grey
> I went out for a walk,
> On a winters day
> If I didn't tell her,
> I could leave today;
> California dreamin'
> On such a winters day.
> --Pop hit 1960's Mommas & Poppas.

I have seen people's dreams shattered. If N. had visions of her Monday Cooking class which she instructed in how to cook cheaply, quickly on appliances plugged in to wall sockets in a one-room, no kitchen, bath-down-the-hall, SRO hotel being televised on public access, it is now gone. Government has slashed funding for all institutions dependent on charity; gay, trans, homeless, etc., and her position has not been renewed. No more cooking class—plus, no more funding even to keep Trans space open on *Mondays* itself—cut back hours. 2 until 5; not 6; Mondays *and* Wednesdays, *closed.* Gawd Almighty what is po' folks gonna do? Persist—and despite all, in the words of Robert – keep stepping on the tail of the monster who enslaves us!

Librarian Heroine Rosé Valland; Champion Of Curators   Will be a title of a painting. This mousy librarian, the bespeckled Valland scuttled around occupied France's museum The Louvre, under the nose of the nazis categorizing great masterpieces they stole and who stole them and where the paintings destination was, shipped out by railroad boxcarby what route; back to Nazi Germany, so they could be traced and reclaimed.

Soon wind down this Journal, 13th book—Well, one of these days, these JOURNEY Journals will be done—and my life over.

Sunday Morning @ Grace. Meeting about Proposition 8. No one here is queer, only gay and lez. Trans is used but often dropped eventually. All are well-heeled, not poor. *These people are not The Lamb! When will small people be empowered? I need to go try a poorer church* Transman thought. He was among those gentry

empowered by society, richer humans. Two Bishops, the Dean, and
several Priests attended the meeting. They were talking into a
microphone:

> Why would we even be surprised; Mormon church, put multi
> million dollars into Prop 8 to advance their agenda; The Catholics
> and Mormons are political patriarchal churches.

Victories of the GLBT struggle over many years salted with many
defeats.

Try to be suppressed Red urged his wild soul; he did not want to burst
out in vitriolic diatribe against those who would erase his presence,
who he was, what he was, his art! Those who would not recognize
his great resources among them! He dared not raise his hand to
speak—because he had so much to say it was confusing to him as
where to start.

This is not a threat, only an observation, but the more we are
downtrodden, and the pressures of the system come down upon our
heads, the more perverted we will become. Some of us will descend
to greater depths of hate & hell unknown.

Noon, Tuesday, November 25
Paint fast, must go to dentist at 2. Time is now five to 12, put
paintbrush to canvass. 1 hour to work!

Wednesday; Noon, November 26
Christmas season comes in with all Kapitalist Korporates pimping the
beautiful traditional Christmas carols to sell products on TV; they
pluck the heartstrings and warm our souls—only to be tossed aside on
the trashheap of falsity and the home you've wanted so long has
come, dwelled with you only briefly then disappeared; instead, there
is grief; so after a long while you see the only purpose is to be near
the Savior; the Spirit, that is the point of our Journey—we will
everlastingly long for, miss the loving family of Christmas time; but
where did the holiday originate? With Christ, with sacrifice, with
greater love, with higher love—for this is a love that does not
disappoint.

A fugitive shadow in the night-deserted park; an angry bent-over
figure performs combat kicks, punches, karate stances.

Noon
Daydream fantasies of fake situations, all which illustrated his own predicament.

184.
Trans. Bad coffee. But it keeps you awake.

Leaving Trans Wednesday; Thanksgiving eve; down the steps from the 2nd floor; he never ceased being amazed at his trans family; we are such a rare breed, coming & going in this place, different specimens of us males-to-females, females-to-males, those in-between; those who will transition; those who won't and be content to represent their secret gender thru fantasy and minor cross-dressing.

PM
4 freaken' hours of jerking off—insane. Too much coffee at Trans. Red was freaking out on Thanksgiving Eve. These emotion-laden holidays, these submerged mental problems and repressed depression of not having family or lover all boils over to surface. Arrived home at 6; began jerking off and finally at quarter to ten, *came* to my senses. Body shaking with coffee, and physical exertion. What a mess I am!

Been alone too long; and not supported in very many ways, shapes or form.

I think one mistake men make and maybe women too, is to think we are stronger then we truly are. The self, the real self asserts itself thru years of bravado and the person begins to melt down; they weren't strong enough to withstand the world, despite that they assumed they could; the fragile structure of the castle walls break apart under the assault—of loneliness, of the concept that maybe we have failed. This Thanksgiving season is the roughest I can remember—and I didn't think it would be! Because I had scheduled a lovely T-Day with Jasmin and others; a day after w/Dr. Sam; however health, stress related problems make me uneasy. All this medicine needed to keep me sane and feeling well. Realize it is imperative that I begin building up more friends, family relationships as forts--but I don't know how, never did know how and my world seems at odds with this; no way to do these things.

--I'm sure I'm not alone in this!

November 29, Day-After Thanksgiving blues; Saturday Noon
For the same reason grief-struck lovers write poetry, art is my bank
account against grief, trouble, death. Spiritual fortresses in which
humans find solace. —They consult priests, rabbis, mystics, gypsy
fortune tellers, psychics, gurus. Some of us do high art; we dance on-
point, we elucidate dramatic lines on-cue; our pain motivates us to
heights formerly out of reach. Art is my personal trust fund against
the days of pain, the bad days, the blues.

Early AM Thursday November 27, Thanksgiving Day.
I am grateful for this life, for my gifts, pets, loved ones. For medical,
and psychiatric, help.

For tens of thousands of years people went out to their art, painting in
depths of caves. The idea to take art with you, this movable piece of
wood, or poetry; later canvass was a great idea.

He had decided to gamble with his life; for greatness & mastery of
art; great art; but what a price!

Freedom of spirit shall not be discouraged; which is the source of
artistic endeavor, which is great art; it will not be denied. It will
assert itself again, again in the human soul; a green shout growing
thru concrete wastelands, thru all sorts of adversity.

I stand before you, the despised of the human world, hands open with
all I have done, and left undone. I 'm glad my crimes were petty.

> You made a fence around me with Torah.
> You comfort me with Your Word.

This earth will pass away. Only My Word will remain. Our
hydrogen sun burning itself out, gone in 500 thousand years.

> Remember My Arms are everlasting & far reaching.

282

Well all I know is God created this beautiful little garden, with all we could want in it—and here we are in these grey, grimy, streets with nothing; looking for a dime or a quarter dropped in the gutter.

To live to be old you have to tell the Lord(ess)—no matter what happens, what disasters, betrayals, sicknesses, I'm in it for the distance.

—Dear Jesus, keep me in your care; watch over me.

And as always call upon Jesus to cleanse my mind so that I might be acceptable in God's sight, and acceptable in my own insight that God has given me.

  & S/He will wipe every tear from their eyes.

Yalla!

Red Jordan Arobateau
November 29, 2008
2PM Pacific Standard Time
San Francisco, CA
USA